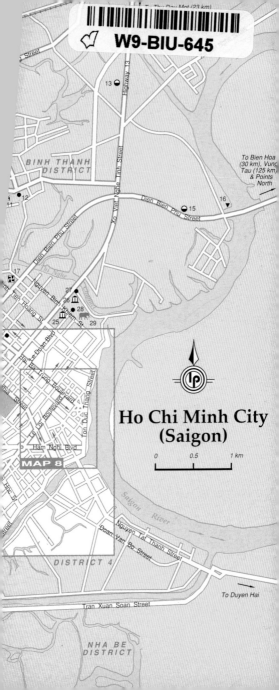

W9-BIU-645

To Thu Dau Mot (23 km)

13

Highway 13

BINH THANH
DISTRICT

To Bien Hoa
(30 km), Vung
Tau (125 km)
& Points
North

Xo Viet Nghe Tinh Street

Dien Bien Phu Street

15

16

17

Thi Nghe

Nguyen Binh

Dien Bien Phu Blvd

Dinh Tien Hoang St

21
26
25
28
29

Hai Ba Trung Boulevard

Le Duan Boulevard

Ton Duc Thang Street

Ham Nghi Blvd

MAP 8

Saigon River

Ho Chi Minh City
(Saigon)

0   0.5   1 km

DISTRICT 4

Nguyen Tat Thanh Street

Doan Van Bo Street

To Duyen Hai

Tran Xuan Soan Street

NHA BE
DISTRICT

Ho Chi Minh City (Saigon)

Robert Storey

Ho Chi Minh City (Saigon)
   1st edition

Published by
   Lonely Planet Publications
   Head Office: PO Box 617, Hawthorn, Vic 3122, Australia
   Branches: 155 Filbert St, Suite 251, Oakland,
                 CA 94607, USA
                 10 Barley Mow Passage, Chiswick,
                 London W4 4PH, UK
                 71 bis rue du Cardinal Lemoine,
                 75005 Paris, France

Printed by
   SNP Printing Pte Ltd., Singapore

Photographs by
   Glenn Beanland (GB)   Sara Jane Cleland (SJC)
   Mick Elmore (ME)   Richard Everist (RE)
   Patrick Horton (PH)   Richard I'Anson (RI)
   Karen O'Connor (KO)   Simon Rowe (SR)
   Helen Savory (HS)   Phil Weymouth (PW)

   Front cover: Bicycle commuters wearing ao dais (RE)
   Front Gatefold: Top: Street barber (SJC)
                    Bottom: Young boy (GB)
   Back Gatefold: Boating, Saigon River (PW)

First Published
   October 1995

**Although the authors and publisher have tried to make the
information as accurate as possible, they accept no responsibility for any loss, injury or inconvenience sustained by any
person using this book.**

National Library of Australia Cataloguing in Publication Data

Storey, Robert
   Ho Chi Minh city

   Includes index.
   ISBN 0 86442 311 X.

   1. Ho Chi Minh City (Vietnam) – Guidebooks. I. Title.
   (Series : Lonely Planet city guide).

   915.97

text & maps © Lonely Planet 1995
photos © photographers as indicated 1995
climate chart compiled from information supplied by Patrick
J Tyson, © Patrick J Tyson, 1995

Robert Storey

After graduating from the University of Nevada with a worthless liberal arts degree, Robert pursued a distinguished career as a slot machine repairman in a Las Vegas casino. He later worked for the government bureaucracy, though he is not quite sure what his job was. Seeking the meaning of life, Robert became a backpacker and drifted around Asia before he finally 'found himself'. These days he can mostly be found cruising the Internet.

From the Author

I first went to Vietnam for Lonely Planet in 1992, fell in love with the place and went back again in 1993 to update the Vietnam chapter of Lonely Planet's shoestring guide to *South-East Asia*. I was back again in 1994 and 1995 for more updating work, and to produce this city guide which you now hold in your hands.

Researching and writing a travel guide is never an individual effort. Information comes from numerous sources, and many people contributed their input. With apologies to anyone left out, some of the contributors I wish to thank include Adrian Bloch, Marcus Dolby, Mike Romano, Patrick Morris, Suz Grumet and Brigitte Wirtz. There are a number of Vietnamese people who served as guides, translators and travelling companions – I'd love to thank them all, but I feel it's prudent to keep their contributions anonymous. However, I am especially grateful to them.

From the Publisher

This first edition of the *Ho Chi Minh City* guide was edited by Ian Ward at the Lonely Planet office in Melbourne. Louise Keppie was responsible for map production, book design and layout. Thanks go to Chris Klep for mapping assistance and David Kemp for artistic guidance. Cover design by Simon Bracken and Adam McCrow. Also to Louise Callan for tidying up the

Vietnamese texts, Kerrie Williams for the index, Dan Levin for solving the computer problems and Greg Alford for assistance beyond the call of duty.

Warning & Request

A travel book is like a snapshot – it represents the way things were for a brief moment in time. Before the ink is dry on a new book, things change, and few places change more quickly than bustling Ho Chi Minh City. Prices go up, new hotels open, old ones burn down, others get renovated and renamed, good places can go bad, bus routes change, buildings collapse and recommended travel agents get indicted for fraud. Carry this book as a guide, not a gospel – since things go on changing we can't tell you exactly what to expect all the time.

At Lonely Planet we get a steady stream of mail from travellers and it all helps – whether it's a few lines scribbled on the back of a used paper plate or a stack of neat typewritten pages spewing forth from our fax machine. And in these days of the information super-highway, we get more and more messages from cyberspace. Despite the ever-increasing volume of mail, all this correspondence actually gets read – we even employ two full-time staff just to scrutinise the mountain of letters and direct them to the appropriate authors.

So if you find things aren't like they're described herein, don't get upset – get out your pen, typewriter or word processor and write to us. Your input will help make the next edition better. As usual, the writers of useful letters will score a free copy of the next edition, or another Lonely Planet guide if you prefer. We give away plenty of books, though obviously not every letter-writer receives one.

Contents

Introduction

The name 'Saigon' has for decades etched itself into the Western consciousness. For the French, it was the capital of colonial Indochina, the tropical Paris of the Orient. In 1950, Norman Lewis described Saigon thus: 'its inspiration has been purely commercial and it is therefore without folly, fervour or much ostentation...a pleasant, colourless and characterless French provincial city'.

The French got the boot in 1954 and the Americans had a go at remodelling Saigon for about 15 years. When the Communists took over in 1975, they renamed the place Ho Chi Minh City and set about creating their own version of utopia. Little did they realise that the city they had hoped to change would eventually change them.

While Hanoi can claim the title of 'national capital', Ho Chi Minh City is still Vietnam's heart and soul, the nation's largest city, economic capital and cultural trendsetter. And with 'new thinking' in Hanoi now remaking the economic life of the whole country in the mould of pre-reunification Saigon, people have been remarking that, in the end, Saigon really won the war.

For the Vietnamese, Ho Chi Minh City exerts a kind a magnetic pull, an irresistible force that sucks in people and rarely lets them go. During the war, the city's population increased enormously as civilians sought refuge from the fighting in the countryside. But when the war ended, the former rural peasants decided that they

Looking up Le Loi Boulevard (SR)

would rather be urbanites and stayed put. The government's efforts to persuade them to leave proved fruitless – the sin and glitter of the city was too attractive. Attempts to forcibly move them back to their rural homes failed – the urban pioneers simply sneaked back into the city at the first opportunity. And although the nation has been at peace for over two decades now, the 'rural refugees' keep coming. They come not to escape war, but to seek their fortunes.

Many do not readily find the proverbial 'pot of gold at the end of the rainbow' and wind up sleeping on the pavement. Yet, very few Vietnamese who come to live in Ho Chi Minh City ever leave it. For better or worse, it is the place to be. Oddly enough, they are now being joined by a small but steady trickle of foreigners who feel the same way. Some get discouraged and soon leave, but there is an emerging community of long-term expats. A few learn to speak Vietnamese, set up a business, marry a local, have children and try to blend into their exotic new surroundings. It takes a special sort of person to do that – but increasingly, such people are finding their way to Ho Chi Minh City.

Ironically enough, some of the most enthusiastic foreign tourists, investors and expatriates are Vietnam's former enemies, the French and the Americans. Even the veterans come back, to see old battlefields, find old friends, relive old experiences and wonder why such tragic wars ever happened. Also returning are Overseas Vietnamese (Viet Kieu), many of whom risked their lives in flimsy boats to flee their homeland – some come to visit family, others come as tourists and investors, but a surprising number are staying on.

The hustle and bustle is to be seen everywhere, and there is something invigorating about it all. Images of the exotic and mundane are everywhere. There are the street markets, where bargains are struck and deals are done. The pavement cafés, where stereo speakers fill up the surrounding streets with a melodious thumping beat. The sleek new pubs where tourists chat over beer, pretzels, coffee and croissants. A young female office worker manoeuvres her Honda through rush-hour traffic, long hair flowing, high-heels working the brake pedal. The sweating Chinese businessman chats on his cellular telephone, cursing his necktie which is so absurdly disfunctional in the tropical heat. A desperate beggar suddenly grabs your arm, rudely reminding you that this is still a Third World city despite the tinsel and trimmings.

The traffic roars. The jackhammers of progress pound the past into pulp, to make way for the new. The city churns, ferments, bubbles and fumes. Yet within the teeming metropolis are the timeless traditions and beauty of an ancient culture. There are the pagodas, where monks pray and incense burns. Artists create their masterpieces on canvas or in carved wood. Puppeteers entertain children in the parks. In the back alleys where tourists seldom venture, acupuncturists poke needles into patients and students learn to play the violin. A seamstress carefully creates an *ao dai*, the graceful Vietnamese costume that could make the fashion designers of Paris envious.

Beyond the metropolis is another world. The Mekong Delta, where canoes ply the canals and young boys harvest coconuts. The Dong Tam Snake Farm where you watch cobras from a respectful distance, or literally pet a giant python. The Caodai Holy See, an otherworldly temple like no other on earth. Or the tropical beaches at Long Hai, where commercial tourism has yet to wash ashore.

Vietnam's situation is far from settled. Party conservatives shriek that opening the door to the West will lead the nation to counter-revolutionary ruin, and urge a retreat from economic liberalism. Meanwhile, the liberals are contemplating where to house the new stock market, and how to finance the proposed subway system. Down at the street level, the masses toil away, creating their own revolutionary society while the politicians debate. Despite official pronouncements and bureaucratic 'five-year plans', no one is quite sure what the future will bring. That Ho Chi Minh City is developing is without question. The big question is, 'developing into what?'.

Facts about Ho Chi Minh City

HISTORY

In the Beginning

From the 1st to the 6th centuries AD, the south of what is now Vietnam was part of the Indianised kingdom of Funan, which produced notably refined art and architecture. The Funanese constructed an elaborate system of canals which crisscrossed the Mekong Delta and may have extended to the site of present-day Ho Chi Minh City. The canals were used for both transportation and the irrigation of wet rice agriculture. The principal port of Funan was Oc-Eo, close to what is now the city of Rach Gia in the Mekong Delta.

In the mid-6th century, Funan was attacked by the Khmer kingdom of Chenla, which gradually absorbed the territory of Funan into its own (the Khmer are thought to have originally moved southwards from China before 200 BC).

Throughout the 17th and 18th centuries, Vietnam was divided between the Trinh Lords who ruled in the north, and the Nguyen Lords who controlled the south. During this period the Nguyen extended Vietnamese control into the Khmer (Cambodian) territories of the Mekong Delta, including the site of present-day Ho Chi Minh

Woman in traditional dress (PH)

City. Cambodia was forced to accept Vietnamese suzerainty in the mid-17th century. Vietnamese settlers moved into the area in the 17th century and founded the city of Saigon on an ancient Khmer site.

About 700,000 Khmer people remain in Vietnam to this day, most now living in the Mekong Delta. A look at the map still reveals that a large finger of Cambodia (called the 'Parrot's Beak' because of its shape) extends very close to the border of present-day Ho Chi Minh City. Many Khmer people still refer to Ho Chi Minh City's present site as 'Lower Cambodia'. Resentment over Vietnam's historical annexation of ancient Khmer territory was the excuse given by the Khmer Rouge when they massacred Vietnamese villagers living near the Cambodian border, triggering a war with Vietnam in late 1978.

French Era

Saigon was captured by the French in 1859, and was made the capital of the French colony of Cochinchina (southern Vietnam) a few years later. In 1887 the French expanded their colony to include all of Indochina (present-day Vietnam, Laos and Cambodia), with Saigon as its capital.

The French tried to mould Saigon in their own image and succeeded to the extent of installing wide boulevards and some beautiful French architecture, and converting a sizeable minority of the locals to Catholicism.

The French colonial authorities carried out ambitious public works, constructing the Saigon-Hanoi railway as well as ports, extensive irrigation and drainage systems and improved dykes. They also established various public services and set up research institutes.

Where the French failed was in winning the hearts and minds of the locals. Indochina was ruthlessly run as a money-making enterprise, and the Vietnamese watched in dismay as their incomes fell while the French became wealthy. The government heavily taxed the peasants, devastating the traditional rural economy. The colonial administration also ran alcohol, salt and opium monopolies for the purpose of raising revenues. In Saigon, they produced a quick-burning type of opium which helped increase addiction and thus earn hefty profits.

French capital was invested for quick returns in mining and in tea, coffee and rubber plantations, all of which became notorious for the abysmal wages they paid and the subhuman treatment to which their

Vietnamese workers were subjected. Farmers lost their land and became little more than indentured servants.

It was a stage set for rebellion. The French colonial administration spent much of its time putting down one small revolt after another, and often publicly guillotined the perpetrators.

Ultimately, the Communists proved to be the most successful of the anti-colonial groups. Communist successes in the late 1920s included major strikes by urban workers. A 1940 uprising in the south was brutally suppressed, however, seriously damaging the Party's infrastructure. French prisons, filled with arrested cadres, were turned by the captives into revolutionary 'universities' in which Marxist-Leninist theory was taught.

WW II

When France fell to Nazi Germany in 1940, the Indochinese government of Vichy-appointed Admiral Jean Decoux concluded an agreement to accept the presence

---

Ho Chi Minh

Ho Chi Minh is the best known of some 50 aliases assumed over the course of his long career by Nguyen Tat Thanh (1890-1969), founder of the Vietnamese Communist Party and President of the Democratic Republic of Vietnam from 1946 until his death. The son of a fiercely nationalistic scholar-official of humble means, he was educated in the Quoc Hoc Secondary School in Hué before working briefly as a teacher in Phan Thiet. In 1911, he signed on as a cook's apprentice on a French ship, sailing to North America, Africa and Europe. He remained in Europe where, while working as a gardener, snow sweeper, waiter, photo retoucher and stoker, his political consciousness began to develop.

After living briefly in London, Ho Chi Minh moved to Paris, where he adopted the name Nguyen Ai Quoc (Nguyen the Patriot). During this period, he mastered a number of languages (including English, French, German and Mandarin Chinese) and began to write about and debate the issue of Indochinese independence. During the 1919 Versailles Peace Conference, he tried to present an independence plan for Vietnam to US President Woodrow Wilson. Ho was a founding member of the French Communist Party, which was established in 1920. In 1923, he was summoned to Moscow for training by the Communist International, which later sent him to Guangzhou (Canton), where he founded the Revolutionary Youth League of Vietnam, a precursor to the

of Japanese troops in Vietnam. For their own convenience the Japanese, who sought to exploit the area's strategic location and its natural resources, left the French administration in charge of the day-to-day running of the country.

In 1941, Ho Chi Minh formed the League for the Independence of Vietnam (Viet Nam Doc Lap Dong Minh Hoi), better known as the Viet Minh, which resisted the Japanese occupation (and thus received Chinese and American aid) and carried out extensive political organising during WW II. Despite its broad nationalist programme and claims to the contrary, the Viet Minh was, from its inception, dominated by Ho's Communists.

Vietnam (American) War

With the defeat of the Japanese in 1945, the Vietnamese had high hopes of achieving true independence. But France had different ideas, and tried to reassert control over all Indochina. The Franco-Viet Minh War started in

Indochinese Communist Party and the Vietnamese Communist Party.

After spending time in a Hong Kong jail in the early '30s and more time in the USSR and China, Ho Chi Minh returned to Vietnam in 1941 for the first time in 30 years. That same year – at the age of 51 – he helped found the Viet Minh Front, the goal of which was the independence of Vietnam from French colonial rule and Japanese occupation. In 1942, he was arrested and held for a year by the Nationalist Chinese. As Japan prepared to surrender in August 1945, Ho Chi Minh led the August Revolution, which took control of much of the country; and it was he who composed Vietnam's Declaration of Independence (modelled in part on the American Declaration of Independence) and read it publicly very near the eventual site of his mausoleum.

The return of the French shortly thereafter forced Ho Chi Minh and the Viet Minh to flee Hanoi and take up armed resistance. Ho spent eight years conducting a guerrilla war until the Viet Minh's victory against the French at Dien Bien Phu in 1954. He led North Vietnam until his death in September 1969 – he never lived to see the North's victory over the South. Ho Chi Minh is affectionately referred to as 'Uncle Ho' (Bac Ho) by his admirers.

Uncle Ho may have been the father of his country, but he wasn't the father of any children, at least none that are known. Like his erstwhile nemesis, South Vietnamese President Ngo Dinh Diem, Ho Chi Minh never married. ∎

1946 and culminated in the dramatic French defeat at Dien Bien Phu (north-western Vietnam) in 1954.

A peace agreement between France and the Viet Minh was negotiated in Geneva. The Geneva Accords provided for the temporary division of Vietnam into two zones (thus creating North and South Vietnam) and the holding of nationwide elections on 20 July 1956.

After the signing of the Geneva Accords, the South was ruled by a government led by Ngo Dinh Diem, a fiercely anti-Communist Catholic. His power base was significantly strengthened by some 900,000 refugees – many of them Catholics – who fled the Communist North.

In 1955 Diem, convinced that if elections were held Ho Chi Minh would win, refused to implement the Geneva Accords; instead, he held a rigged referendum on his continued rule. Diem declared himself president of the Republic of Vietnam and Saigon became its capital in 1956.

In December 1960, Hanoi announced the formation of the National Liberation Front (NLF), whose aim was to 'liberate' the South through all means (including military) and reunify the country. In the South, the NLF came to be known as the 'Viet Cong' or just the 'VC'; both are abbreviations for Viet Nam Cong San, which means 'Vietnamese Communist'. The Viet Cong were also joined by regular troops from the North Vietnamese Army (NVA).

Diem's tyrannical rule earned him many enemies. In the early 1960s, Saigon was rocked by anti-Diem unrest led by university students and Buddhist clergy, including several self-immolations by monks. These acts, and the indifference to them shown, notoriously, by Diem's sister-in-law Tran Le Xuan, shocked the world. In November 1963, Diem was assassinated by his own troops in Saigon.

The first American soldiers to die in the Vietnam War were killed at Bien Hoa (30 km from Saigon) in 1959 at a time when about 700 US military personnel were in Vietnam. As the military position of the South Vietnamese government continued to deteriorate, the USA sent more and more military advisors and troops to Vietnam. In April 1969, the number of US soldiers in Vietnam reached an all-time high of 543,400.

In order to extract itself from this guerilla war without end, the USA began a policy of 'Vietnamisation' in which the Army of the Republic of Vietnam (ARVN) was equipped and trained to do the fighting without direct American involvement. US troops were slowly withdrawn while the Americans pursued peace negotiations with the North Vietnamese.

Top : War Memorial, Cao Lanh (RS)
Bottom : American tank (SR)

The Paris Agreements, signed by the USA, North Vietnam, South Vietnam and the Viet Cong on 27 January 1973, provided for a cease-fire, the total withdrawal of US combat forces and the release of 590 American POWs.

In March 1975, the NVA quickly occupied a strategic section of South Vietnam's Central Highlands in a surprise attack. In the absence of US military support or advice, South Vietnamese President Nguyen Van Thieu personally decided on a strategy of tactical withdrawal to more defensible positions. This proved to be a spectacular military blunder. The totally unplanned withdrawal turned into a rout as panicked ARVN soldiers deserted en masse in order to try to save their families.

President Thieu, in power since 1967, resigned on 21 April 1975 and fled the country. He was replaced by Vice President Tran Van Huong, who quit a week later, turning the presidency over to General Duong Van Minh. He, in turn, lost his post after less than 43 hours in office, surrendering on the morning of 30 April 1975 in Saigon's Independence Palace (now Reunification Palace). The first official act of the North Vietnamese was to change the name of Saigon and vicinity to Ho Chi Minh City.

Since Reunification

Whatever else can be said, the North Vietnamese troops (*bo doi*) were well disciplined. Saigon residents had feared that their enemy would engage in an orgy of rape, murder and looting, but this never happened. Not that revenge for the war wasn't on the agenda – it would come later – but during the first three weeks of the occupation the NVA behaved impeccably. Indeed, the only incidents of theft were those committed by the South Vietnamese themselves. The bo doi were treated as country bumpkins by the arrogant Saigonese. Unfortunately, these country bumpkins had AK-47s.

By the third week, the crackdown on crime began. Suspected thieves were simply rounded up and shot. But even this was only the beginning of a harsh new reality. Reunification (officially called 'liberation') was accompanied by large-scale political repression which destroyed whatever trust and goodwill the Southerners might have felt towards the North. Despite promises to the contrary, hundreds of thousands of people who had ties to the previous regime came under suspicion. Their property, which the Northerners viewed as having been gained through capitalist exploitation, was confiscated, and they were subsequently rounded up and imprisoned without trial in forced-labour camps or 're-education camps'. Others simply fled abroad. However many of the prisoners were released in 1979.

The purges affected not only former opponents of the Communists, but also their descendants. More than a decade after the war, the children of former 'counter-revolutionaries' were still treated as if they had some hereditary disease and were thus prevented from receiving an education or employment. This desire to take revenge against the children of the former regime has now saddled Ho Chi Minh City with a huge new set of social problems – it may take decades to eradicate the resultant poverty, illiteracy and crime.

Opening the Door

After reunification, Vietnam set up an economic system closely modelled on that of the former Soviet Union. The economy shrank and billions of roubles of Soviet aid were needed in order to stave off complete economic collapse. When the Soviet Union itself collapsed in 1991, Vietnam had little choice but to seek reconciliation with the Western world.

The decision to experiment with capitalist-style economic reforms quickly revived the fortunes of Ho Chi Minh City. Indeed, bureaucrats from Hanoi have come south to seek out their former capitalist enemies and learn from them the art of doing business. As the 20th century draws to a close, Ho Chi Minh City stands poised to become one of Asia's great metropolises.

GEOGRAPHY

Ho Chi Minh City is in fact an enormous municipality covering an area of 2029 sq km. It stretches from the South China Sea almost to the Cambodian border. Most of this vast territory is overwhelmingly rural, dotted with villages and groups of houses set amidst rice paddies. Rural regions make up about 90% of the land area of Ho Chi Minh City and hold around 25% of the municipality's population. The other 75% of the population is crammed into the remaining 10% that constitutes the urban centre.

The word 'city' is of course English, and the official name in Vietnamese is Thanh Pho Ho Chi Minh. This is often abbreviated as TP Ho Chi Minh or TP HCM.

Politically, Ho Chi Minh City is divided into 12 urban districts (quan, derived from the French quartier) and six rural districts (huyen). District 1 is now the official name for Saigon proper and District 5 is the old Chinese city of Cholon.

The 12 urban districts are as follows: District 1, District 3, District 4, District 5, District 6, District 8, District 10, District 11, Binh Thanh, Go Vap, Phu Nhuan and Tan Binh. The six rural districts are Binh Chanh, Can Gio, Cu Chi, Hoc Mon, Nha Be and Thu Duc.

The city rests on very flat terrain, and the chief geographical feature is the Saigon River which flows into the even larger Nha Be River. The largest but least populated district of Ho Chi Minh City is Can Gio, which is one vast mangrove swamp near the sea.

CLIMATE

Being only 10.5° north of the equator and five to 10 metres above sea level, Ho Chi Minh City has a very tropical climate. There are two main seasons: wet and dry. The wet season (summer) lasts from May to November (June to August are the wettest months). During this time, there are heavy but short-lived downpours almost daily, usually in the afternoon. The dry season (winter) runs from December to April. Late February through May are the hottest months and it's also very humid, but things cool down slightly when the summer rainy season begins.

Between July and November, violent and unpredictable typhoons often develop over the ocean east of Vietnam, hitting central and northern Vietnam with devastating results. Fortunately, Ho Chi Minh City is so far south that it is spared most of the damage, but these big storms can still generate several days of heavy rains.

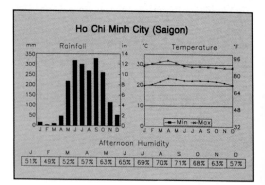

Temperatures vary little with the seasons, averaging 26°C in January and 28°C in July. Summer daily highs are usually in the low 30s, while in January the overnight lows are about 21°C. Average humidity is 80%. Annual rainfall averages 1979 mm, most of which occurs during summer. The coldest temperature ever recorded in Ho Chi Minh City was 14°C.

ENVIRONMENT

As in much of the world, economic development gets priority over environmental protection in Ho Chi Minh City. Recent economic growth has worsened the situation considerably as the newly affluent purchase polluting motorbikes and automobiles. Throwaway plastic containers and other detritus are finding their way into the city's once-charming canals, which are choked by raw sewage. The rapidly increasing population also puts strains on the city's environment.

While there seems little doubt that cleaning up the environment of Ho Chi Minh City will be a considerable challenge, the situation is not hopeless. There is a surprisingly high level of awareness of what the problems are and what should be done about them. The local newspapers continually rail against plans to put up new high-rises which will spoil the skyline, and engineers will soon undertake a study of the feasibility of building a mass-transit system to alleviate the traffic mess. The city plans to put the sewage canals into underground pipes and install a modern sewage-treatment plant. Furthermore, the government wants to push factories and

Paddy fields (KO)

other new economic developments to areas away from the city centre.

The problem, of course, is that most of these plans will cost money and funds are in short supply. It's almost certain that the environment will get worse before it gets better.

By contrast, the outlying districts of the city are still amazingly rural. Even a 30-minute drive from the centre can bring one to areas of surprisingly rural charm and tranquillity.

GOVERNMENT

Vietnam's political system is dominated by the 1.8-million-member Communist Party, centred in Hanoi, whose influence is felt at every level of the country's social and political life.

Nevertheless, the Party has a relatively decentralised structure which allows local leaders considerable leeway for initiative. Every one of Vietnam's 50 provinces and three municipalities, including Ho Chi Minh City, is headed by a People's Committee. Most of the various People's Committees are dominated by cadres from northern Vietnam, a hangover from the Vietnam War which still causes considerable resentment. Nevertheless, it can be said that the People's Committee of Ho Chi Minh City is more enterprising and forward-looking than almost any other local government in the country.

Candidates to the municipal People's Committee are elected to office. The voting age is 18. Everyone of voting age is required to vote, though proxy-voting is allowed (and is very common). This permits the government to boast that elections produce 100% voter participation, thus conferring legitimacy on the process.

Elections are held with great fanfare and it all appears very democratic on the surface. In practice, most Vietnamese are highly cynical about their 'democracy'. To a large extent, election results are mostly decided before the voting takes place. Only Party-approved candidates are permitted to run and opposition parties are prohibited. Some 'independents' have appeared on the slate in Ho Chi Minh City (and nowhere else), but they must also have the government's approval to run. During elections, the number of candidates running in a given constituency usually exceeds the number of contested seats by 20% to 30%.

With the national government based in Hanoi, visitors wishing to talk to officials may have to go there. However, some possible government contacts in Ho Chi Minh City are given under Useful Organisations in the Facts for the Visitor chapter.

ECONOMY

I have been over to the future, and it works.
Lincoln Steffens, 1920, after returning from Russia

Long before it was called Ho Chi Minh City, Saigon was the most prosperous place in Vietnam by far. The city reached its zenith of economic stardom during the Vietnam War when US aid poured into the country. US assistance was not only economic and military, but also technical. The Vietnamese proved to be fast learners, absorbing everything from engineering to cost accounting.

The sudden success of the 1975 North Vietnamese offensive surprised the North almost as much as it did the South. As a result, Hanoi had not prepared specific plans to deal with integrating the two parts of the country, whose social and economic systems could hardly have been more different.

Until the formal reunification of Vietnam in July 1976, the South was nominally ruled by a Provisional Revolutionary Government (PRG). One thing the PRG did was to cancel South Vietnam's currency and issue a new PRG banknote, at a swap rate of 500:1 in favour of the new money. This instantly wiped out the savings of millions of South Vietnamese and sent the economy into a tailspin. In an attempt to implement a rapid transition to socialism, an anti-capitalist campaign was launched in March 1978 during which most private property and businesses were seized. The goal was to set up a centrally planned economy based on the Soviet model. The economy plunged into an abyss and Vietnam became one of the poorest countries in the world. Famine was probably only averted by massive assistance from the former Soviet Union.

Vietnam's efforts to restructure the economy really got started with the Sixth Party Congress held in December 1986. Immediately upon the legalisation of limited private enterprise, family businesses began popping up all over the country. But it is in Ho Chi Minh City, with its previous experience of capitalism, that the entrepreneurial skills and managerial dynamism needed to effect the reforms are to be found.

Privatisation of large state industries has not yet begun but is being considered. At the present time, Vietnam has no stock market – establishing one would be a prerequisite for any privatisation moves. In 1995, the government promised to open a capital market by year's end.

Swords into Market Shares

The word is out – it's time to put away the guns and beat the swords into ploughshares. Yes, the Vietnam War is over, but the battle for market share is just beginning. And everyone wants a piece of the action. Joint-venture capitalists from Japan, Korea, Taiwan, France, Germany, England and Australia have been flocking to Vietnam since the beginning of the 1990s.

The most recent arrivals in town have been the Americans, and they bring with them several competitive advantages. As with the French, there is this strange nostalgia for doing business with those who were just yesterday Vietnam's enemy. Aside from that, the fact is that Vietnamese love anything American, be it Mickey Mouse or Michael Jackson. Long prohibited from doing business in Vietnam by a US-imposed embargo (only lifted in 1994), American companies are now beating a path to what they hope will be Asia's newest economic tiger.

The new American warriors don't wear green uniforms or carry M-16s. Rather, they come in pressed suits, carrying Gucci luggage and laptop computers. Their weapons of choice are cola drinks, Hollywood celluloid and compact discs. Their battle cry is 'Stocks, bonds and rock 'n' roll!'.

Consumerism is now rampant in Vietnam, at least among the relatively affluent. Being called a member of the 'upper crust' (once defined as 'a lot of crumbs held together by dough') is no longer an insult. Making money is OK now. And so is spending it. It's this consumer boom that keeps foreign investors awake at night.

American companies have already splashed ashore. Computers sporting the label 'Intel Inside' are on display in newly opened hi-tech electronic shops. Chrysler has formed a joint-venture to produce its gas-guzzling Jeep Cherokee in Vietnam. Motorola pagers can be heard beeping in the pockets and handbags of Saigon's well-to-do. Pepsi was the first American soft drink vendor to return to Vietnam, but Coke was not far behind.

American fast food should find a ready market among Vietnam's trendy urban elite. McDonald's, when it finally opens a branch in Saigon, will be an instant hit. That is, of

Sign of the times (RE)

course, if nobody clones the name first. Already, Ho Chi Minh City has two fake 7 Elevens.

The Americans, for their part, are displeased with the lack of protection for intellectual property rights. Trademarks, patents and copyrights are violated with impunity by the Vietnamese. The proliferation of pirated music tapes and fake Rolex watches are potential bones of contention. Nothing is sacred – even downsized copies of the Statue of Liberty have popped up in Vietnam's newest avant-garde cafés. Vietnamese who know their history point out that the original Statue of Liberty was a gift to America from France – 'Why', they ask, 'shouldn't we have one too?'. Why not indeed.

On the other hand, the Vietnamese government has so far refused anyone permission to capitalise on Ho Chi Minh's name. A proposal to open an American joint-venture called *Uncle Ho's Hamburgers* went up like a lead balloon. Nor were the Vietnamese persuaded when the American business reps pointed out that Ho Chi Minh does vaguely resemble Colonel Sanders. 'No', said the frowning Vietnamese, 'Ho Chi Minh was a general'. ∎

Speakers for sale (PW)

The government is intent on limiting Vietnam's restructuring *(doi moi)* to the economic sphere, keeping ideas such as pluralism and democracy from undermining the present power structure.

Foreign investors say that their biggest obstacles include the formidable bureaucracy, official incompetence, corruption, nepotism, the high rents which foreigners must pay and the ever-changing rules and regulations. On paper, intellectual property rights are protected, but enforcement is lax – patents, copyrights and trademarks are openly pirated. Tax rates and government fees are frequently revised.

POPULATION & PEOPLE

Population

Officially, Ho Chi Minh City claims a population of 4½ million. In reality, six to seven million is the true figure. The wide discrepancy is explained by the fact that the government census-takers only count those who have official residence permits, but probably one-third of the population lives here 'illegally'. Many of the illegal residents actually lived legally in Saigon prior to 1975 but their residence permits were transferred to rural re-education camps after liberation. Not surprisingly, these people (and now their children and grandchildren) have simply sneaked back into the city, though without a residence permit they cannot own property or a business.

People

Ethnic-Vietnamese The Vietnamese people (called 'Annamites' by the French) developed as a distinct ethnic group between 200 BC and 200 AD through the fusion of a people of Indonesian stock with Viet and Tai immigrants from the north and Chinese who arrived, along with Chinese rule, as of the 2nd century AD. Vietnamese civilisation was profoundly influenced by China and, via Champa and the Khmers, India; but the fact that the Vietnamese were never absorbed by China indicates that a strong local culture existed prior to the 1000 years of Chinese rule, which ended in 938 AD.

Over the past two millennia, the Vietnamese have slowly pushed southward along the narrow coastal strip, defeating the Chams in the 15th century and taking over the Mekong Delta (including present-day Ho Chi Minh City) from the Khmers in the late 17th century.

Ethnic-Chinese The ethnic-Chinese (Hoa) constitute the largest single minority group in Vietnam. Today, most of them live in and around District 5 of Ho Chi Minh City, an area called Cholon before 1975.

The Chinese have organised themselves into communities, known as 'congregations' *(bang)*, according to their ancestors' province of origin and dialect. Important congregations include Fujian (Phuoc Kien in Vietnamese), Cantonese (Quang Dong in Vietnamese or Guangdong in Chinese), Hainan (Hai Nam), Chaozhou (Tieu Chau) and Hakka (Nuoc Hue in Vietnamese or Kejia in Mandarin Chinese).

Indians Almost all of South Vietnam's population of Indians, most of whose roots were in southern India, left in 1975. The remaining community in Ho Chi Minh City worship at the Mariamman Hindu temple and the Central Mosque.

Khmers The number of Khmers (ethnic-Cambodians) is estimated at about 700,000 in Vietnam, but most live south of Ho Chi Minh City in the Mekong Delta region. They practise Hinayana (Theravada) Buddhism.

Chams Vietnam's 60,000 Chams are the remnant of the once-vigorous Indianised kingdom of Champa which flourished from the 2nd to the 15th centuries and was destroyed as the Vietnamese expanded southward. Most of them live along the coast between Nha Trang and Phan Thiet and in the Mekong Delta province of An Giang. The Chams were profoundly influenced by both Hinduism and Buddhism, but most are now Muslims.

The Chams are best known for the many brick sanctuaries (known as 'Cham towers') they constructed all over the southern half of the country. In Ho Chi Minh City, you can see a downsized reproduction of a Cham tower in Cong Vien Van Hoa Park.

Hill Tribes Approximately 55 minority groups occupy the highlands of Vietnam, many of whom are related to Thailand's hill tribes. You may occasionally encounter some of these people in Ho Chi Minh City, but mostly they are rural inhabitants. The French called them *montagnards* (which means 'highlanders'), a term they still use themselves. The Vietnamese often refer to the hill-tribe people as *moi*, a derogatory word meaning 'savages' that unfortunately reflects all-too-common popular attitudes. The present government prefers the term 'national minorities'.

Top : Old man (RI)
Bottom : Flower lady (KO)

Facts about Ho Chi Minh City

Top : Market seller (PW)
Bottom : Young woman with balloons (PW)

ARTS

Film

One of Vietnam's first cinematographic efforts was a newsreel of Ho Chi Minh's 1945 proclamation of independence. After Dien Bien Phu, parts of the battle were restaged for the benefit of movie cameras.

Prior to reunification, the South Vietnamese movie industry concentrated on producing sensational, low-budget flicks using techniques learned from Hollywood. Until recently, most North Vietnamese film-making efforts have been dedicated to 'the mobilisation of the masses for economic reconstruction, the building of socialism and the struggle for national reunification'. Predictable themes include 'workers devoted to socialist industrialisation', 'old mothers who continuously risk their lives to help the people's army' and 'children who are ready to face any danger'.

The relaxation of ideological censorship of the arts has proceeded in fits and starts, but the last few years has seen a gradual easing of restrictions. However, paranoia about evil foreign influence means the government still keeps the film industry on a tight leash. One film worth seeing that has been successful overseas is *The Scent of Green Papaya*.

Music & Dance

Each of Vietnam's ethnic minorities has its own musical and dance traditions which often include colourful costumes and instruments such as reed flutes, lithophones (similar to xylophones), bamboo whistles, gongs and stringed instruments made from gourds. Ho Chi Minh City has a music conservatory teaching both traditional Vietnamese and Western classical music.

Bizarrely, most of the world's Vietnamese pop music originates in California, the home of numerous Overseas Vietnamese. One reason why Vietnam itself produces so few local music tapes is because all music tapes are instantly pirated, thus depriving the singing stars of the revenue they would need to survive. As a result, only Overseas Vietnamese are economically secure enough to pursue a career in music.

Theatre & Puppetry

There are many kinds of Vietnamese theatre featuring singing, dancing and storytelling. However, foreigners are most interested in that uniquely Vietnamese art form, water puppetry *(roi nuoc)*, in which lacquered wooden puppets, around 50 cm high, are manipulated by rods to make them appear to be walking on the water surface. It is thought that water puppetry developed when determined puppeteers in the Red River Delta (northern Vietnam) managed to carry on with the show despite flooding. Often shows were performed in village ponds, which greatly enhanced their magical effect. These days, the various forms of Vietnamese theatre are performed by dozens of state-funded troupes and companies around the country. In Ho Chi Minh City, water puppetry can be seen at the History Museum, which is within the grounds of the zoo.

Architecture

The Vietnamese have not been great builders like their predecessors, the Chams, whose brick towers grace many parts of the southern half of the country. Most Vietnamese architecture has used wood and other materials that proved highly vulnerable in the tropical climate.

Plenty of pagodas and temples founded hundreds of years ago are still functioning but their physical plan has usually been rebuilt many times, with little concern for making the upgraded structure an exact copy of the original. As a result, modern elements have been casually introduced into pagoda architecture; neon haloes for statues of the Buddha are only the most glaring example of this.

Because of the Vietnamese custom of ancestor-worship, many graves from previous centuries are still extant. These include temples erected in memory of high-ranking mandarins, members of the royal family, emperors and, most recently, Ho Chi Minh.

Sculpture

Vietnamese sculpture has traditionally centred on religious themes and functioned as an adjunct to architecture, especially that of pagodas, temples and tombs. Many inscribed stelae, erected hundreds of years ago to commemorate the founding of a pagoda or important national events, can still be seen.

Lacquerware

The art of making exquisite lacquerware was brought to Vietnam from China in the mid-15th century. Before that time, the Vietnamese used lacquer solely for practical

Top : Lacquered box (GB)
Middle : Water puppets (PW)
Bottom : Modern architecture (RS)

Top : Sculpture, Art Museum (RS)
Bottom : Revolutionary art, Art Museum (RS)

purposes such as making things watertight. Designs are routinely added by engraving in low relief, by painting, or by inlaying mother-of-pearl, eggshell, silver or even gold.

Ceramics

The production of ceramics has a long history in Vietnam. In ancient times, ceramic objects were made by coating a wicker mould with clay and baking it. Later, ceramics production became very refined, and each dynastic period is known for its particular techniques and motifs.

Painting

Traditional Painting done on frame-mounted silk dates from the 13th century. Silk-painting was at one time the preserve of scholar-calligraphers, who also painted scenes from nature. Before the advent of photography, realistic portraits for use in ancestor-worship were produced. Some of these – usually of former head monks – can still be seen in Buddhist pagodas.

Modern During this century, Vietnamese painting has been influenced by Western trends. Much of the recent work done in Vietnam has had political rather than aesthetic or artistic motives. According to an official account, the fighting of the Vietnam War provided painters with 'rich human material: people's army combatants facing the jets, peasant and factory women in the militia who handled guns as well as they did their production work, young volunteers who repaired roads in record time...old mothers offering tea to anti-aircraft gunners...'. There's lots of this stuff at the Art Museum in Ho Chi Minh City.

Recent economic liberalisation has convinced many young artists to abandon the revolutionary themes and concentrate on producing commercially saleable paintings. Some have gone back to the traditional silk paintings, while others are experimenting with new subjects. Nudes are popular, which might indicate either an attempt to appeal to Western tastes or an expression of long-suppressed desires.

The cheaper stuff (US$10 to US$30) gets spun off to gift shops and street markets. Higher-standard works are put on display in some of the government-run art galleries such as the Ho Chi Minh City Association of Fine Arts (☎ 230025), 218 Nguyen Thi Minh Khai, District 1. Typical prices are in the US$30 to US$100 range, though the artists may ask 10 times that. It's important to know that there are quite a few forgeries around – just because you spot a painting by a 'famous Vietnamese artist' does not mean that it's an original, though it may still be an attractive work of art.

SOCIETY & CONDUCT

Traditional Culture

Geomancy Geomancy is the art (or science if you prefer) of manipulating or judging the environment. If you want to build a house or find a suitable site for a grave, then you call in a geomancer. The orientation of houses, communal meeting halls, tombs and pagodas is determined by geomancers, which is why cemeteries have tombstones turned every which way. The location of an ancestor's grave is an especially serious matter – if the grave is in the wrong spot or facing the wrong way, then there is no telling what trouble the spirits may cause.

Businesses that are failing call in a geomancer. Sometimes the solution is to move the door or a window. If this does not do the trick, it might be necessary to move an ancestor's grave. Distraught spirits may have to be placated with payments of cash (donated to a temple), especially if one wishes to erect a building or other structure which blocks the spirits' view.

The concept of geomancy is believed to have originated with the Chinese. Although the Communists (both Chinese and Vietnamese) have disparaged geomancy as superstition, it still has an influence on people's behaviour.

Lunar Calendar The Vietnamese lunar calendar closely resembles the Chinese one. Year 1 of the Vietnamese lunar calendar corresponds to 2637 BC, and each lunar month has 29 or 30 days, resulting in years with 355 days. Approximately every third year is a leap year; an extra month is added between the third and fourth months to keep the lunar year in sync with the solar year. If this weren't done, you'd end up having the seasons gradually rotate around the lunar year, playing havoc with all elements of life linked to the agricultural seasons. To find out the Gregorian (solar) date corresponding to a lunar date, check any Vietnamese or Chinese calendar.

The Vietnamese animal zodiac has 12 signs, based on the lunar year rather than the solar month (as in Western astrology). This text was written in 1995, the Year of the

Pig. Children born in this year are said to be noble and chivalrous, with lifelong friends but frequent marital strife. For more details, see a fortune-teller.

To give you an idea of what's coming, consider the following:

Rat 1996, Ox/Cow 1997, Tiger 1998, Rabbit 1999, Dragon 2000, Snake 2001, Horse 2002, Goat 2003, Monkey 2004, Rooster 2005, Dog 2006, Pig 2007.

Appearance & Conduct

Dress The graceful national dress of Vietnamese women is known as the ao dai (pronounced 'ow-yai'). It consists of a close-fitting blouse with long panels in the front and back that is worn over loose black or white trousers.

Ao dais have been around a long time, and in the beginning they were anything but revealing. But in the past few years partially see-through ao dais have become all the rage – it's doubtful that even Western women would wear something so provocative.

Traditionally, men have also worn ao dais, but nowadays you are only likely to see this in the theatre or at traditional music performances.

Beauty Concepts The Vietnamese consider pale skin to be beautiful. On sunny days trendy Vietnamese women can often be seen strolling under the shade of an umbrella in order to keep from tanning. As in 19th-century Europe, peasants get tanned and those who can

Women dressed in ao dais (HS)

afford it do not. Women who work in the fields will go to great lengths to preserve their pale skin by wearing long-sleeved shirts, gloves, a conical hat and wrapping their face in a towel.

Name Cards Name cards are very popular in Ho Chi Minh City and, like elsewhere in east Asia, exchanging business cards is an important part of even the smallest transaction or business contact. Get some printed before you arrive in Vietnam and hand them out like confetti.

Deadly Chopsticks Leaving a pair of chopsticks sticking vertically in a rice bowl looks very similar to the incense sticks which are burned for the dead. This is a powerful death sign and is not appreciated anywhere in the Orient.

Mean Feet It's rude to let the bottom of your feet point towards other people except maybe with close friends. When sitting on the floor, you should fold your legs into the lotus position so you're not pointing your soles at others. And most importantly, never point your feet towards anything sacred such as figures of the Buddha.

In formal situations, when sitting on a chair do not sit with your legs crossed.

Keep Your Hat in Your Hand As a form of respect to the elderly or other people regarded with respect (monks etc), take off your hat and bow your head politely when addressing them.

Pity the Unmarried Telling the Vietnamese that you are single or divorced and enjoying a life without children will disturb them greatly. Not having a family is regarded as bad luck, and such people are to be pitied, not envied. Almost every Vietnamese will ask if you are married and have children. If you are young and single, simply say you are 'not yet married' and that will be accepted. If you are not so young (over 30) and unmarried, it's better to lie. Divorce is scandalous.

Also, don't be too inquisitive about other people's family problems such as divorce, death, etc (even if they are inquisitive about yours). Failure in family life is a major loss of face, and loss of family members through death is the ultimate tragedy. The discussion of such tragedies is to be avoided.

Face Having 'big face' is synonymous with prestige, and prestige is important in the Orient. All families, even poor ones, are expected to have big wedding parties and throw around money like water, in order to gain face. This is often ruinously expensive, but the fact that the wedding results in bankruptcy for the young couple is far less important than losing face.

A certain amount of generosity would also be expected of foreigners in a business context, such as holding banquets for potential business partners, though gratuitous displays of largesse would not be appreciated.

Smile Asians say that Westerners tend to speak too frankly and are rude and inconsiderate of the feelings of others. Perhaps this is unfair criticism, but you can certainly find Westerners flying off the handle when things go wrong (as they inevitably do) when travelling in Vietnam.

In most of the Orient, including Vietnam, people put much value on being pleasant and smiling a lot. Gruff criticism and complaints are to be avoided. Be sure that you don't make others lose face. But if you want to criticise someone, do it in a joking manner to avoid confrontation. Expect delays – build them into your schedule. And never show anger. Getting visibly upset is not only rude – it will cause you to lose face.

And finally, don't act as though you deserve service from anyone. If you do, it's likely that you will be delayed.

RELIGION

Three great philosophies and religions, Confucianism, Taoism and Buddhism, have fused with Vietnamese animism and popular Chinese beliefs such as ancestor-worship to form what is known collectively as the 'Triple Religion', or Tam Giao. About 90% of the population could be considered in this category. The pagodas in Ho Chi Minh City thus contain a mixture of deities, with Chinese gods and the various manifestations of the Buddha predominating.

Today, Vietnam has the highest percentage of Catholics in Asia (8% to 10% of the population) outside the Philippines, and there is also a small minority of Protestants.

The Hoa Hao sect, which is strictly Buddhist, constitutes 2% of the population.

Caodaism is an indigenous Vietnamese sect that claims roughly 2% of the population as its members.

Muslims – mostly ethnic-Khmers and Chams – constitute about 0.5% of Vietnam's population. Champa was profoundly influenced by Hinduism, but after the fall of Champa in the 15th century, most Chams who remained in Vietnam became Muslims. However, they continue to practise various Brahmanic (high-caste Hindu) rituals and customs.

LANGUAGE

The Vietnamese language is a fusion of Mon-Khmer, Tai and Chinese elements. For centuries, the Vietnamese language was written in standard Chinese characters. The Latin-based quoc ngu script, in wide use since WW I, was developed in the 17th century by Alexandre de Rhodes, a brilliant French Jesuit scholar who first preached in Vietnamese only six months after arriving in the country in 1627. By replacing Chinese characters with quoc ngu, de Rhodes facilitated the propagation of the gospel to a wide audience.

The Vietnamese treat every syllable as an independent word, so 'Saigon' gets spelled 'Sai Gon' and 'Vietnam' is written as 'Viet Nam'.

The most widely spoken foreign languages in Vietnam are Chinese (Cantonese and Mandarin), English and French, more or less in that order. Many of the Vietnamese who speak fluent English learned it while working with the Americans during the Vietnam War. These days, almost everyone has a desire to learn English. If you're looking to make contact with English students, the best place is at the basic food stalls around university areas.

Phrasebooks

A phrasebook can be very useful at crucial moments – don't leave home without it!

Lonely Planet has a *Vietnamese phrasebook*, with complete lists of useful words and phrases in Vietnamese, so you can make the most of your travels.

Lonely Planet also has a *Vietnamese audio pack*, companion to the phrasebook, available on CD or cassette.

Pronunciation & Tones

Most of the names of the letters of the quoc ngu alphabet are pronounced in the same way as the letters of the French alphabet. Dictionaries are alphabetised as in English except that each vowel/tone combination is treated as a different letter. The consonants of the

Romanised Vietnamese alphabet are pronounced more or less as they are in English with a few exceptions, and Vietnamese makes no use of the Roman letters f, j, w and z.

c	like a 'k' but with no aspiration
đ	with a crossbar; like a hard 'd'
d	without a crossbar; like a 'y'
gi-	like a 'y'
kh-	like '-ch' in the German *Buch*
ng-	like the '-nga-' in 'long ago'
nh-	like Spanish 'ñ' (as in *mañana)*
ph-	like an 'f'
s	like a 'sh'
th-	like a strongly aspirated 't'
x	like an 's'
-ch	like a 'k'
-ng	as in 'long', but with lips closed
-nh	like '-ng' in 'sing'

The hardest part of studying Vietnamese for Westerners is learning to differentiate between the tones. There are six tones in spoken Vietnamese. Thus, every syllable in Vietnamese can be pronounced six different ways. For example, depending on the tone, the word *ma* can be read to mean phantom, but, mother, rice seedling, tomb or horse. *Ga* can mean railroad station and chicken as well as several other things.

The six tones of spoken Vietnamese are indicated with five diacritical marks in written form (the first tone is left unmarked). These should not be confused with the four other diacritical marks used to indicate special consonants (such as the 'd' with a cross through it).

ma	phantom
má	mother
mà	but
mả	tomb
mã	horse
mạ	rice seedling

A visual representation of these looks something like this:

Proper Names

Most Vietnamese names consist of a family name, a middle name and a given name, in that order. Thus, if Henry David Thoreau had been Vietnamese, he would have been named Thoreau David Henry. He would have been addressed as Mr Henry – people are called by their given name, but to do so without the title Mr, Mrs or Miss is considered as expressing either intimacy or arrogance of the sort a superior would use with an inferior.

In Vietnamese, Mr is *Ong* if the man is of your grandparents' generation, *Bac* if he is of your parents' age, *Chu* if he is younger than your parents and *Anh* if he is in his teens or early 20s. Mrs is *Ba* if the woman is of your grandparents' age and *Bac* if she is of your parents' generation or younger. Miss is *Chi* or *Em* unless the woman is very young, in which case *Co* might be more appropriate. Other titles of respect are for a Buddhist monk *(Thay)*, Buddhist nun *(Ba)*, Catholic priest *(Cha)* and Catholic nun *(Co)*.

There are 300 or so family names in use in Vietnam, the most common of which is Nguyen (pronounced something like 'nwyen'). About half of all Vietnamese have the surname Nguyen!

To get you started, following are some useful survival words and phrases.

Pronouns

(The word *các* indicates the plural form of 'you.')

I	*tôi*
you (to an older man)	*(các) ông*
you (to an older woman)	*(các) bà*
you (to a man your age)	*(các) anh*
you (to a woman your age)	*(các) chị*
you (to a woman, formal)	*(các) cô*
you (to a younger person)	*(các) em*
he	*ông ấy/anh ấy*
she	*chị ấy/cô ấy*
we	*chúng tôi*
they	*họ*

Greetings & Civilities

Hello.	*Xin chào.*
Goodbye.	*Chào* (+ pronoun).
How are you?	*Có khoẻ không*
Fine, thank you.	*Khoẻ, cám ơn.*
Thank you (very much).	*Cám ơn (rất nhiều).*
Excuse me	*Xin lỗi.*

Useful Words & Phrases

What is your name?
Tên ông là gì?
My name is...
Tên tôi là...
I am from...
Tôi đến từ...
What does this mean?
Cái này nghĩa là gì?
I (don't) like...
Tôi (không) thích...
I (don't) understand.
Tôi (không) hiểu.
I need...
Tôi cần...

Yes.	*Dạ.*
No.	*Không.*
understand	*hiểu*
to change money	*đổi tiền*
man	*nam*
woman	*nữ*

Getting Around

I want to go to...
Tôi muốn đi...
What time does the bus arrive?
Mấy giờ xe buýt đến?
What time does the train depart?
Mấy giờ xe lửa khơi hành?
to hire an automobile
muớn xe hơi

Where is the...	*... ơ đâu?*
bus station	*bến xe*
railway station	*ga xe lửa*
airport	*phi trường*
How much is...?	*Già bao nhiêu...?*
a return fare	*vé khử hồi*
a one-way ticket	*vé một chuyến*

to go	*đi*
cyclo (pedicab)	*xe xích lô*
map	*bản đồ*
sleeping berth	*giường ngủ*
timetable	*thời biểu*
1st class	*hạng nhất*
2nd class	*hạng nhì*

Accommodation

Where is there a (cheap) hotel?
O đâu có khách sạn (rẻ tiền)?
How much does a room cost?
Giá một phòng là bao nhiêu?
I would like a cheap room.
Tôi thích một phòng loại rẻ.
I don't like this room.
Tôi không thích phòng này.

air-conditioning	*máy lạnh*
bathroom	*phòng tắm*
blanket	*mền*
fan	*quạt máy*
guesthouse	*nhà khách*
hotel	*khách sạn*
hot water	*nước nóng*
laundry	*giặt ủi*
mosquito net	*mùng*
reception	*tiếp tân*
room	*phòng*
room key	*chìa khóa phòng*
sheet	*ra trãi giường*
toilet	*nhà vệ sinh*
toilet paper	*giấy vệ sinh*
towel	*khăn tắm*

Around Town

I'm looking for the...	*Tôi đang tìm...*
bank	*ngân hàng*
embassy	*tò đại sứ*
market	*chợ*
office	*văn phòng*
post office	*bưu điện*
restaurant	*nhà hàng*
telephone	*điện thoại*
street	*đường, phố*
boulevard	*đại lộ*
bridge	*cầu*
city square	*công viên*
public toilet	*nhà vệ sinh công cộng*
tourist info office	*phòng hướng dẫn du lịch*

east	*đông*
north	*bắc*
south	*nam*
west	*tây*

Shopping

I would like to buy...
Tôi muốn mua...
How much is this?
Cái này giá bao nhiêu?
I want to pay in dong.
Tôi muốn trả bằng tiền Việt Nam.

too big	*quá lớn*
too small	*quá nhỏ*
cheap	*rẻ tiền*
expensive	*mắc tiền*
very expensive	*mắc quá*
bookshop	*nhà sách*
clothing store	*tiệm áo quần*
pharmacy	*nhà thuốc tây*
souvenir shop	*tiệm bán đồ kỷ niệm*
mosquito coils	*nhang chống muỗi*
insect repellent	*thuốc chống muỗi*
sanitary pads	*băng vệ sinh*
condoms	*bao ngừa thai*
film (camera)	*phim*
cigarettes	*thuốc lá*
newspaper	*báo*

Numbers

1	*một*
2	*hai*
3	*ba*
4	*bốn*
5	*năm*
6	*sáu*
7	*bảy*
8	*tám*
9	*chín*
10	*mười*
11	*mười một*
19	*mười chín*
20	*hai mươi*
21	*hai mươi mốt*
30	*ba mươi*
90	*chín mươi*
100	*một trăm*
1000	*một ngàn*
10,000	*mười ngàn*
1 million	*một triệu*
first	*thứ nhất*
second	*thứ hai*

Health

I'm sick.
Tôi bị đau.
Please take me to the hospital.
Làm ơn đưa tôi bệnh viện.
Please call a doctor.
Làm ơn gọi bác sĩ.

I'm allergic to...   *Tôi bị dị ứng với...*
  antibiotics   *thuốc kháng sinh*
  penicillin   *thuốc pê-ni-xi-lin*

backache	*đau lưng*
dentist	*nha sĩ*
doctor	*bác sĩ*
diarrhoea	*ỉa chảy*
dizziness	*chóng mặt*
fever	*cảm, cúm*
headache	*nhức đầu*
hospital	*bệnh viện*
malaria	*sốt rét*
pharmacy	*nhà thuốc tây*
stomachache	*đau bụng*
toothache	*nhức răng*
vomiting	*ói, mửa*

Emergencies

Help!	*Cứu tôi với !*
Thief!	*Cướp, cắp!*
Pickpocket!	*Móc túi!*
I didn't do it.	*Tôi không là việc ấy.*
I'm sorry.	*Xin lỗi.*
police	*công an*
immigration police	*phòng quản lý ngườ nước ngoài*

Facts for the Visitor

ORIENTATION

The downtown section of Ho Chi Minh City, now officially called District 1, is still known as Saigon. In the south, most people use the terms 'Saigon' and 'Ho Chi Minh City' interchangeably. In the north, people toe the official line and almost everyone will 'correct' you if you say 'Saigon'. Since most government officials are from the north, you'd be wise to say 'Ho Chi Minh City' whenever dealing with them.

To the west of the centre is District 5, the huge Chinese neighbourhood called Cholon which some people will tell you means 'Chinatown'. In fact, Cholon means 'Big Market' in Vietnamese, though its Chinese name *(di an)* means 'embankment'. Cholon rose to prominence after Chinese merchants began settling there in 1778. These days it's also known as Ho Chi Minh City's 'copy centre', the source of pirated videos and counterfeit 'Swiss' watches.

Urban orienteering is very easy in Ho Chi Minh City since Vietnamese is written with a Latin-based alphabet. Street names are sometimes abbreviated on street signs to just the initials ('DBP' for 'Dien Bien Phu St' etc). Unfortunately, the numbering can be a problem. In some places, consecutive buildings are numbered 15A, 15B, 15C and so forth, while elsewhere, consecutive addresses read 15D, 17D, 19D, etc. Most streets have even numbers on one side and odd numbers on the other, but number 75 can be three blocks down the street from number 76. Often, two numbering systems – the old confusing one and the new confusing one – are in use simultaneously, so that an address may read '1743/697'. In some cases several streets, numbered separately, have been run together under one name so that as you walk along, the numbers go from one into the hundreds (or thousands) and then start over again.

Many restaurants are named after their street addresses. For instance, 'Nha Hang 51 Nguyen Hue' *(nha hang* means restaurant) is at No 51 Nguyen Hue St.

MAPS

Reasonably detailed colour maps of Ho Chi Minh City are on sale everywhere. One popular map shows modern Ho Chi Minh City on one side, while the reverse side is a map of old Saigon as it appeared before liberation. If you buy one of these maps for navigation, be careful about reading the wrong side – quite a few things have changed since 1975.

TOURIST OFFICES

Local Tourist Offices

The municipal and national governments operate profitable travel agencies masquerading as tourist offices. While you might be able to squeeze some useful information out of these agencies, their sole reason for existence is to separate tourists from their cash.

Saigon Tourist is Ho Chi Minh City's official government-run travel agency. Saigon Tourist owns or is a joint-venture partner in nearly 100 hotels and numerous high-class restaurants, plus tourist traps such as the Cu Chi Tunnel site and Binh Quoi Tourist Village, to name a few. The agency also rents out cars, boats, tour guides and drivers.

The way Saigon Tourist got so big is simple: the hotels and restaurants were 'liberated' from their former capitalist (mostly ethnic-Chinese) owners after 1975, most of whom subsequently fled the country. The upper-level management of this state company are entirely former Viet Cong (no kidding) and their attitude towards foreigners is still decidedly cool. None of this is to say that Saigon Tourist doesn't know how to do business. Indeed, the company keeps growing bigger – if Vietnam ever establishes a stock market, Saigon Tourist shares will be blue chip.

Vietnam Tourism is the national government's tourist agency. While Vietnam Tourism operates branch offices all over the country, Saigon Tourist holds the lion's share of the tourist business in Ho Chi Minh City. Both agencies do their best to overcharge for their mediocre service.

You can contact Saigon Tourist or Vietnam Tourism at the following locations:

Saigon Tourist
   49 Le Thanh Ton St, District 1 (☎ 298914; fax 224987)
Vietnam Tourism
   234 Nam Ky Khoi Nghia St, District 3 (☎ 290776; fax 290775)

Tourist Offices Abroad

France
Vietnam Tourism, 4 rue Cherubini, 75002 Paris (☎ (01) 42.86.86.37; fax 42.60.43.32)
Saigon Tourist, 24 rue des Bernadins, 75005 Paris (☎ (01) 40.51.03.02; fax 43.25.05.70)

Germany
Saigon Tourist, 24 Dudenstrasse 78 W, 1000 Berlin 61 (☎ (030) 786-5056; fax 786-5596)

Japan
Saigon Tourist, IDI 6th floor, Crystal Building, 1-2 Kanda Awaji-cho, Chiyoda-ku, Tokyo 101 (☎ (03) 3258-5931; fax 3253-6819)

Singapore
Vietnam Tourism, 101 Upper Cross St, No 02-44 People's Park Centre, Singapore 0105 (☎ 532-3130; fax 532-2952; pager 601-3914)
Saigon Tourist, 131 Tanglin Rd, Tudor Court, Singapore 1024 (☎ 735-1433; fax 735-1508)

DOCUMENTS

Visas

In most cases you are better off getting your visa from a travel agent rather than from the Vietnamese embassy directly. This is because all visas issued by embassies will be stamped directly into your passport, while travel agencies will get them on a separate piece of paper (as long as you don't hand over your passport to the agency). In most cases, having your visa on a separate paper will prove safer. The reason is because within Vietnam itself you will often be required to leave your visa with the hotel reception desk, the immigration police or with bureaucratic ministries of every sort. Replacing a lost visa will be a major hassle but still *much* easier than replacing your entire passport.

The travel agency doing your visa needs a photocopy of your passport (you keep the original!) and three photos.

Bangkok (especially Khao San Rd) has always been the most convenient place to get Vietnamese visas. In Bangkok, single-entry tourist visas cost US$40 at budget travel agencies. Beijing, by contrast, is known to be the worst place to apply for a Vietnamese visa.

Tourist Visas Processing a visa application takes five working days in Bangkok and most other Asian countries, though it takes 10 days in Taiwan because of a lack of official diplomatic relations. In most Western countries, 10 days will also be required.

Visas are normally valid for 30 days from the date you specify, so you must let your travel agent know just when you plan to enter Vietnam. You must also decide on your port of entry (Ho Chi Minh City or Hanoi, but your visa can be stamped for both) because this will be written on the visa. Vietnamese visas also specify where you must exit the country, though this can be changed within Vietnam at the immigration police, Interior Ministry or the Foreign Ministry.

Theoretically, you can enter Vietnam with a sponsor's letter and get your visa stamped into your passport on arrival for US$25. This 'visa on arrival' process is fraught with risks and not recommended. There have been many cases of travellers arriving with these letters which were then arbitrarily rejected by the immigration authorities. Many airlines will not accept these sponsor's letters in lieu of a visa and deny you permission to board the aircraft. But if you want to try it, you need the right cash (US dollars only in the exact amount) because there is no place to change money before you pass through immigration.

Airport immigration staff have complete authority to decide on how long you can stay. Don't uncork the champagne until you've passed immigration and checked what they stamped on the back of your visa – the staff may arbitrarily give you a shorter stay than what your visa calls for! Your 30-day visa might only be validated for one week, or a three-month visa for just one month. If you've only been given a week, sometimes you can get it changed right at the immigration queue – otherwise, you will be forced to visit the immigration police and apply for an extension.

Always have some photos with you because immigration officials have been known to inexplicably give travellers more forms to fill out and photos are required. However, there is a photographer at the airport to serve you – for a substantial fee.

Business Visas Business visas have three advantages: they are usually valid for three months, can be issued for multiple-entry journeys and automatically give you the right to legally seek employment in Vietnam. At least, that is the situation at the time of this writing – the rules could change tomorrow.

The same travel agencies which do tourist visas can also arrange business visas. These are easy to get, but a business visa costs about four times what you'd pay for a tourist visa. Immigration officials may arbitrarily validate your visa for one month upon arrival even though a business visa is good for three months.

There is another category of business visa which remains valid for six months. To get these, you must apply in Vietnam. If approved, you must then go abroad (most travellers go to Phnom Penh) to pick up the visa from a Vietnamese embassy.

Student Visas A student visa is something you usually arrange after arrival. It's acceptable to enter Vietnam on a tourist visa, enrol in a Vietnamese language course and then apply at the immigration police for a change in status. Of course, you do have to pay tuition and are expected to attend class. A minimum of 10 hours of study per week is needed to qualify for student status.

Resident Visas Only a few foreigners can qualify for a resident visa. Probably the easiest way to do this is to marry a local, though anyone contemplating doing this had best be prepared for mountains of paperwork. Spouses of Vietnamese nationals gain a few other legal advantages besides a resident visa – for example, they can own 50% of the couple's property (including real estate).

Resident visas currently cost US$170 for six months, plus US$170 for each extension.

Visa Extensions

You can legally extend your visa in any provincial capital, and in some places the authorities are considerably easier to deal with than the Ho Chi Minh City immigration police. Vung Tau authorities have a better reputation than those in Ho Chi Minh City, and the police in isolated backwaters have sometimes proven to be amazingly helpful and efficient.

In Ho Chi Minh Cit,y first-time visa extensions cost US$20 and subsequent ones are US$35. You must apply through a travel agency, not directly to the police. There is in fact no law which says you must use the services of a travel agency, but the Ho Chi Minh City police will not cooperate if you apply to them directly.

For what it's worth, the immigration police office is at 254 Nguyen Trai St. It's open from 8 to 11 am and 1 to 4 pm.

The extension procedure takes one or two days and one photo is needed. You can apply for your extension several weeks before it's necessary. Official policy is that you are permitted two visa extensions, each one for the same length of time as your original visa. So, that means a 30-day visa can be extended twice, permitting you 90 days in total before you leave the country. If you entered Vietnam on a 90-day visa, you should be able to extend twice for a total of 270 days.

Usually the first extension goes OK if you work through an agent who has good connections and knows which palms to grease. Sometimes things inexplicably go wrong. The Ho Chi Minh City immigration police have been known to refuse a second extension unless you also got your first extension from them. Again, no law says it is supposed to be this way – the immigration police make their own laws:

I got my visa extension in Vinh which only cost US$2, but in Ho Chi Minh City I was later told that this was invalid. The police cancelled my first extension, forced me to buy a second one plus I had to pay a US$10 fine for overstaying 13 days. I also lost three days dealing with the bureaucracy.

Gerhard Heinzel

The official word is that even if you do get your visa extension in some obscure backwater (such as Vinh), the airport immigration police *will* accept it and allow you to depart with no problems.

Re-Entry Visas

If you wish to visit Cambodia, Laos or any other country, it is possible to do this and then re-enter Vietnam using your original single-entry Vietnamese visa. However, you must apply for a re-entry visa before departing Vietnam. If you do not have a re-entry visa, then you will have to go through the whole expensive and time-consuming procedure of applying for a new Vietnamese visa.

Re-entry visas are easy enough to arrange in Ho Chi Minh City, but you will almost certainly have to ask a travel agent to do the paperwork for you. Travel agents charge about US$10 to US$20 for this service and can complete the procedure in one or two days. Although travellers can theoretically secure the re-entry visa without going through a travel agent, Vietnamese bureaucrats usually thwart such individual efforts.

Remember that your re-entry visa also must show the point where you intend to re-enter Vietnam. So if you fly from Vietnam to Cambodia and want to re-enter overland, your re-entry visa must indicate this. However, the Vietnamese Embassy in Cambodia can amend this if you didn't get it right the first time.

If you already have a valid multiple-entry visa for Vietnam, you do not need a re-entry visa.

Travel Insurance

Although you may have insurance in your own country, it is probably not valid in Vietnam. A travel insurance policy is a very good idea – to protect you against cancellation penalties on advance purchase flights, against medical costs through illness or injury, against theft or loss of possessions, and against the cost of additional air tickets if you get really sick and have to fly home. Read the small print carefully since it's easy to be caught out by exclusions.

If you undergo medical treatment, be sure to collect all receipts and copies of your medical report, in English if possible, for your insurance company. If you get robbed, you'll need a police report (good luck) if you want to collect from your insurance company.

Driver's Licence

If you plan to be driving abroad, get an International Driver's Licence from your local automobile association or motor vehicle department. In many countries, these are valid for one year only. However, some countries will issue International Driver's Licences valid for several years – it just depends on where you live. Make sure that your licence states that it is valid for motorcycles if you plan to drive one.

Student & Youth Cards

These cards are of no use whatsoever within Vietnam, but are sometimes useful for extracting discounts from international airlines. To qualify, you need to prove you are a full-time student (some sort of official letter is needed). The most widely recognised card is the International Student Identity Card (ISIC). There are also Teacher Cards (ISTC). To get these cards, inquire at your campus.

STA Travel issues STA Youth Cards to persons aged 13 to 26 years.

Health Certificates

Useful (though not essential) is an International Health Certificate to record any vaccinations you've had. These can also be issued in Vietnam.

Miscellaneous

Make photocopies of your passport and Vietnamese visa. The reason for doing this is that in Vietnam you are almost certain to encounter people who want to take your documents away from you. This is particularly true of hotel clerks – they say they need your passport to register you with the police. In Ho Chi Minh City such police registration is *not* required. In most cases the only motive is to make sure you pay your hotel bill and don't steal the towels. Some hotels will accept photocopies, but most will not. Once you've handed over your passport and/or visa, this leaves you with no documentation at all.

At least photocopies give you something to show to the authorities (the police, the railway ticket office, etc) while the hotel holds your original documents. And if the worst comes to the worst, photocopies are helpful if the hotel manages to lose them. When police stop you on the street and ask to see your passport, give them the photocopy rather than the original, and explain that the hotel has your original. Entrusting your documents to the police always puts you in a very vulnerable position.

If you're travelling with your spouse, a photocopy of your marriage licence just might come in handy should you become involved with the law, hospitals or other bureaucratic authorities.

If you're planning on working or studying in Vietnam, it could be helpful to have copies of transcripts, diplomas, letters of reference and other professional qualifications.

A collection of small photos for visas (about 10 should be sufficient) will be useful for dealing with the bureaucracy. These photos must have a neutral background.

Local enterprise (PW)

EMBASSIES

Vietnamese Embassies Abroad

Australia
    6 Timbarra Crescent, O'Malley, Canberra, ACT 2603 (☎ (06) 286-6058; fax 286-4534)
Belgium
    Ave de la Floride 130, 1180 Brussels (☎ 374-9370; fax 374-9376)
Cambodia
    Son Ngoc Minh area (opposite 749 Achar Mean Blvd), Phnom Penh (☎ 25481)
Canada
    695 Davidson Drive, Gloucester, Ottawa, Ontario K1J 6L7 (☎ 744-0698; fax 744-1709)
China
    32 Guangua Lu, Jianguomen Wai, Beijing (☎ 532-1125)
    Canton Consulate: (☎ (020) 776-9555 ext 101, 604; fax 767-9000)
Egypt
    Omar Tasson Mormdeoine, Cairo, Kitkattmail (☎ 344-2123)
France
    62-66 rue de Boileau, Paris 16 (☎ 45.24.50.63; fax 45.24.39.48)
Germany
    Konstantinstrasse 37, Bonn (☎ 357-0201)
India
    17 Kautilya Marg Chanakyapury, Delhi (☎ 301-7714)
Indonesia
    Jalan Teuku Umar 25, Jakarta (☎ 310-0358; fax 310-0350))
Italy
    Piazza Barberini 12, 00187 Rome (☎ 475-5286)
Japan
    50-11 Moto Yoyogi-cho, Shibuya-ku, Tokyo 151 (☎ 3466-3311)
Korea (South)
    33-1 Hannam-dong, Yong-gu, Seoul (☎ 794-3570)
Laos
    1 Thap Luang Rd, Vientiane (☎ 5578)
Malaysia
    4 Pesiaran Stonor, Kuala Lumpur (☎ 484036; fax 483270)
Myanmar (Burma)
    30 Komin Kochin Rd, Yangon (☎ 50361)
Philippines
    54 Victor Cruz, Malate, Metro Manila (☎ 500364, 508101)
Thailand
    83/1 Wireless (Withayu) Rd, Bangkok (☎ 251-7201)
UK
    12-14 Victoria Rd, London W8 5RD (☎ 937-1912; fax 9376108)
USA
    Vietnamese Liaison Office, Washington DC (☎ (800) 874-5100)

Foreign Consulates

Australia
    Landmark Building, 5B Ton Duc Thang St, District 1
    Trade Office: 4 Dong Khoi St, District 1 (☎ 299387)
Belgium
    236 Dien Bien Phu St, District 3 (☎ 294527)
Cambodia
    124 Nguyen Dinh Chieu St, District 3 (☎ 295818)
    Trade Office: 180 Dien Bien Phu St, District 3 (☎ 296814)
Canada
    No 303, 203 Dong Khoi St, District 1 (☎ 242000 ext 3320)
China
    39 Nguyen Thi Minh Khai St, District 3 (☎ 292457, 292463)
France
    27 Xo Viet Nghe Tinh St, District 3 (☎ 297231)
    Trade Office: 75 Tran Quoc Thao St, District 3 (☎ 296056)
Germany
    126 Nguyen Dinh Chieu St, District 3 (☎ 291967)
Indonesia
    18 Phung Khac Khoan St, District 1 (☎ 223799)
Italy
    4 Dong Khoi St, District 1 (☎ 298721)
Japan
    13-17 Nguyen Hue St, District 1 (☎ 225314)
Korea (South)
    107 Nguyen Du St, District 1 (☎ 225757)
Laos
    181 Hai Ba Trung St, District 3 (☎ 297667)
Malaysia
    53 Nguyen Dinh Chieu St, District 3 (☎ 299023)
Singapore
    5 Phung Khac Khoan St, District 1 (☎ 225173)
Switzerland
    270A Bach Dang St, Binh Thanh District (☎ 442568)
Taiwan
    Trade Office: Taipei Economic & Cultural Office, 68 Tran
    Quoc Thao St, District 3
    Visa section: ☎ 299348
    Commercial section: ☎ 299349
Thailand
    Rex Hotel, Room 662 (☎ 293115)
UK
    261 Dien Bien Phu St, District 3 (☎ 298433)

CUSTOMS

You are permitted to bring in duty-free 200 cigarettes, 50
cigars or 250 grams of tobacco; two litres of liquor; gifts
worth up to US$50; and a reasonable quantity of luggage
and personal effects. Items which you cannot bring in
include opium (competes with local suppliers?),
weapons, explosives and 'cultural materials unsuitable

to Vietnamese society'. That last category seems to include videos about the Vietnam War, and pornographic photos.

Tourists can bring an unlimited amount of foreign currency into Vietnam but they are required to declare it on their customs form upon arrival. Theoretically, when you leave the country you should have exchange receipts for all the foreign currency you have spent if you spent more than US$300. In practice, though, the authorities rarely check.

When entering Vietnam, visitors must also declare all precious metals (especially gold), jewellery, cameras and electronic devices in their possession. Customs is liable to tax you on gold bars, jewellery and diamonds – if you don't need this stuff, then don't bring it.

The import and export of Vietnamese currency and live animals is forbidden.

Most travellers have more trouble exiting the country than entering. The great stumbling block seems to be what the authorities call 'cultural materials'. This includes video tapes, which must be screened in advance by 'experts' from the Department of Culture. This is to make sure that you haven't somehow snatched Vietnamese culture and found a way to smuggle it out of the country on a video tape. A similar hassle occurs if you've bought antiques (or something which looks antique) unless you have an official export certificate.

MONEY

Cash

It's not a bad idea to bring at least US$300 (or more) in cash, while the rest of your funds are kept in travellers' cheques. In emergencies (like when banks are closed), only cash transactions will be possible. It's best to keep these emergency funds in a well-hidden money belt or in pockets sewn on the inside of your clothing to thwart pickpockets.

Without a doubt, US dollars are the most useful foreign banknotes to have. Although you can at least theoretically convert French francs, German marks, UK pounds, Japanese yen and other major currencies, the reality is that US dollars are still much preferred. The Vietnamese like new crisp ones – tattered notes may not be accepted, even at a bank. Large-denomination bills (US$100 notes) are quite OK, but also keep a small stash of US$20 notes for those odd occasions when you can't unload the big ones.

Since 1995, it has been illegal for hotels, restaurants, shops or anyone else to demand payment in US dollars or other foreign currencies. You are supposed to pay for everything in Vietnamese currency. Anyone who demands payment in US dollars is breaking the law. This having been said, many places will ask for payment in US dollars but 'exchange' these on the spot for Vietnamese currency.

Travellers' Cheques

Major foreign exchange banks can cash travellers' cheques, but private money changers will not. The foreign exchange counter at the airport also changes travellers' cheques.

Travellers' cheques denominated in US dollars can be exchanged for US dollars cash. A 2% commission is charged for this service. No commission is charged if you exchange travellers' cheques for Vietnamese currency.

Tax Department Store (RE)

If your cheques are denominated in other currencies besides US dollars, you may find banks unwilling to accept them because they don't know the latest exchange rate. If you insist, the banks may exchange non-US dollar cheques for local currency, but charge a hefty commission (perhaps 10%) to protect themselves from any possible exchange rate fluctuations.

Because there has been a sharp increase in the number of stolen travellers' cheques, many banks will demand to see your original purchase receipt. If you don't have it, that could be a problem. In that case, the bank staff *might* be willing to cash just one cheque for you if the amount isn't large. Save yourself a hassle and bring the receipt, but keep it separate from your original cheques. If you're stuck, try the foreign-run banks – they seem to be more easygoing, though they often charge a 1% commission.

As with cash, the Vietnamese are loath to accept any travellers' cheques that are crumpled or dirty. In other words, keep your cheques well protected in some sort of plastic holder or envelope (or both).

ATMs

Ho Chi Minh City has no ATM machines yet, but that will probably change soon. Most likely, the early ATMs will not accept foreign ATM cards, so don't count on this means of securing cash.

Credit Cards

Visa, MasterCard, American Express and JCB cards are now acceptable in all major touristy hotels. However, you will usually be charged a 3% commission every time you use a credit card to purchase something or pay a hotel bill.

Getting a cash advance from a credit card is possible at Vietcombank, but you will be charged a 4% commission.

International Transfers

Money can be cabled into Vietnam quickly and cheaply and the recipient can be paid in US dollars or Vietnamese currency. Right now, only Vietcombank is authorised to handle wire transfers. Money should be cabled to 'Vietcombank Ho Chi Minh City' (see the Changing Money section below for its address). The cable needs to include the recipient's name and passport number.

Vietcombank's telex number in Ho Chi Minh City is 811.234 VCB.VT or 811.235 VCB.VT.

Bank Accounts

Foreigners can open accounts at Vietcombank and these can be denominated in local currency or US dollars. Both demand-deposit (savings) and time-deposit (long-term) accounts are available and interest is paid. A number of other banks allow foreigners to open accounts, including Saigonbank, Indovina and the State Bank of Vietnam.

Vietcombank can arrange letters of credit for those doing import and export business in Vietnam, and it is even possible to borrow money from them.

Currency

The currency of Vietnam is the dong (abbreviated to a 'd' following the amount). Banknotes in denominations of 200d, 500d, 1000d, 2000d, 5000d, 10,000d, 20,000d and 50,000d are presently in circulation. It can be difficult to get change for the 50,000d notes in small backwaters, so keep a stack of small bills handy.

Now that Ho Chi Minh has been canonised, his picture appears on every banknote. There are no coins currently in use in Vietnam, though the dong used to be subdivided into 10 hao and 100 xu. All dong-denominated prices in this book are based on US$1 being worth 11,053d.

Country	Unit		Dong
Australia	A$1	=	8140d
Canada	C$1	=	8158d
China	Y1	=	1294d
France	FFr1	=	2144d
Germany	DM1	=	7352d
Hong Kong	HK$1	=	1430d
Japan	¥1	=	113d
New Zealand	NZ$1	=	6740d
Philippines	P1	=	434d
Singapore	S$1	=	7498d
South Korea	W1	=	14d
Switzerland	SFr1	=	8826d
Taiwan	NT$1	=	423d
Thailand	B1	=	443d
UK	£1	=	17,754d
USA	US$1	=	11,053d

Changing Money

The airport bank gives the official exchange rate. The only problem is that the staff work banker's hours, which means it's closed when at least half of the flights arrive. For this reason, you'd be wise to have sufficient US dollar notes in small denominations to get yourself into the city.

Outside the airport, foreign currency can be exchanged for dong at four kinds of places: at foreign exchange banks, through authorised exchange bureaus, at hotel reception desks and on the black market.

The best rates are offered by banks, though some foreign-owned banks charge a 1% commission. Exchange bureaus are more convenient – they tend to be located just where you need them, and they stay open at times when banks are closed. The reception counters of upmarket hotels often change money, but their exchange rates are usually the worst around. Furthermore, they may insist that you be a guest at their hotel.

Vietcombank (☎ 297245; fax 230310), also known as the Bank for Foreign Trade of Vietnam (Ngan Hang Ngoai Thuong Viet Nam), is Vietnam's main foreign exchange bank. In Ho Chi Minh City, Vietcombank occupies two adjacent buildings at the intersection of Ben Chuong and Pasteur Sts. The east building is the one that does foreign exchange, and it's worth a visit even if you don't change money – the ornate interior is stupendous!

There is a smaller branch of Vietcombank at 175 Dong Khoi St, opposite the Continental Hotel.

Choosing a chicken (RE)

Banking hours are normally from 8 am to 3 pm on weekdays, 8 am to noon on Saturdays and closed on Sundays and holidays. Most banks also close for 1½ hours during lunch. The list of banks in Ho Chi Minh City which do foreign exchange follows; travellers have had particularly good things to say about Sacombank and Thai Military Bank:

Bangkok Bank
    117 Nguyen Hue St, District 1 (☎ 223416; fax 223421)
Banque Française du Commerce Extérieur
    11 Me Linh Square, District 1 (☎ 294144; fax 299126)
Banque Indosuez
    39 Nguyen Cong Tru St, District 1 (☎ 296061; fax 296065)
Banque Nationale de Paris
    2nd floor, State Bank Building, 1 Ton That Dam St, District 1 (☎ 299504; fax 299486)
Crédit Lyonnais
    17 Ton Duc Thang St, District 1 (☎ 299226; fax 296465)
Firstvina Bank
    3-5 Ho Tung Mau St (☎ 291566; fax 291583)
Indovina Bank
    36 Ton That Dam St, District 1 (☎ 230130; fax 230131)
Sacombank
    211 Nguyen Thai Hoc St (cnr of Pham Ngu Lao St), District 1
Thai Military Bank
    11 Ben Chuong St, District 1 (☎ 222218; fax 230045)
VID Public Bank
    15A Ben Chuong St, District 1 (☎ 223583; fax 223612)

You can reconvert reasonable amounts of dong back to dollars on departure without an official receipt, though just how one defines 'reasonable' is open to question. You cannot legally take the dong out with you.

Black Market

Private individuals and some shops (particularly jewellery stores) will swap cash US dollars for dong and vice versa. However it's important to realise that black market exchange rates are *worse* than the official exchange rates. In other words, you do not gain anything by using the black market other than the convenience of changing money when and where you please.

If people approach you on the street with offers to change money at rates better than the official bank rate, then you are being set up for a rip-off. Don't even think about trying it. Remember, if an offer sounds too good to be true, that's because it is.

Costs

The cost of travelling in and around Ho Chi Minh City depends on your tastes and susceptibility to luxuries. Ascetics can get by on US$10 a day, for US$15 to US$20 a backpacker can live fairly well, and the average business traveller could get by on US$45 a day. Transport is likely to be the biggest expense if you rent a car and make excursions to the countryside. Such journeys will of course be cheaper if you can deal with Vietnam's decrepit public transport, or at least split the cost of vehicle rentals with others.

Tipping

Tipping according to a percentage of the bill is not expected in Vietnam but it is enormously appreciated. For someone making US$50 per month, 10% of the cost of your meal can go a long way. Government-run hotels and restaurants that specifically cater to tourists usually have an automatic 10% service charge – how much of this (if any) actually goes to the low-paid staff is questionable. It's also a nice gesture to tip the staff who clean your room if you stay a couple of days in the same hotel – US$0.50 to US$1 should be enough. If you hire drivers and guides, also consider tipping them if they worked hard.

Men you deal with will also greatly appreciate small gifts such as a pack of cigarettes (women almost never smoke). But make sure it's a foreign brand of cigarettes; people will be insulted if you give Vietnamese cigarettes. The 555 brand (said to be Ho Chi Minh's favourite) is popular, as are most US brands. Most of the usual kinds of gifts (chocolates, coffee-table books etc) are acceptable, so long as they are foreign-made.

It is considered proper to make a small donation at the end of a visit to a pagoda, especially if the monk has shown you around; most pagodas have contribution boxes for this purpose.

Bargaining

In many places, such as markets, items typically do not have marked prices and foreigners will almost always be overcharged. Your best defence again this is to attempt to bargain.

Remember, 'face' is important in the Orient. Bargaining should be good-natured – smile, don't scream and argue. Many Westerners really blow it big on this point. By no means should you get angry during the bargaining process. And once the money is accepted, the deal is done – if you harbour hard feelings because you later find out that someone else got it cheaper, the only one you are hurting is yourself.

Taxes

On all goods you pay, the marked or stated price includes any relevant taxes. Only in some hotels and restaurants is there an additional 10% tax or service charge, and this should be made clear to you from the beginning (ask if you're not sure).

Expatriates working in Vietnam for six months or more every year are subject to taxes on their total income (including income earned outside Vietnam, which they are supposed to declare). Tax brackets range from 10% to 50%. Vietnam's arbitrary income tax laws change when the moon is full and the tides are high, so don't consider the foregoing to be the final word. If you are planning to work in Vietnam, enquire about taxes at the Ho Chi Minh City Tax Office.

COMMUNICATIONS

Post

Sending & Receiving Mail Saigon's French-style Central Post Office (CPO; Buu Dien Thanh Pho Ho Chi Minh) is at 2 Cong Xa Paris St, next to Notre Dame Cathedral. The structure was built between 1886 and 1891 and is by far the largest post office in Vietnam. The staff at the information desk (☎ 296555, 299615) speak English. Postal services are available daily from 7.30 am to 7.30 pm. To your right as you enter the building is poste restante, which is labelled 'Delivery of Mail – Mail to be Called For'. Pens, envelopes, aerograms, postcards and stamp collections are on sale at the counter to the right of the entrance and outside the CPO along Nguyen Du St.

Letters and parcels airmailed from abroad to Vietnam can be delivered in as little as four days or as long as 10 months! Prolonged delays are almost certainly due to the Vietnamese security apparatus inspecting any documents which have been deemed 'suspicious'. Reliability is greatly enhanced if your envelope or package contains nothing that somebody would want to steal.

Domestic letters cost 400d (less than US$0.04). To send a postcard to Europe costs US$0.55; to the USA it's

US$0.45; to Australia, US$0.40; to east Asia (Hong Kong, Taiwan, etc), the rate is US$0.40.

International postal rates in Vietnam might not seem expensive to you, but just think about how the Vietnamese feel. The tariffs are so out of line with most salaries that locals *literally* cannot afford to send letters to their friends and relatives abroad. If you would like to correspond with Vietnamese whom you meet during your visit, leave them enough stamps to cover postage for several letters.

Vietnamese stamps often have insufficient gum on them; use the paste provided in little pots at post offices.

Saigon Central Post Office (RE)

If practicable, ensure that the clerk cancels them, as some travellers have reported that someone (for whom the stamps are worth a day's salary) has soaked the stamps off and thrown the letters away.

Foreigners sending parcels out of Vietnam sometimes have to deal with time-consuming inspections of the contents. The most important thing is to keep the parcel small. If it's documents only, you should be OK. Sending out video tapes and the like can be problematic.

Express Mail Service (EMS) is available to most developed countries and a few of the less developed ones. It's perhaps twice as fast to use EMS than to use regular airmail, but a bigger advantage is that the letter or small parcel will be registered. There is also domestic EMS between Ho Chi Minh City and other major cities in Vietnam.

Receiving packages from abroad can be a headache. If you're lucky, customs will clear the package and the clerks at the post office will simply let you take it. If you're unlucky, customs will demand an inspection, at which you must be present. In that case, the post office will give you a written notice which you take to the customs office along with your passport. The customs office for incoming parcels is in the rear of the CPO building.

Procedures from this point on can be very tedious; and if you are particularly unlucky, you may have to pay import duty. If your parcel contains books, documents, video tapes, computer disks, or other dangerous goods, it's possible that a further inspection will be required by the Ministry of Culture. This could take from a few days to a few weeks.

Private Couriers DHL Worldwide Express offers express document delivery from the Saigon CPO (☎ 231525) and from their main office (☎ 446203, 444268; fax 445387) at 253 Hoang Van Thu St, Tan Binh District.

The main Federal Express office (☎ 290747; fax 290477) is at 1 Nguyen Hau St, District 1. Outside Ho Chi Minh City you can call Federal Express on their toll-free number (☎ (018) 290747).

United Parcel Service (☎ 243597; fax 243596) has a representative at the CPO, 2 Cong Xa Paris St, District 1.

TNT Express Worldwide has its head office (☎ 446460, 446476, 446478; fax 446592) at 56 Truong Son St, Ward 2, Tan Binh District.

Another alternative is Airborne Express (☎ 294310, 294315; fax 292961), with offices at two locations: the CPO at 2 Cong Xa Paris St, and the main office (☎ 292976) at 80C Nguyen Du St, District 1.

Freight Forwarders Planning on shipping Vietnamese furniture or a used car? Or will you move your entire household and belongings to Vietnam for a long stay? For these you need the services of a freight forwarder. One to contact is Sea & Air Freight International (SAFI; ☎ 241814; fax 231679) at 3-5 Nguyen Hue St, District 1.

You could also contact Saigon Van (☎ 350396, 352676; fax 350397), 6E An Binh, District 5. This company is associated with the international Atlas Van Lines chain.

Telephone

International and domestic long-distance calls can be booked at many hotels, but this is expensive.

It's somewhat less expensive to book long-distance phone calls from the post office. For operator-assisted calls, you will be charged for three minutes even if you only talk for one minute, plus the rate per minute will be higher. As in most countries, the cheapest way to make a long-distance call is to dial direct.

Domestic Calls Local calls can usually be made from any hotel or restaurant phone and are usually free.

Domestic direct-dialling is known as 'subscriber trunk dialling' (STD). To place an STD call, you must first dial the national trunk prefix (01) followed by the area code and local number. For example, to call Hanoi (area code 4) you would dial ☎ 01-4-123456. Area codes in Vietnam are assigned according to province, and the current dispensation is as follows:

Province	Main City	Area Code
An Giang	Long Xuyen	76
Ba Ria	Vung Tau	64
Bac Thai	Thai Nguyen	28
Ben Tre	Ben Tre	75
Binh Dinh	Qui Nhon	56
Binh Thuan	Phan Thiet	62
Cantho	Cantho	71
Cao Bang	Cao Bang	26
Dac Lac	Buon Ma Thuot	50
Dong Nai	Bien Hoa	61
Dong Thap	Cao Lanh	67
Gia Lai	Pleiku	59
Ha Bac	Bac Giang	24
Ha Giang	Ha Giang	19
Ha Tay	Ha Dong	34
Ha Tinh	Ha Tinh	39
Hai Hung	Hai Duong	32
Haiphong	Haiphong	31
Hanoi	Hanoi	4

Ho Chi Minh City	Saigon	8
Hoa Binh	Hoa Binh	18
Khanh Hoa	Nha Trang	58
Kien Giang	Rach Gia	77
Kon Tum	Kon Tum	60
Lai Chau	Dien Bien Phu	23
Lam Dong	Dalat	63
Lang Son	Lang Son	25
Lao Cai	Lao Cai	20
Long An	Tan An	72
Minh Hai	Camau	78
Nam Ha	Nam Dinh	35
Nghe An	Vinh	38
Ninh Binh	Ninh Binh	30
Ninh Thuan	Phan Rang	68
Phu Yen	Tuy Hoa	57
Quang Binh	Dong Hoi	52
Quang Nam	Danang	51
Quang Ngai	Quang Ngai	55
Quang Ninh	Halong City	33
Quang Tri	Dong Ha	53
Soc Trang	Soc Trang	79
Son La	Son La	22
Song Be	Thu Dau Mot	65
Tay Ninh	Tay Ninh	66
Thai Binh	Thai Binh	36
Thanh Hoa	Thanh Hoa	37
Thua Thien	Hué	54
Tien Giang	Mytho	73
Tra Vinh	Tra Vinh	74
Tuyen Quang	Tuyen Quang	27
Vinh Long	Vinh Long	70
Vinh Phu	Viet Tri	21
Yen Bai	Yen Bai	29

Domestic long-distance calls are reasonably priced, but will be cheapest if you dial direct. You can save up to 20% by calling at night (10 pm to 5 am).

International Calls International calls from Vietnam are ridiculously expensive and, outside of major cities, unreliable. To be fair, the phone company has lowered rates slightly in the past two years, but its international rates are easily two to five times higher than in Western countries. The total monopoly enjoyed by the DGPT (Directorate General of Posts & Telecommunications) means that price decreases will come slowly and grudgingly.

Perhaps the most obnoxious example of the greed of the DGPT is the fact that foreigners are not permitted to make international reverse-charge (collect) calls. However, Vietnamese nationals can. Why? Because the DGPT earns less from a reverse-charge call than from

calls paid for in Vietnam. However, since most Vietnamese cannot possibly afford to pay for an international
call, they are permitted to call collect to their overseas
relatives (the assumption being that those relatives will
probably send them money).

This means that if your credit cards or travellers'
cheques are stolen, you will not be able to call collect to
the issuing company to report the loss. At best this is a
major nuisance – it could prove disastrous if you get
robbed of all your cash and need to call abroad to get
some help.

Calling from most countries to Vietnam will be at least
50% cheaper than calling from Vietnam to abroad. So if
you plan to talk more than a few minutes, it's best to
make a very brief call abroad and ask the other party to
call you back.

The cheapest and simplest way by far to make an
international direct-dial (IDD) call is to buy a telephone
card, known as a 'UniphoneKad'. They are on sale at the
telephone company. UniphoneKads can only be used in
special telephones, usually found in the lobbies of major
hotels. The cards are issued in four denominations:
30,000d (US$2.72), 60,000d (US$5.45), 150,000d
(US$10.90) and 300,000d (US$27.27). The 30,000d and
60,000d cards will only work for domestic calls.

To make an IDD call, you must first dial the international prefix (00) followed by the country code, area
code (if any) and the local number. Note that for many
countries (Australia, for example), area codes start with
a zero, but this zero must not be dialled when calling
internationally. So to call Melbourne (area code 03) in
Australia (country code 61) from Vietnam, you would
dial 00-61-3-9123 4567. Some useful country codes
include:

Australia	61	New Zealand	64
Belgium	32	Norway	47
Canada	1	Philippines	63
Denmark	45	Singapore	65
France	33	Spain	34
Germany	49	Sweden	46
Hong Kong	852	Switzerland	41
Italy	39	Taiwan	886
Japan	81	Thailand	66
Korea (South)	82	UK	44
Malaysia	60	USA	1
Netherlands	31	Vietnam	84

Calls are charged by one-minute increments; any fraction of a minute is charged as a full minute. But many
travellers find that international calls cost more than the

advertised rate (is there some sort of hidden tax?) – this applies even when you use a phone card. There is only a 10% discount for calls placed between 11 pm and 7 am.

Useful Telephone Numbers Ho Chi Minh City produces its own version of the Yellow Pages in which you can look up services by subject. For example, to find the phone numbers of hotels look under *khach san*. You can find telephone books at most hotel reception desks, and you can also purchase these directories from the phone company offices.

You'll need the ability to speak Vietnamese to get much use out of the following numbers:

Ambulance	15
Directory Assistance	16
Economic & Social Information	108
Fire	14
Operator-Assisted Calls (domestic)	101
Operator-Assisted Calls (international)	110
Phone Installation	242888
Phone Repair	19
Police	13
Time	17

Pagers Aside from the convenience they offer, using a pager is more economical than having a telephone installed. Pagers also solve the problem posed by being forced to move every time Saigon's police decide you can't stay in the place you just rented. At least if you have to move, the pager goes with you.

Le Duan Boulevard (RE)

PhoneLink is Vietnam's largest paging service, though not necessarily the cheapest. Business travellers who have an account with PhoneLink in Bangkok might be interested to know that someone in Bangkok can page you in Ho Chi Minh City.

There are currently four paging companies operating in Ho Chi Minh City. For additional information, try contacting any of the following:

Di Dong MCC
    125 Hai Ba Trung St, District 1 (☎ 290117)
PhoneLink
    146-150 Pasteur St, District 1 (☎ 243038; fax 223997)
    230 Hai Ba Trung St, District 1 (☎ 251368)
    180 Tran Hung Dao B Blvd, District 5 (☎ 351070; fax 351062)
Radio Paging Centre
    146-150 Pasteur St, District 1 (☎ 351070)
Saigon ABC Paging Centre
    125 Hai Ba Trung St, District 1 (☎ 241338; fax 241340)

Cellular Phones As in other Third World countries, Vietnam is putting a lot of money into the cellular network simply because it's cheaper than laying thousands of km of copper or fibre-optic cables. The day has not yet arrived when travellers visiting Vietnam can make a cellular call using their own mobile phones. However, that day is coming soon. In the meantime, resident foreigners can apply for one in Saigon. This is far more expensive than owning a pager, but you get what you pay for. Aside from offering the obvious advantages of portability and convenience, cellular phones bypass Vietnam's decrepit wiring system which plagues conventional telephone calls with crackling static.

The place to contact is Call-Link, Saigon Mobile Telephone Centre (☎ 288; fax 290666), 5 Nguyen Hau St, District 1. The business office of Call-Link (☎ 355999) is at 2 Hung Vuong St, District 10.

Fax, Telex & Telegraph

Faxes can be sent to you at the CPO (fax 298540, 298546) and these will be delivered to your hotel for a small charge. In order for this to work, the fax should clearly indicate your name, hotel phone number and the address of the hotel (including your room number). The cost for receiving a fax is US$0.60.

Upmarket hotels also have 'business centres', many of which operate 24 hours a day. You can send and receive fax and telex messages at these places. You do not have to be a guest at these hotels to take advantage of these services.

Vietnam still has telex machines, but they are dying off quickly and are mainly used by banks and post offices. You can easily send telexes from major post offices in Vietnam, though this service is useless if the person you need to reach does not have a telex number. Telex messages are charged by the minute with a one-minute minimum. Considering the slow transmission speed of telex (about 50 words per minute), you'd best keep the message short.

The telegraph windows of major CPOs are open 24 hours a day, seven days a week. Telegrams are charged for each word (including each word of the address) and there is a seven-word minimum charge. The cost per word varies from US$0.30 to US$0.60, depending on the country of destination.

Electronic Mail

Getting online from Vietnam is anything but easy and certainly not cheap. The government has so far not permitted any of the popular international e-mail services (CompuServe, Delphi, America Online, MCI-Mail, Prodigy, etc) to open branch nodes in Vietnam. Nor can you access through third-party data-switching networks such as Infonet or Sprint. The only way you can connect to your favourite e-mail service is to dial direct to a foreign country.

Aside from expense, IDD has another drawback – noisy phone lines. You may be disappointed to see your computer screen fill up with meaningless crap, and the only thing you can do to avoid this is to use a high-quality error-correcting modem. Make sure that your modem is high-speed (14,400 baud or more) because time is big money when making international calls from Vietnam.

The final issue is where to call. Most of the major international e-mail providers are based in the USA, though some have branch nodes in Hong Kong, and it is *slightly* cheaper to call Hong Kong than the USA. However, the e-mail services charge you more to use their Hong Kong node, so the net savings over a direct call to the USA will be puny.

Actually, Vietnam does provide access to major e-mail services through its own packet-switching network called Vietpac. Vietpac is a joint-venture with modern equipment and reliable service. The downside is that the service is ridiculously expensive and it takes months to set up an account, thus excluding this option for short-term travellers.

Having said all these negative things, the Vietnamese government *may* soon give students and business people access to the Internet. But for now, aspiring infonauts can only dream of the day when 'surfing the Net' from Ho Chi Minh City will be possible.

BOOKS

Guidebooks

Lonely Planet's travel survival kit to *Vietnam* gives the scoop on the whole country rather than just Ho Chi Minh City. Also worth investing in is Lonely Planet's new travel atlas to *Vietnam*, companion to the travel survival kit, which allows travellers to plan their trip through the country and details sites of interest.

Those travelling further afield should consider taking along Lonely Planet's shoestring guide to *South-East Asia*.

Friendly local (PW)

History

The Fall of Saigon by David Butler (Simon & Schuster, New York, 1985) is one of the best researched and most readable accounts of the Communist takeover of the city in 1975.

General

Graham Greene's 1954 novel *The Quiet American*, which is set during the last days of French rule, is probably the most famous Western work of fiction on Vietnam. Much of the action takes place at Saigon's Continental Hotel and at the Caodai complex in Tay Ninh.

The Lover by Marguerite Duras is a fictional love story set in Saigon during the 1930s. The book has been made into a major motion picture.

Saigon by Anthony Grey (Pan Books) is your standard blockbuster by the author of *Peking*. Not bad.

MEDIA

Newspapers & Magazines

Vietnam has no equivalent to the sleaze circus that characterises the Western tabloid press. Basically, it's self-congratulatory rhetoric and sombre financial news.

The best locally produced English-language magazine is the *Vietnam Economic Times* which is published monthly. For subscription information, contact the magazine direct on ☎ (8) 356717; fax 356716. Or get in touch with the Vietnam Resource Group (☎ (8) 222982; fax

'Smile' (PW)

222983), 92-96 Nguyen Hue Blvd, District 1. In the USA, subscriptions are available through the Vietnam Resource Group (☎ (202) 6518007; fax 4844899), 955 L'Enfant Plaza SW, No 4000, Washington DC 20024.

The best English-language newspaper is the *Vietnam Investment Review* which is published weekly. Subscription and advertising information is available at (☎ (8) 222440, 243111, 243112; fax 231699), 122 Nguyen Thi Minh Khai St, District 1.

What's On in Saigon is produced monthly by expats living in Ho Chi Minh City. The magazine is free – look for copies in hotel lobbies and expat pubs. For subscription information, call (☎ (8) 357673) or write to PO Box 571, Central Post Office, Ho Chi Minh City.

The *Vietnam News* is published daily, but that's about the only good thing one can say for it. The blank space left over from the lack of news is filled in with harangues on the joys of Marxism-Leninism or the life and times of Ho Chi Minh.

Radio & TV

The Voice of Vietnam broadcasts on shortwave, AM and FM for about 18 hours a day. The broadcasts are mostly music, but there are also news bulletins in Vietnamese, English, French and Russian. The broadcast programmes are printed daily in the Vietnam News.

Vietnamese domestic national radio broadcasts news and music programmes from 7 am until 11 pm. Visitors may want to bring along a small short-wave receiver to hear foreign broadcasts.

Vietnamese TV began broadcasting in 1970 and it's fair to say that the content hasn't improved much since then. There is currently only one channel in Ho Chi Minh City. Broadcast hours from Monday through Saturday are from 9 to 11.30 am, and from 7 to 11 pm. On Sunday there is an extra broadcast from 3 to 4 pm. English-language news comes on in the evenings as the last broadcast at some time after 10 pm. Sometimes soccer or other sports come out at strange hours like 1.30 am.

Satellite TV is now widely available, though you're not likely to see it except in the large hotels catering to foreigners. Hong Kong's Star TV is most popular.

PHOTOGRAPHY & VIDEO

X-Rays

The feared x-ray machines at Tan Son Nhat Airport have been upgraded and are now film-safe. At least it says so on the machines.

Film

Fresh colour print film is widely available. Popular brands available in Vietnam include Kodak, Fuji and Konica. The prices charged are at least as cheap or cheaper than in the West.

Western-made slide film can easily be bought in Ho Chi Minh City, but is difficult to find elsewhere. If you have no luck at photoprocessing stores, look for slide film in hotel gift shops.

Check the expiry date on film, especially if the film has been stored in a warm environment (which is likely). The metal floors of minibuses get very hot, but you might not notice if the vehicle is air-conditioned – leaving your bag or camera on the vehicle floor could result in cooked film.

Photoprocessing shops have become ubiquitous and are equipped with the latest Japanese one-hour colour-printing machines.

There are a few back-alley shops in Ho Chi Minh City which try to develop slide film by hand using basic equipment. Quality is erratic, but your only other choice is to send the film abroad. Cost for processing is US$5 per roll, but most places do not mount the slides. However, you can buy the frames for around US$0.15 a piece and mount them yourself.

Restrictions

The Vietnamese police usually don't care what you photograph, but on occasion they get persnickety. Obviously, don't photograph something that is militarily sensitive (airports, seaports, border checkpoints etc). Photography from aircraft is permitted. However, many museums have restrictions. Taking pictures inside pagodas and temples is *usually* all right, but it's always better to ask permission first from the monks.

Laminating

Plastic laminating is cheap and ubiquitous. Just look for the signs saying 'Ep Plastic'. It's particularly advisable to laminate photos intended as presents to protect them from Vietnam's tropical climate. Unlaminated photos deteriorate and go mouldy.

Camera Fees

Many of the touristy sites now charge a 'camera fee' of at least US$0.50, or a 'video fee' of US$2 to US$5. If the staff refuses to issue a receipt for the camera fee, then you should refuse to pay – the 'fee' in that case is likely to go into their pocket.

TIME

Ho Chi Minh City (like Bangkok) is seven hours ahead of GMT/UTC. Daylight saving time (summer time) is *not* observed. When it's noon in Ho Chi Minh City it is 10 pm the previous day in San Francisco, 1 am in New York, 5 am in London, 1 pm in Perth and 3 pm in Sydney. When Western countries are on daylight saving time, subtract one hour from the times listed for the foregoing cities.

ELECTRICITY

Electric current in Vietnam is mostly 220 volts at 50 Hz (cycles), but occasionally you'll still find 110 volts (also at 50 Hz). Looking at the shape of the outlet on the wall gives no clue as to what voltage is flowing through the wires. If the voltage is not marked on the socket try finding a light bulb or appliance with the voltage written on it. In Ho Chi Minh City, most outlets are US-style flat pins but you'll also see Russian-inspired round pins. All sockets are two-prong only – in no case will you find a third wire for ground (earth).

Vietnam's electrical power is often unstable. Sudden voltage drops can cause computers to 'crash', meaning that you'll have to shut it down and restart it again. Even worse is a high-voltage surge which can actually damage the sensitive electronics. A voltage surge suppressor can help solve this problem – many portable computers already come with these built into the power supply.

LAUNDRY

It is usually easy to find a hotel attendant who will get your laundry spotlessly clean for the equivalent of US$1 or slightly more. Clothes are dried on the line, which can be problematic during the wet season.

WEIGHTS & MEASURES

Vietnam uses the international metric system. In addition, there are two measurements for weight borrowed from the Chinese, the *tael* and the *catty*. A catty is 0.6 kg (1.32 lb). There are 16 taels to the catty. One tael is 37.5 grams (1.32 oz). Gold is always sold by the tael.

HEALTH

Pre-Departure Preparations

Vaccinations Various health authorities recommend that travellers get the following vaccines: meningitis, rabies, hepatitis A, hepatitis B, BCG (tuberculosis), Japanese encephalitis, polio, TABT (for typhoid, paratyphoid A and B, and tetanus) and diphtheria. On the health form you fill out upon arrival in Vietnam, it's suggested that you should be vaccinated for yellow fever if your arrival in Vietnam is within six days of leaving or transiting a yellow fever area. A vaccine exists for cholera, but it is not very effective. Measles and polio require booster shots (polio every five years), even though you may have been immunised against them as a child.

Plan ahead for getting your vaccinations: some of them require an initial shot followed by a booster, while some vaccinations should not be given together. If you are travelling with children, it's especially important to be sure that they've had all necessary vaccinations. The period of protection offered by vaccinations differs widely and some, including cholera, are contraindicated for pregnant women.

See under Medical Facilities at the end of this section for places in Ho Chi Minh City to get vaccines or treatment.

Aural hygiene (PH)

Other Precautions Sunburn can be more than just uncomfortable. It can lead to possible skin cancer in later years. Bring sunscreen (UV) lotion and wear something to cover your head. Protect your eyes with decent sunglasses.

It's wise to get your teeth checked and any necessary dental work done before you leave home. Carry a spare pair of glasses or your prescription in case of loss or breakage.

Sweating makes you lose a lot of salt and that can lead to fatigue and muscle cramps. Putting extra salt in your food (a teaspoon a day is probably too much) will solve this, but increase your water intake if you do. Using soy sauce is another method of increasing salt intake.

Cuts and scratches can easily get infected in the tropical climate. Wash cuts out with boiled or bottled water, use an antiseptic, keep them dry and keep an eye on them; nasty cases require use of an antibiotic cream. Cuts on your feet and ankles are particularly troublesome – a new pair of sandals can quickly give you an abrasion which can be difficult to heal. Try not to scratch mosquito bites for the same reason.

Leaving a fan and/or air-conditioner on at night when you go to sleep might give you a cold. To cure it, rest, drink lots of liquids, keep warm (easy to do in Ho Chi Minh City!) and wait it out.

Food & Water

In Ho Chi Minh City, tap water is not too bad (it's chlorinated) but it's still recommended that you boil it before drinking. In the nearby countryside, the water varies from pretty safe to downright dangerous. After a typhoon and subsequent flooding, there is a problem with sewers overflowing into reservoirs. Do not even brush your teeth with unboiled water after flooding.

Bottled water or soft drinks are generally fine. Milk should be treated with suspicion, as it is often unpasteurised or kept unrefrigerated. Yoghurt should be OK if it's been kept refrigerated and is not too old. Tea and coffee should both be OK since the water should have been boiled.

While boiling will kill nasty microbes, freezing will not. In Ho Chi Minh City, ice is delivered daily to restaurants from a factory which has to meet certain standards of hygiene (the water is at least chlorinated). In rural areas the ice could be made from river (sewer?) water. Another problem is that even clean ice often makes its way to its destination in a filthy sack. Completely avoiding ice would be a good idea, but that's not easy advice to follow in a hot, tropical country.

Food should be thoroughly cooked. Raw foods like salads and unpeeled fruit can give you dysentery. Ice cream is usually OK but beware of ice cream that has melted and been refrozen. Take great care with shellfish or fish – if it tastes extremely soft, that is a clear warning sign of spoilage. Unfortunately, even fresh fish can make you ill if the creature was raised in contaminated water.

Medical Problems & Treatment

Diarrhoea Diarrhoea is often due simply to a change of diet. If you do get diarrhoea, the first thing to do is wait – it rarely lasts more than a few days.

Diarrhoea will cause you to dehydrate. Water mixed with oral rehydration salts will help. Dissolve the powder in *cool* water (never hot!), but don't use it if the powder is wet. Rehydration salts are also useful for treating heat exhaustion caused by excessive sweating.

If the diarrhoea persists then the usual treatment is Lomotil or Imodium tablets. Activated charcoal, not technically a drug, can also provide relief. These don't cure anything but they do give symptomatic relief, though you should be careful not to get dependent on them. Furthermore, the diarrhoea serves one useful purpose – it helps the body expel unwanted bacteria. On the other hand, letting a diarrhoea problem go untreated for weeks or months can lead to irritable bowel syndrome, which is hard to cure.

If you feel extremely ill or can't get rid of diarrhoea, it's possible you may have a nastier disease like dysentery or giardia. Seek medical advice fast.

Fruit juice, tea and coffee can aggravate diarrhoea, as can vegetables, fruits and greasy foods. Basically, eat a light, fibre-free diet, such as yoghurt or boiled eggs with salt; later you should be able to handle white bread.

Japanese Encephalitis Although still rare, this disease is spreading. Recently, there have been outbreaks in the Mekong Delta and in District 4 of Ho Chi Minh City.

As with other mosquito-borne diseases, Japanese encephalitis can be prevented if you can avoid getting bitten by mosquitos. See the section on malaria below for some advice on how to do this.

Malaria Considered one of the greatest health risks to travellers, this potentially fatal disease is spread by mos-

Poisonous Wind

In the countryside, you will no doubt see Vietnamese covered with long bands of red welts on their necks and backs. This is not some kind of horrid skin disease, but rather a treatment. In traditional Vietnamese folk medicine, many illnesses are attributed to 'poisonous wind' *(trung gio)*. The bad wind can be released by scraping the skin with spoons, coins, etc, thus raising the welts. The results aren't pretty, but the locals say this treatment is good for what ails you. Try it at your own peril.

Another way to fight poisonous wind is a technique – borrowed from the Chinese – that employs suction cups made of bamboo placed on the patient's skin. A burning piece of alcohol-soaked cotton is briefly put inside the cup to drive out the air before it is applied. As the cup cools, a partial vacuum is produced, leaving a nasty-looking but harmless red circular mark on the skin. ■

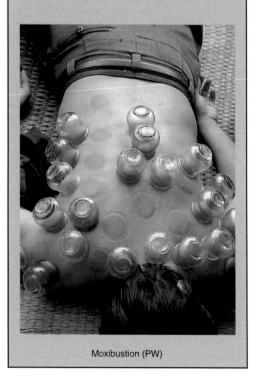

Moxibustion (PW)

quitos. The risk is highest in the rainy season, but you can catch it any time of the year.

While it is not yet possible to be inoculated against malaria, limited protection can be gained from either a daily or weekly tablet. You should consult a doctor before taking anti-malarial drugs. Common drugs used to prevent malaria include chloroquine, maloprim, daraprim, doxycycline and artemesinine. Pregnant women in particular should consult a doctor before taking these.

Most Vietnamese hotels are equipped with mosquito nets and you'd be wise to use them. In the evenings when mosquitos are most active, cover bare skin, particularly the ankles. Use an insect repellent which contains diethyl-toluamide ('deet') – Autan and Off! are widely available in Asia. The 'green oil' (a Vietnamese cure-all sold in every pharmacy) works well. Mosquito coils are effective, though the smoke is irritating. There are also small, efficient 'electric mosquito incense' machines which are widely available in Vietnam.

Treating malaria is complicated and you should not try to undertake it yourself.

Prickly Heat & Fungus Prickly heat is a common problem for people from temperate climates. Small red blisters appear on the skin where your sweat glands have become swollen and blocked from the heavy workload. To prevent or cure it, wear light loose-fitting clothes; synthetic clothing can't absorb the sweat. Dry well after bathing and use a zinc-oxide-based talcum powder.

Fungal infections also occur more frequently in this sort of climate – often on the inside of the thigh (known as 'jock itch'). It itches like hell but is easy to clear up with an anti-fungal cream or powder.

Fungal ear infections usually result from swimming or washing in unclean water. Aquaear drops are a preventative to be used before you enter or wash in the water. A broad-spectrum antibiotic like Septrim can cure fungal infections, but check with a doctor.

Athlete's foot is also a fungal infection, usually occurring between the toes. Wearing open-toed sandals will often solve the problem. It also helps to clean between the toes with warm soapy water and an old toothbrush.

Sexually Transmitted Diseases (STDs) Sexual abstinence is the only 100% preventative. Travellers with uncontrollable hormones should at least use condoms. Gonorrhoea and syphilis are the most common STDs –

the latter can have fatal complications over time. There is no vaccine for gonorrhoea but there is one for syphilis. Both diseases can be treated with antibiotics.

There are numerous other sexually transmitted diseases, for most of which effective treatment is available. However, there is neither a cure nor a vaccine for herpes and AIDS.

AIDS can also be spread through infected blood transfusions; most developing countries cannot afford to screen the blood used for transfusions. It can also be spread by dirty needles, for example in vaccinations, acupuncture, ear-piercing and tattooing, not to mention drug-taking.

Cuts, Bites & Stings

Venomous snakes *are* found within the urban parts of Ho Chi Minh City. A nasty surprise can be baby snakes which are hard to see but are still venomous. Fortunately, snakes tend to avoid contact with creatures larger than themselves. Be careful about walking through grass and underbrush.

If you get bitten, try to remain calm (sounds easier than it really is) and not run around. Keep still and allow the poison to be absorbed slowly. Don't try to cut off circulation from the bitten area. Sucking out the poison has been widely discredited; immersion in cold water is also considered useless. Treatment in a hospital with an antivenin would be ideal. However, getting the victim to a hospital is only half the battle – you will also need to identify the snake.

Be careful, especially in rural areas, of insect and spider bites and stings. Bring an antihistamine if you are allergic to them. Down at the beach, take the usual precautions against jellyfish and other seaborne dangers.

Medical Facilities

Travel Medical Consultancy (☎ 357644), 10 Nguyen Canh Chan St, District 1, is one of the newest medical facilities in Ho Chi Minh City. It's staffed by foreign doctors, and they can even perform surgery if necessary. This clinic is open only during regular office hours, so you should go elsewhere if you have an emergency at night or on weekends.

Cho Ray Hospital (Benh Vien Cho Ray; ☎ 554137, 554138, 558074; 1000 beds), one of the best medical facilities in Vietnam, is at 201B Nguyen Chi Thanh Blvd, District 5. There is a section for foreigners on the

10th floor. About a third of the 200 doctors speak English. There are 24-hour emergency facilities. Spending the night in the foreigners' ward would cost about US$25. The hospital was built in the 1970s before reunification and some of the equipment still dates from around that period.

The Emergency Centre (☎ 225966, 291711, 292071), 125 Le Loi St, District 1, operates 24 hours. Doctors speak English and French. A visit typically costs US$10.

The French Consulate operates a clinic (☎ 297231, 297235) at 27 Nguyen Thi Minh Khai St, District 3. You do not need to be a French national, and the doctor speaks English and French. Call for an appointment. This is *not* a 24-hour clinic and is closed on weekends.

Asia Emergency Assistance (☎ 298520; fax 298551), Hannam Office Building, 65 Nguyen Du St, District 1, has a medical services programme for resident expats. The payment of an annual fee buys you regular treatment, emergency medical care and evacuation 24 hours a day. You can also contact International SOS Assistance (☎ 242866) for information about their health plan and evacuation services.

The Pasteur Institute (☎ 230252), 167 Pasteur St, District 3, has the best facilities in Vietnam for doing medical tests. However, you need to be referred here first by a doctor.

The Cardiology Institute is a speciality clinic at 520 Nguyen Tri Phuong, District 10. Another specialised medical facility is Phu San (☎ 392722), 284 Cong Quynh St, District 1, which treats only women.

Binh Dan Hospital is said to have belonged to President Thieu during the days when he ruled South Vietnam. This hospital is still one of the best in Vietnam but it's too far from the centre to be of much use to visitors. It's approximately 13 km north-west from the centre in Tan Binh District.

Pharmacies *(nha thuoc)* are everywhere. One good one is at 678 Nguyen Dinh Chieu St, District 3. The owner there speaks excellent English and French and can even get unusual medicines not normally kept in stock (someone delivers the medicines by motorbike within a couple of hours).

WOMEN TRAVELLERS

Sexual Harassment

Like other predominantly Buddhist countries, Vietnam is relatively free of the problem of sexual harassment. At least, that applies to women who are easily recognised

Newly-wed Vietnamese couple (RS)

as foreigners. But it's a different story for women who are Vietnamese, or look like they could be Vietnamese. To better understand this, see the following section on Prostitute Vigilantes.

Prostitute Vigilantes

An Asian woman accompanied by a Western male will automatically be labelled a 'Vietnamese whore'. The fact that the couple could be married (or just friends) doesn't seem to occur to anyone, nor does it seem to register that the woman might not be Vietnamese at all. If she's Asian then she's Vietnamese, and if she's with a Western male then she must be a prostitute. It will be difficult to convince most Vietnamese otherwise.

A woman in this situation can expect daily verbal abuse, though it will be spoken entirely in Vietnamese which means she may not realise that insults are being hurled at her. However, there will be no mistaking the hateful stares and occasional obscene gestures. Most of this abuse will come from Vietnamese men (including teenagers) – Vietnamese women will usually say nothing, regardless of what they think.

Verbal abuse is one thing, but there is the real possibility that the woman in question will become a target for occasional physical abuse, too. Women labelled 'whores' have reported having had rocks thrown at them, being hit by sticks, being spat upon, etc. Fortunately, this is rarely a group activity – the vigilante is usually a sole low-life greased with a bit of alcohol. Cyclo drivers (always male) are some of the worst offenders, though teenage boys are fond of rock-throw-ing. Interestingly, all the abuse is directed at the woman – the Western male standing by her side will be ignored unless he physically intervenes on his companion's behalf.

So far, the Vietnamese government has made no attempt to educate the masses to stop this primitive behaviour. For racially mixed couples wanting to visit Vietnam, no easy solution exists. Of course, public intimacy (holding hands etc) is best avoided, but even just walking down the street together invites abuse. Four people travelling together are less likely to encounter trouble than just two, but this isn't guaranteed. In an actual confrontation, the woman should shout some abuse at the antagonist in any language *other* than Vietnamese – this might make the low-life realise that he is confronting a foreigner rather than a 'Vietnamese whore'. If this revelation sinks in, he might suddenly apologise!

The Western male might be strongly tempted to physically assault a Vietnamese man who is insulting his Asian wife or girlfriend, but this could lead to a brawl with serious consequences. Before hitting anyone, remember that some of the spectators could be the man's brothers and they may violently retaliate.

Toilets

The scarcity of public toilets is a much greater problem for women than for men. Vietnamese males can often be seen urinating in public, but this seems to be socially unacceptable for women. It is not very clear how Vietnamese women handle this situation, but about the best advice one can give is to not drink too much.

DISABLED TRAVELLERS

Remember that Vietnam is still very much a Third World country, and such concerns as 'handicapped rights' are just not hot political issues. Disabled travellers will have to deal with such things as multi-storey hotels lacking lifts, pavements blocked by street vendors, high kerbs and motorbike riders who only slow down when they hit something.

SENIOR TRAVELLERS

Ho Chi Minh City poses no special problems for the elderly beyond the chaotic traffic and (possibly) pickpockets who may view older people as 'soft targets'.

Senior travellers should be extra careful about keeping all vaccinations up-to-date. Any special medications required should also be brought along. Asthmatics might experience unpredictable reactions to the food, air pollution, humidity or pollen, though the same warning would apply in developed countries as well.

THE CITY FOR CHILDREN

The Vietnamese absolutely adore children, and if you bring the kids you can expect that everyone will want to play with them.

The main risk to children comes from Ho Chi Minh City's horrendous traffic. It's bad enough for adults to deal with the reckless driving, but for children this is an especially serious hazard.

Daycare centres are notable for their absence, though it will not be difficult to hire a babysitter if you need one. Finding a babysitter who can speak English will be a little more difficult, but certainly not impossible.

Keeping the children happy and entertained can prove challenging at times. Playgrounds are scarce – one of the few is in Cong Vien Van Hoa Park. The zoo, circus and water puppet shows might be of interest to kids, including adult kids.

USEFUL ORGANISATIONS

Commercial Organisations

The following are some government and trade organisations that may be worth contacting for any business dealings in the city:

Chamber of Commerce & Industry of Vietnam (also called Vietcochamber), 171 Vo Thi Sau St, District 3 (☎ 230331, 230339; fax 294472)

Foreign Affairs Office 6 Thai Van Lung St, District 1 (☎ 223032, 224311, 24124)

Foreign Economic Relations Service 45-7 Ben Chuong Duong St, District 1 (☎ 92991)

People's Committee of Ho Chi Minh City 86 Le Thanh Ton St, District 1 (☎ 91056, 92991)

State Committee for Cooperation & Investment 178 Nguyen Dinh Chieu St, District 3 (☎ 94674, 223905)

Vietnam Trade Information Centre 35-7 Ben Chuong Duong St, District 1 (☎ 298734)

Tan Thuan Industrial Promotion Company 260 Tran Phu St, District 5 (☎ 350780; fax 351564); also operating from the Tan Thuan Export Processing Zone (☎ 728193; fax 725575) in the outlying Nha Be District. The Taiwanese joint-venture partner in this 'one stop shop for foreign investors' is CT&D Group (☎ (02) 3119933; fax 3881116) in Taipei.

For information regarding the development of Vietnam's legal code, contact the Vietnam Law & Legal Forum, at 21C Ton Duc Thang St, District 1.

Aid Organisations

Vietnam needs all the help it can get, and there are a number of international aid organisations filling that role. Unfortunately, most of the relief organisations do not accept donations or volunteers. One which does is the Rehabilitation Centre for Malnourished Children.

FAO
  (UN Food & Agriculture Organisation; TC Luong Thuc Va Nong Nghiep) 2 Phung Khac Khoan St, District 1 (☎ 290781)
ICRC
  (International Committee of the Red Cross; UB Chu Thap Do Quoc Te) 70 Ba Huyen Thanh Quan St, District 3 (☎ 222965)
Rehabilitation Centre for Malnourished Children
  38 Tu Xuong St, District 3
UNDP
  (UN Development Programme; Chuong Trinh Cua LHQ Ve Phat Trien) 2 Phung Khac Khoan St, District 1 (☎ 295821, 295865)
UNHCR
  (UN High Commission for Refugees; Cao Uy LHQ Ve Nguoi Ti Nan) 257 Hoang Van Thu St, Tan Binh District (☎ 445895, 445896)
UNICEF
  (UN Children's Fund; Quy Nhi Dong LHQ) 2 Phung Khac Khoan St, District 1 (☎ 291006)

DANGERS & ANNOYANCES

Women travellers, especially those of Asian appearance, should note also the section on Prostitute Vigilantes under the Women Travellers heading earlier in this chapter.

Theft

The Vietnamese are convinced that their cities are very dangerous and full of criminals. Although the danger is generally exaggerated, crime rates have risen significantly in the past couple of years.

Especially watch out for drive-by thieves on motorbikes – they specialise in snatching handbags and cameras from tourists riding in cyclos. Many are also proficient at grabbing valuables from the open window of a car and speeding away with the loot. Foreigners have occasionally reported having their glasses and hats snatched too.

Pickpocketing often involves the most unlikely kinds of people. Even cute little kids, women with babies and newspaper vendors seem to be practitioners of the art. It is currently a serious problem, especially in tourist areas of Saigon such as Dong Khoi and Pham Ngu Lao Sts. The children often wander right into cafés and restaurants where foreigners are eating, ostensibly to sell newspapers or postcards. In the process – and often with the help of another child accomplice – they can relieve you of your camera or handbag if you've set it down on an adjacent seat. If you must set things down while you're eating, at least take the precaution of fastening these items to your seat with a strap or chain. Remember, any luggage that you leave unattended for even a moment will grow legs and vanish.

There have been recent reports of people getting drugged and then robbed on long-distance public buses. The way it usually works is that a friendly fellow passenger offers you a free Coke, which in reality turns out to be a chloryl hydrate cocktail. You wake up hours later to find your valuables and new-found 'friend' gone. If you're unlucky, you don't wake up at all because an overdose of chloryl hydrate can easily be fatal.

Despite all this, you should not be overly paranoid. Although crime certainly exists and you need to be aware of it, theft in Vietnam does not seem to be any worse than elsewhere in the Third World (including 'Third World' cities in the West). Don't assume that everyone's a thief – most Vietnamese are very poor but reasonably honest.

And finally, there is the problem of your fellow travellers. It's a nauseating reality that some backpackers subsidise their journey by ripping off whoever they can, including other backpackers. This is most likely to happen if you stay in a dormitory, though in this regard Ho Chi Minh City is relatively safe since dormitories are rare.

Top : Street corner (RE)
Bottom : Funeral procession (RE)

To avoid theft, probably the most sensible advice one can follow is to not bring anything valuable that you don't need. Expensive watches, jewellery and electronic gadgets invite theft, but do you really need these things while travelling?

If robbed, should you turn to the friendly local police for help? There is often not a lot they can do in such cases except write a report for the insurance company. Some people have found that an offer to cover costs can elicit a more positive result.

Violence

Unlike in some Western cities, recreational homicide is not a popular sport in Ho Chi Minh City. In general, violence against foreigners is extremely rare. Vietnamese thieves prefer to pick your pocket or grab your bag and then run away – knives, guns, sticks and other weapons are almost never used. However, Vietnamese newspapers have started reporting a recent upsurge in violent robberies. So far, the victims have been overwhelmingly Vietnamese – the thieves seem to be reluctant to get involved with foreigners. That, of course, is almost certain to change.

Con Artists

Compared to some other countries (the Philippines and Thailand come to mind), Vietnam is relatively free of con artists who try to draw travellers into 'practice' card games, 'sure-fire investments' and great bargains on 'rare gems' which can always be 'resold at a profit'. But the Vietnamese are starting to learn some of the tricks which can be played on naive tourists in order to separate them from their money. You can never anticipate every scam you might encounter, so perhaps the best advice is to maintain a healthy scepticism and be prepared to walk away when unreasonable demands are made for your money.

There have been persistent reports in the tourist zones (especially Dong Khoi and Nguyen Hue Sts) of single male travellers being approached in the evening by women who appear to be prostitutes. Those foreigners foolish enough to even talk to these 'prostitutes' for a couple of minutes may suddenly be approached by a very angry, screaming 'husband' claiming that the foreigner is trying to rape his wife. He makes a big scene, a crowd gathers and he demands US$100 or so in 'compensation'.

Beggar Fatigue

Just as you're about to dig into the scrumptious Vietnamese meal you've ordered, you feel someone gently tugging on your shirtsleeve. You turn around to deal with this latest 'annoyance' only to find it's someone who looks like he or she hasn't eaten for a week.

You are looking into the face of poverty. How do you deal with these situations? If you're like me, not very well. On occasion, I've given food to a couple of beggars and watched in horror as they fought over it.

So what can you do to help these street people, many of whom are malnourished, illiterate and have no future? Good question – please send me your suggestions. Give or refuse as you wish, and spare a moment to think just how lucky you are.

Rats

Even cockroach enthusiasts are generally reluctant to share a hotel room with rats. If you encounter rats in Ho Chi Minh City hotels, they are not likely to be the cute, fluffy white creatures forced to smoke cigarettes and drink Diet Coke in Western medical experiments. Rather, they are the grey, decidedly less friendly variety.

Avoiding nocturnal visits by uppity rodents is fairly simple: don't keep any food in your hotel room.

Noise

One thing that can be insidiously draining on your energy during a visit to Ho Chi Minh City is noise. At night, there is often a competing cacophony from motorbikes, dance halls, cafés, video parlours, karaoke lounges, restaurants and so on. Taxis might as well have a permanent siren attached.

The Vietnamese themselves are immune to noise. Fortunately, most of the racket subsides around 10 or 11 pm, as few clubs stay open later than that thanks to the midnight curfew. Unfortunately, though, the Vietnamese are very early risers; most people are up and about from around 5 am onwards. This not only means that traffic noise starts early, but you're likely to be woken up by the crackle of café speakers, followed by very loud (and often atrocious) music. It's worth trying to get a hotel room at the back so that the effect of street noise is diminished. Other than that, perhaps you could consider bringing a set of earplugs.

BUSINESS HOURS

The Vietnamese rise early (and consider sleeping in to be a sure indication of illness). Offices, museums and many shops open between 7 and 8 am and close between 4 and 5 pm. Lunchtime is sacred, and virtually everything shuts down for 1½ hours between noon and 1.30 pm. Government workers tend to take longer breaks, so figure on getting nothing done from 11.30 am to 2 pm.

Most government offices are open on Saturday until noon. Sunday is a holiday. Most museums are closed on Mondays. Temples are usually open all day every day. Vietnamese tend to eat their meals by the clock regardless of whether or not they are hungry, and disrupting someone's meal schedule is considered very rude. This means that you don't visit people during lunch (unless invited). It also means that if you hire somebody for the whole day (a cyclo driver, for example), delaying the lunch break until 1 pm will earn you a reputation as a sadistic employer.

Many small privately owned shops, restaurants and street stalls stay open seven days a week, often until late at night – they need the money.

Consulates are notorious for keeping absurdly short business hours and for closing on every holiday, from Shakespeare's birthday to National Girl Guide Week.

PUBLIC HOLIDAYS

Politics affects everything, including public holidays. As an indication of Vietnam's new openness, Christmas, New Year, Tet (the lunar new year) and Buddha's birthday have been added as holidays after a 15-year lapse. The following are Vietnam's public holidays:

1 January
New Year's Day (Tet Duong Lich)
1st to 7th days of the 1st moon (late January to mid-February)
Tet (Tet Nguyen Dan), the Vietnamese lunar new year
3 February
Anniversary of the Founding of the Vietnamese Communist Party (Thanh Lap Dang CSVN) The Vietnamese Communist Party was founded on this date in 1930.
30 April
Liberation Day (Saigon Giai Phong) The date on which Saigon surrendered is commemorated nationwide as Liberation Day.
1 May
International Workers' Day (Quoc Te Lao Dong) Also known as May Day, this falls back to back with Liberation Day giving everyone a two-day holiday.

19 May
> *Ho Chi Minh's Birthday (Sinh Nhat Bac Ho)* Ho Chi Minh is said to have been born on this date in 1890 near Vinh, Nghe An Province.

8th day of the 4th moon (usually June)
> *Buddha's Birthday (Dan Sinh)*

2 September
> *National Day (Quoc Khanh)* This commemorates the proclamation in Hanoi of the Declaration of Independence of the Democratic Republic of Vietnam by Ho Chi Minh on 2 September 1945.

25 December
> Christmas *(Giang Sinh)*

FESTIVALS

Special prayers are held at Vietnamese and Chinese pagodas on days when the moon is either full (on the 14th and 15th days of the lunar month) or just the thinnest sliver (on the 29th/30th day of the month just ending and the first day of the new month). Many Buddhists eat only vegetarian food on these days.

The Tet Festival (ME)

The following major religious festivals are listed by lunar date:

1st to 7th days of the 1st moon
> *Tet (Tet Nguyen Dan)* The Vietnamese New Year is the most important festival of the year and falls in late January or early February. This public holiday is officially three days, but many people take off an entire week.

5th day of the 3rd moon
> *Holiday of the Dead (Thanh Minh)* People pay solemn visits to graves of deceased relatives – specially tidied up a few days before – and make offerings of food, flowers, incense sticks and ghost money.

8th day of the 4th moon
> *Buddha's Birth, Enlightenment & Death (Phat Dan)* This day is celebrated at pagodas and temples which, like many private homes, are festooned with lanterns. Processions are held in the evening.

5th day of the 5th moon
> *Summer Solstice Day (Doan Ngu)* Offerings are made to spirits, ghosts and the God of Death to ward off epidemics. Human effigies are burned to satisfy the requirements of the God of Death for souls to staff his army.

15th day of the 7th moon
> *Wandering Souls Day (Trung Nguyen)* This is the second-largest festival of the year. Offerings of food and gifts are made in homes and pagodas for the wandering souls of the forgotten dead.

15th day of the 8th moon
> *Mid-Autumn Festival (Trung Thu)* This festival is celebrated with moon cakes of sticky rice filled with such things as lotus seeds, watermelon seeds, peanuts, the yolks of duck eggs, raisins and sugar. Colourful lanterns in the form of boats, unicorns, dragons, lobsters, carp, hares, toads, etc are carried by children in an evening procession accompanied by drums and cymbals.

28th day of the 9th moon
> *Confucius' Birthday*

LANGUAGE COURSES

Universities require that you study 10 hours per week. Lessons usually last for two hours per day, for which you pay tuition of around US$5.

The regional dialects between northern and southern Vietnam are very different, and most foreigners who want to study in the south would prefer to learn the southern dialect. But the majority of the teachers at universities in the south have been imported from the north, and will tell you that the northern dialect is the 'correct one'! So even if you study at a university in the south, you may find that you need to hire a local private tutor (cheap at any rate) to help rid you of a northern accent.

The vast majority of foreign language students enrol at the General University of Ho Chi Minh City (Truong Dai Hoc Tong Hop) at 12 Binh Hoang, District 5. It's near the south-west corner of Nguyen Van Cu Blvd and Tran Phu Blvd.

WORK

Vietnam's opening to capitalist countries has suddenly created all sorts of work opportunities for Westerners. However, don't come to Ho Chi Minh City looking for big money. The most well-paid Westerners living in Vietnam are those working for official foreign organisations such as consulates, or hired by private foreign companies attempting to set up joint-venture operations. People with certain high-technology skills may also find themselves much in demand and able to secure high pay and cushy benefits.

Nice work if you can get it, but such plum jobs are thin on the ground. For the vast majority of travellers, the most readily available work opportunities will be teaching a foreign language.

English is by far the most popular foreign language with Vietnamese students. About 10% of foreign language students in Vietnam also want to learn French. There are also many Vietnamese who want to learn Chinese, but many ethnic Chinese live in Vietnam so there is little need to import foreign teachers. There is also some small demand for teachers of Japanese, German, Spanish and Korean.

Government-run universities in Vietnam hire some foreign teachers. Pay is generally around US$2 per hour, but certain benefits like free housing and unlimited visa renewals are usually thrown in. Teaching at a university requires some commitment – you may have to sign a one-year contract, for example.

There is also a budding free market in private language centres and home tutoring, and this is where most newly arrived foreigners seek work. Pay in the private sector is slightly better than what the government offers – figure on perhaps US$4 per hour to start. At private schools, free housing and other perks are usually not included. A business visa is required to be legally employed, and the school may not be in a good position to help you out with the authorities. One possible way around the visa hurdles is to sign up for Vietnamese language lessons at a university (see the Language

Courses section above), but be aware that you may actually be expected to attend class and study.

Private tutoring pays even better, around US$5 per hour and more. Flakiness is a problem – students can and do cancel without warning. As a private tutor, you are in business for yourself. The authorities may or may not turn a blind eye to such activities.

Everyone who has become a foreign language teacher in Vietnam will have a different story to tell. There is no one way to do it. It's generally *not* worth signing a contract unless the school is very reputable (ie other foreigners are working there and happy). Agreements mean little – your salary might be lowered without your consent, you might get underpaid (count the money in that envelope carefully) and you might find upon arriving for class that the director has decided that the lesson you have prepared has been replaced by another. The classes are huge (up to 60). You might find yourself yelling into a microphone, competing with the roar of traffic noise a few metres away and with the other teachers shouting into microphones in the adjoining classrooms.

The main hassle is finding a place to live. Landlords will tell you they're licensed to house foreigners, and then the cops will come by and kick you out a few days after you've moved in.

Getting There & Away

AIR

Many major airlines now have direct flights to Ho Chi Minh City. If there are no direct flights from your nearest major airport to Vietnam, the next best thing is to go via Bangkok or Hong Kong. These two places have emerged as the main transport hubs for getting to Ho Chi Minh City, as well as being ideal for accessing the rest of Asia.

To/From Asia

Cambodia There are daily flights between Phnom Penh and Ho Chi Minh City (US$50 one way; US$100 return) on either Cambodia Airlines or Vietnam Airlines. There is a US$5 airport tax to fly out of Cambodia. Visas for Cambodia are available upon arrival at Phnom Penh Airport for free if you stay less than 15 days.

China China Southern Airlines and Vietnam Airlines fly the China-Vietnam route using fuel-guzzling Soviet-built Tupolev 134 aircraft. The only direct flight between Ho Chi Minh City and China is to Guangzhou (Canton). All other flights are via Hanoi, though Ho Chi Minh City is the southern terminus of these flights. The Guangzhou-Hanoi flight (US$140 one way) takes 1½ hours; Guangzhou-Ho Chi Minh City (US$240 one way) takes 2½ hours. Return airfares cost exactly double.

The Beijing-Hanoi-Ho Chi Minh City flight on China Southern Airlines stops at Nanning (capital of China's Guangxi Province) en route – you can board or exit the plane there.

Hong Kong Hong Kong-Ho Chi Minh City flights run daily and require 2½ hours' flying time.

A travel agent in Hong Kong specialising in discount air tickets and customised tours to Vietnam is Phoenix Services (☎ 2722-7378; fax 2369-8884), in Room B, 6th floor, Milton Mansion, 96 Nathan Rd, Tsimshatsui, Kowloon.

Hong Kong's flag carrier, Cathay Pacific, and Vietnam Airlines offer joint service between Hong Kong and Ho Chi Minh City (one-way/return US$291/436).

Discount Flights
If you're looking for discounts or bargain airfares to Ho Chi Minh City, you will need to go to a travel agent rather than directly to the airlines, which can only sell fares at the full list price. A number of discount schemes are available. Remember when consulting your travel agent about discounts to make sure you know what kinds of restrictions apply to your ticket (journey to be completed within a certain time, no flights during holidays, and so on). If, later, you want to make changes to your route (before you go) or get a refund on an unused ticket, you need to see the original agent again, not the airline.

Group Tickets One way in which you can get a significant discount on fares to Ho Chi Minh City is to buy a group ticket. In theory, this means that you will arrive and depart with a tour group; in practice, you may never see the group or the tour guides. These tickets cannot be altered once issued, nor can you obtain a refund on the unused portion of such tickets. Since travellers often extend their stay in Vietnam, buying such a ticket could be a false way to economise.

APEX Tickets APEX (Advance Purchase Excursion) tickets are a variation on the theme, but such tickets must be purchased two or three weeks ahead of departure. They do not permit stopovers and may have minimum and maximum stays as well as fixed departure and return dates. It may be best to purchase an APEX ticket on a one-way basis only; there are stiff cancellation fees if you decide not to use it.

Open-Ended There are plenty of discount tickets valid for 12 months, allowing multiple stopovers with open dates. Though these tickets are not readily available to Ho Chi Minh City, you can easily get one to Bangkok, and getting from there to Ho Chi Minh City is both easy and cheap.

Round-the-World (RTW) Tickets These may be offered by one or more airlines. They let you take your time (six months to a year) moving from point to point on their routes for the price of one ticket, but they often work out more expensive overall, as well as limiting your flexibility.

Student If you are a student, you can usually get a discount on your ticket of up to 25%, providing you hold an Interna-

Indonesia Vietnam Airlines does not fly to Indonesia, but Garuda Airlines flies to Vietnam. A Jakarta-Ho Chi Minh City ticket costs US$437 each way. Round-trip excursion fares (good for 30 days) cost from US$705.

tional Student Identity Card (ISIC). An official-looking letter from the school is required by some airlines. Many airlines also require you to be aged 26 or younger to qualify for this discount.

Frequent Flyer These deals can earn you a free air ticket or other goodies if you accumulate enough mileage with one airline. First, you must apply to the airline for a frequent flyer account number. Every time you buy an air ticket and/or check in for your flight, inform the clerk of your account number. Save your tickets and boarding passes too; you should receive monthly statements, and can check against these how much mileage you've accumulated. Once you've built up sufficient mileage, you are supposed to receive vouchers by mail. However, frequent-flyer programmes tend to lock you into one airline, they have 'blackout' periods when you cannot fly for free (eg Christmas and Tet) and they may not always offer the cheapest fares or the most convenient schedule for your trip.

Children Airlines usually carry babies up to two years of age at 10% of the relevant adult fare; a few may carry them free of charge. Reputable international airlines usually provide nappies (diapers), tissues, talcum powder and all the other paraphernalia needed to keep babies clean, dry and half-happy. For children between the ages of four and 12 the fare on international flights is usually 50% of the regular fare or 67% of a discounted fare.

Couriers Courier flights can be a bargain if you're fortunate enough to find one. The way it works is that an air-freight company takes over your entire checked baggage allowance; you are permitted to bring along a carry-on bag, but that's all. In return, you get a steeply discounted ticket. Be aware that such tickets are sold for a fixed date and can be difficult or impossible to alter. Courier flights are occasionally advertised in the newspapers; or contact air-freight companies listed in the phone book.

Hint Some travellers might offer to sell you a ticket they haven't used or the return portion of a partially used ticket. Most airlines will absolutely refuse to honour a ticket if the name does not match the one on your passport. ■

Japan Arranging visas and air tickets in Japan is so outrageously expensive and time-consuming that you might consider taking a boat to Korea instead and doing it from there. Even better is to go to Bangkok.

If you've got no choice and must fly from Japan, Vietnam Airlines flies between Osaka and Ho Chi Minh City three times weekly. At present, there are no direct flights from Tokyo though that is expected to change. Osaka-Ho Chi Minh City flights take approximately 5½ hours. Japanese travel agents want US$150 to US$250 for a visa which takes two to three weeks to process. Compare this to Bangkok where the cost is US$45 and processing time is five days.

Tickets purchased in Vietnam are cheaper than those available in Japan. Low-end prices in Vietnam for Ho Chi Minh City-Osaka one-way/return are US$500/800.

Korea Korean Air and Vietnam Airlines offer joint service between Seoul and Ho Chi Minh City daily except Tuesdays. Asiana Airlines also flies to Vietnam. Flying time between Ho Chi Minh City and Seoul is 4¾ hours. The cheapest one-way/return fares are currently US$350/500.

Seoul is also a useful transit point connecting Vietnam to the USA.

Laos Lao Aviation and Vietnam Airlines offer joint service between Vientiane and Ho Chi Minh City (US$170/340).

Malaysia Malaysian Airline System (MAS) and Vietnam Airlines have joint service from Kuala Lumpur to Ho Chi Minh City (US$150/300 one-way/return). Flying time for Kuala Lumpur-Ho Chi Minh City is 1¾ hours.

Philippines Philippine Airlines and Vietnam Airlines fly from Manila to Ho Chi Minh City. Economy one-way/return tickets start at US$185/280. Flying time from Manila to Ho Chi Minh City is 2½ hours.

Singapore Singapore Airlines and Vietnam Airlines offer daily joint service on the Ho Chi Minh City-Singapore route. Flight time between Singapore and Ho Chi Minh City is 1¾ hours. The one-way fare is US$213 and return fares are exactly double.

Taiwan Taiwan's China Airlines flies between Ho Chi Minh City and the Taiwanese cities of Taipei and Kaohsiung. Flight time between Ho Chi Minh City and Taiwan is around three hours. The cheapest return fares are 90-day excursion tickets – one-way/return excursion fares are US$350/525.

Pacific Airlines offers the cheapest fares Ho Chi Minh City-Taipei for US$461 return.

EVA Air claims to be Taiwan's luxury airline and charges accordingly. On a Taipei-Ho Chi Minh City excursion return ticket, figure on around US$560.

Travel agents in Taiwan advertise return fares as low as US$423, but these are group tickets which must be booked well in advance and no changes are permitted.

A long-running discount travel agent with a good reputation is Jenny Su Travel (☎ (02) 5947733, 5962263; fax 5920068), 10th floor, 27 Chungshan N Rd, Section 3, Taipei.

There are no diplomatic relations between Taiwan and Vietnam, and visa processing can take up to 10 days.

Thailand Bangkok, only 80 minutes' flying time from Ho Chi Minh City, has emerged as the main port of embarkation for air travel to and from Vietnam.

Thai Airways International (THAI), Air France and Vietnam Airlines offer daily Bangkok-Ho Chi Minh City service for US$150 one way; round-trip tickets cost exactly double.

Khao San Rd in Bangkok is the budget travellers' headquarters and the place to look for bargain ticket deals. There are many agencies here milking the backpacker market, but one which has received frequent recommendations from travellers is Vista Travel Service (☎ 2800348), 24/4 Khao San Rd. Another place that does all right for tickets and visas is Exotissimo Travel (☎ 2535240; fax 2547683).

Airport workers (RS)

To/From Australasia

Australia Qantas and Vietnam Airlines offer joint service from Ho Chi Minh City to both Melbourne (9½ hours) and Sydney (eight hours). Rock-bottom excursion fares are US$600/1000 for one-way/return tickets.

Ethnic-Vietnamese living in Australia are known to have the inside scoop on ticket discounts. The weekend travel sections of papers like *The Age* (Melbourne) or the *Sydney Morning Herald* are good sources of travel information. Also look at *Escape*, a free magazine published by STA Travel. STA Travel has offices all around Australia (check your phone directory).

Among the cheapest regular tickets available are APEX tickets. The cost depends on your departure date from Australia. The year is divided into 'peak', 'shoulder' and 'low' seasons; peak season, the most expensive, is December to January. It's possible to get reductions on the cost of APEX and other fares by going to the travel agents in Australia that specialise in discounting.

Also well worth trying is the Flight Centres International (☎ (03) 9670-0477), 386 Little Bourke St, Melbourne. They also have branches elsewhere in Australia, including Sydney (☎ (02) 233-2296) and Brisbane (☎ (07) 229-9958).

New Zealand You'll have to go via Australia or through an Asian gateway, such as Bangkok, Singapore or Hong Kong, to get to Vietnam from New Zealand. A low-season excursion will cost about NZ$1650. There are currently no direct flights, although this is likely to change in the not-too-distant future.

To/From Europe

France Vietnam Airlines cooperates with Air France. Flights between Paris and Ho Chi Minh City (usually via Dubai and sometimes Berlin) run three times weekly. One-way/return fares are US$830/1245.

Germany Germany's Lufthansa and Vietnam Airlines offer joint service between Berlin and Ho Chi Minh City. There are two flights weekly which go via Dubai, and flying time is at least 14½ hours. Bottom-end one-way/return fares are US$830/1245.

Netherlands Vietnam Airlines has a joint operation with KLM and flies Amsterdam-Ho Chi Minh City nonstop. The best prices you can hope to get on one-way/return tickets are currently US$825/1240.

Russia Aeroflot flies Ilyushin IL86s and IL62s from Moscow to Hanoi and Ho Chi Minh City with numerous stopoffs along the way. The whole hopscotch across Asia can take over 20 hours.

Vietnam Airlines flies twice weekly between Ho Chi Minh City and Moscow via Dubai. This airline uses Boeing 767s and the flight takes 14 hours. Tickets purchased in Russia cost more than those bought in Vietnam. The best prices you can get in Vietnam for one-way/return Ho Chi Minh City-Moscow tickets are US$640/1280.

UK There are no direct flights between the UK and Vietnam, but cheap tickets are available on the London-Hong Kong run. From Hong Kong, it's easy enough to make onward arrangements to Vietnam.

Air-ticket discounting is a legitimate business in the UK but do be careful about handing over large sums of cash to potential fly-by-night operators.

To find out what's going, there are a number of magazines in Britain which have good information about flights and agents. These include *Trailfinder*, free from the Trailfinders Travel Centre in Earls Court, and *Time Out*, a London weekly entertainment guide. Discount tickets are almost exclusively available in London.

To/From North America

Canada There are currently no direct flights between Canada and Vietnam. Most Canadian travellers transit at Hong Kong.

Getting discount tickets in Canada is much the same as in the USA – go to the travel agents and shop around until you find a good deal.

CUTS is Canada's national student bureau and has offices in a number of Canadian cities including Vancouver, Edmonton, Toronto and Ottawa – you don't necessarily have to be a student. There are a number of good agents in Vancouver for cheap tickets.

USA It's not advisable to send money (even cheques) through the post unless the agent is very well established – some travellers have reported being ripped off by fly-by-night mail-order ticket agents. Nor is it wise to hand over the full amount to Shady Deal Travel Services unless they can give you the ticket straight away – most

US travel agencies have computers that can spit out the ticket on the spot.

Council Travel is the largest student travel organisation, and though you don't have to be a student to use them, they do have specially discounted student tickets. Council Travel has an extensive network in all major US cities and is listed in the telephone book. There are also Student Travel Network offices which are associated with STA Travel.

One of the cheapest and most reliable travel agents on the west coast is Overseas Tours (☎ (800) 222-5292), 475 El Camino Real, Room 206, Millbrae, CA 94030. Another good agent is Gateway Travel (☎ (214) 960-2000, (800) 878-2828; fax 490-6367), 4201 Spring Valley Rd, Suite 104, Dallas, TX 75244. Both of these places seem to be trustworthy for mail-order tickets.

China Airlines (of Taiwan, not China) currently offers the cheapest fares on US-Vietnam flights, all of which transit Taipei. Low-season San Francisco-Ho Chi Minh City one-way/return tickets cost US$464/837; New York-Ho Chi Minh City is US$573/1047.

Other possible but slightly pricier US-Vietnam tickets are available from EVA Air (also via Taipei), Cathay Pacific (via Hong Kong), THAI (via Bangkok) and Asiana (via Seoul).

At the time of this writing, no US air carriers were flying into Vietnam. However, this is expected to change shortly. Airlines to watch include Northwest and United.

Within Vietnam

Domestic flights from Ho Chi Minh City on Vietnam Airlines with one-way ticket prices are as follows:

Destination	Frequency	Price (US$)
Buon Ma Thuot	two daily	60
Cantho	suspended	50
Dalat	three weekly	40
Danang	three daily	85
Haiphong	two daily	150
Hanoi	five daily	150
Hué	two daily	85
Nha Trang	two daily	60
Phu Quoc	five weekly	65
Pleiku	one daily	60
Qui Nhon	five weekly	60

Pacific Airlines also flies the Ho Chi Minh City-Hanoi route (daily except Sundays) and charges the same fare as Vietnam Airlines.

Airline Offices

The representative offices of airlines in Ho Chi Minh City are as follows:

Aeroflot
    4B Le Loi Blvd, District 1 (☎ 293489)
Air France
    127 Tran Quoc Thao St, District 3 (☎ 293770)
Asiana
    141-143 Ham Nghi Blvd, District 1 (☎ 222665)
Cambodia Air
    343 Le Van St, Tan Binh District (☎ 440126)
Cathay Pacific
    49 Le Thanh Ton St, District 1 (☎ 223272)
China Airlines (Taiwan)
    132 Dong Khoi St (Continental Hotel), District 1 (☎ 251387)
China Southern Airlines
    52B Pham Hong Thai St, District 1 (☎ 291172, 298417)
EVA Air
    129 Dong Khoi St, District 1 (☎ 224488)
Garuda Indonesia
    106 Nguyen Hue Blvd (☎ 293644)
KLM
    244 Pasteur St, District 3 (☎ 231990)
Korean Air
    141 Nguyen Hue Blvd, District 1 (☎ 296042)
Lao Aviation
    39/3 Tran Nhat Duat St (☎ 442807)
Lufthansa
    132-134 Dong Khoi St (Continental Hotel), District 1 (☎ 298529)
Malaysian Airline System (MAS)
    116 Nguyen Hue Blvd, District 1 (☎ 230695)
Pacific Airlines
    77 Le Thanh Ton St, District 1 (☎ 231285, 290844)
Philippine Airlines
    4A Le Loi Blvd, District 1 (☎ 292113)
Qantas
    311 Dien Bien Phu St, District 3 (☎ 396194)
Singapore Airlines
    6 Le Loi Blvd, District 1 (☎ 231583)
Thai Airways
    65 Nguyen Du St, District 1 (☎ 223365)
Vietnam Airlines
    116 Nguyen Hue Blvd, District 1 (☎ 292118)
    15B Dinh Tien Hoang Rd (☎ 299910)

Leaving Vietnam

Be aware that Vietnamese visas specify from which point(s) – usually Ho Chi Minh City's Tan Son Nhat Airport and/or Hanoi's Noi Bai Airport – you are permitted to leave the country. If you are departing from Ho Chi Minh City, be sure your visa says Tan Son Nhat, or else visit the immigration police and get it straightened out before departure. Some foreigners who failed to do this have managed to bribe their way out, but that is expensive and uncertain.

You *must* reconfirm all flights out of Vietnam even if you purchased a return ticket with a fixed departure date. Reconfirmation is best done by paying a visit to the office of the relevant airline in Ho Chi Minh City (woe to anyone who thinks they can accomplish anything at Tan Son Nhat Airport). Theoretically, it can also be done by telephone, but you are always better off to go in person and have the airline affix a reconfirmation sticker to your ticket. This gives you some clout should the airline decide to bounce you and claim that it is your fault because 'you didn't reconfirm'. You should also visit the airline office if you need to make any modifications to your date of departure, or if you want to upgrade to business class, etc.

Departure tax at Ho Chi Minh City is US$8 for all international flights. The tax is payable in either dong or US dollars.

BUS

To/From Cambodia

Vietnam requires a special visa for entering the country overland. These visas cost more and take longer to issue than the normal tourist visas needed for entering by air. Travellers who have tried to use a standard visa for entering Vietnam overland have fared poorly, but sometimes they manage after paying the Vietnamese border guards a considerable bribe.

Exiting from Vietnam to Cambodia is much simpler. The Cambodians don't require anything more than a standard tourist visa, and Cambodian visas do not indicate entry or exit points. However, your Vietnamese visa must have the correct exit point marked on it. This is a change which can easily be made in Ho Chi Minh City.

Although land travel through Cambodia is not especially recommended due to attacks by the Khmer Rouge, the situation is considered relatively safe on the main highway between Ho Chi Minh City and Phnom Penh. However, it would still be wise to make enquiries before proceeding, and realise that flying is safest of all.

The only frontier crossing between Cambodia and Vietnam which is open to Westerners is at Moc Bai.

Buses run every day between Ho Chi Minh City (via Moc Bai) and Phnom Penh. The cost is US$5 or US$12 depending on whether you take the air-con coach or an old De Soto rattletrap. In Ho Chi Minh City, you purchase tickets from the Phnom Penh Bus Garage at 155 Nguyen Hue Blvd, adjacent to the Rex Hotel, but the bus departs at 5 am from 145 Nguyen Du St. The biggest disadvantage of this bus is that you must wait for everybody to clear customs at the border, a procedure which can take hours.

There is a faster and cheaper way, although it's a bit more complicated. You can board one of the many bus tours heading for the Caodai Great Temple at Tay Ninh (for as little as US$5). But instead of going to Tay Ninh, you get off sooner at Go Dau where the highway forks. There will be motorcycle taxis waiting here, and for as little as US$0.50 you can get a ride to the border crossing at Moc Bai. At the border you must walk across, and you will find air-conditioned share taxis waiting on the Cambodian side to take you to Phnom Penh for US$5 per person.

There are also share taxis direct from Saigon to the Moc Bai border crossing, some costing as little as US$20 for three persons. In Saigon, Kim Café at 270-272 De Tham St, District 1, is one place to book these, but also check at other travel agencies.

To do this overland crossing, you will need a Cambodian visa (which takes seven working days to process) and a re-entry visa for Vietnam if you are going back to Vietnam rather than flying on to a third country. If you are entering or exiting Vietnam by this route, your Vietnamese visa (or re-entry visa) must indicate the Moc Bai crossing. If you forgot to do that in Saigon, amendments to Vietnamese re-entry visas can also be made at the Vietnamese Embassy in Phnom Penh.

Foreigners making the crossing at Moc Bai have reported attempts by Vietnamese customs agents to solicit bribes.

To/From Laos

There is a cross-border bus running between Danang (central Vietnam) and Savannakhet (Laos) via the Vietnamese bordertown of Lao Bao. This journey is beyond the scope of this city guide. Travellers should refer to Lonely Planet's guide to *Vietnam* for further details.

Within Vietnam

Long-Distance Bus Inter-city buses depart from and arrive at a variety of stations around Ho Chi Minh City. In general, you will find that these buses are nearly always extremely crowded, as well as being unreliable and unsafe, but at least they are dirt cheap.

Cholon Station is the most convenient place to get buses to Mytho and other Mekong Delta towns. The Cholon Bus Station is at the very western end of Tran Hung Dao B Blvd in District 5, close to the Binh Tay Market.

Less conveniently located than Cholon Station, Mien Tay Station has even more buses to points south of Ho Chi Minh City (basically the Mekong Delta). This enormous station is about 10 km west of Saigon in An Lac, a part of Binh Chanh District. There are buses from central Saigon to Mien Tay Bus Station from the Ben Thanh Bus Station (near Ben Thanh Market).

Buses to places north of Ho Chi Minh City leave from Mien Dong Bus Station, which is in Binh Thanh District about five km from central Saigon on National Highway 13 (the continuation of Xo Viet Nghe Tinh St). To get there, you can take a bus from Ben Thanh Bus Station near Ben Thanh Market.

Vehicles departing from Van Thanh Bus Station serve destinations within a few hours of Ho Chi Minh City, mostly in Song Be and Dong Nai provinces. For travellers, most important are probably the buses to Dalat and Vung Tau. Van Thanh Bus Station is in Binh Thanh District about 1.5 km east of the intersection of Dien Bien Phu and Xo Viet Nghe Tinh Sts.

Buses to Tay Ninh, Cu Chi and points north-west of Ho Chi Minh City depart from the Tay Ninh Bus Station in Tan Binh District. To get there, head all the way out on Cach Mang Thang Tam St. The station is about one km past where Cach Mang Thang Tam St merges with Le Dai Hanh St.

Minibus Privately owned minibuses are more comfortable than the huge public buses. However, the level of comfort varies – only with a charter can you be assured that the driver won't pack the passengers in like sardines.

Just next to the Saigon Hotel and the mosque on Dong Du St is where you catch minibuses to Vung Tau. This is an unofficial bus stop and there is always the possibility that the location will be suddenly moved. In other words, enquire first.

TRAIN

The main thing to remember about Vietnamese trains is that the odd-numbered ones travel southward, and even-numbered trains travel northward. The one which runs between Ho Chi Minh City and Hanoi is known as the *Reunification Express*. Travel times on this run are 37 to 44 hours for the 1726-km trip. Slow local trains go from Ho Chi Minh City to such places as Nha Trang and Qui Nhon. To the Chinese border from Hanoi, there are spur trains to two points, Dong Dang and Lao Cai.

Timetables change frequently but are posted at major stations and you can copy these down. It's important to realise that the train schedule is bare bones during Tet. Even the *Reunification Express* is suspended for nine days, starting four days before Tet and continuing four days after.

Petty crime is a problem on trains, especially if you travel in budget class where your fellow passengers are likely to be dirt poor. Thieves have become proficient at

Reunification Express (PW)

grabbing packs through the open windows as trains pull out of stations.

Another hazard is that children frequently throw rocks at the train. Many conductors will insist that you keep down the metal window shields to prevent injury to passengers. Unfortunately, these shields obstruct the view.

One disadvantage of rail travel is that foreigners are supposed to pay a surcharge of around 400% over and above what Vietnamese pay. It works out to about US$100 for a Saigon-Hanoi ticket in a hard-sleeper compartment. This is compared to US$150 to fly the same route.

Reservations for all trips should be made at least one day in advance. For sleeping berths, you may have to book passage three or more days before the date of travel. Bring your passport and visa when buying train tickets, and hang onto your ticket until you've exited the railway station at your final destination. There is a 20-kg limit for luggage carried on Vietnamese trains.

There are six classes of train travel: half-seat, hard-seat, soft-seat, hard-berth, soft-berth and super-berth. Since it's all that the vast majority of Vietnamese can afford, half-seat and hard-seat are usually packed and are very uncomfortable.

Saigon Railway Station (Ga Sai Gon; ☎ 230105) is in District 3 at 1 Nguyen Thong St. Trains from here serve cities along the coast north of Ho Chi Minh City. The ticket office is open from 7.15 to 11 am and 1 to 3 pm daily.

BOAT

From Abroad

Vietnam has 3451 km of intriguing coastline, so it's a shame that there's so little chance of arriving on these scenic shores by boat. If you have connections in the shipping industry, you might get on a freighter. A number of luxury cruise liners offer stopovers in Ho Chi Minh City.

Long-Distance Boats

Passenger and goods ferries to the Mekong Delta depart from a dock at the river end of Ham Nghi Blvd. There is daily service to Mytho (six hours; departs daily at 11 am). Buy your tickets on the boat. Simple food might be available on board. Be aware that these ancient vessels lack the most elementary safety gear, such as life jackets.

TRAVEL AGENTS

There are heaps of these in Ho Chi Minh City. Most of their revenue comes from the business of doing car rentals and local tours, but a few can arrange international airline tickets. Fiditourist on Pham Ngu Lao St has some of the cheapest prices we've seen, but ring up a few others before putting down your hard-earned cash. A few agencies to try include the following:

Art Tourist
    63 Ly Tu Trong St, District 1 (☎ 230234; fax 293289)
Atlas Travel & Tours
    41 Nam Ky Khoi Nghia St, District 1 (☎ 210300, 224122; fax 298604)
Ben Thanh Tourist
    121 Nguyen Hue St, District 1 (☎ 298597; fax 296269)
CESAIS Tourism
    17 Pham Ngoc Thach St, District 3 (☎ 296750)
Eden Tourist
    104-106 Nguyen Hue St, District 1 (☎ 293651; fax 230783)
Fiditourist
    195 Pham Ngu Lao St, District 1 (☎ 353018)
    71-73 Dong Khoi St, District 1 (☎ 296264)
Hacotours
    8 Nguyen Binh Khiem St, District 1 (☎ 299360; fax 231302)
NHABEXIM
    31 Dong Khoi St, District 1 (☎ 298272)
OSC
    65 Nam Ky Khoi Nghia St, District 1 (☎ 296658; fax 290195)
Peace Tours
    (Cong Ty Du Lich Hoa Binh) 60 Vo Van Tan St, District 3 (☎ 290923; fax 294416)
Sao Viet Tour
    59 Dong Du St, District 1 (☎ 294561)
TNT
    9 Dong Khoi St, District 1 (☎ 299363; fax 295832)
Vietlink Trading Travel & Tour Company
    411 Tran Hung Dao Blvd, District 5 (☎ 555849; fax 555852)
Vietnam Veteran Tourism
    97 Nguyen Dinh Chieu St, District 3 (☎ 241627; fax 248268)
Youth Tourist Company
    292 Dien Bien Phu St, District 3 (☎ 294580)

ORGANISED TOURS

Even if you're not the sort of person inclined to take organised tours, there are good reasons to consider doing so on excursions around Ho Chi Minh City. First of all, there is Vietnam's decrepit transport system to contend with. Slugging it out on the buses is bad enough, but many of the places worth seeing are not even accessible by bus. Then there is the issue of cost – labour is cheap, so by choosing your tour operator carefully you need not spend a large pile of money. There is also the benefit of having a guide and interpreter who can add value to your trip, as well as making good travelling companions.

And you can forget the image of big tour buses and hordes of camera-clicking tourists – it's easy to arrange tours for small groups (three to 10 persons is typical). Even if you've come to Vietnam by yourself, you should have no difficulty finding other travellers to accompany you and split the cost – indeed, the travel agencies in Ho Chi Minh City can arrange this too.

From Abroad

Package tours of Ho Chi Minh City are sold by agencies in Bangkok and elsewhere, but nearly all these tours, which usually follow one of a dozen or so set itineraries, are run by the omnipresent government tourism authorities, Vietnam Tourism and Saigon Tourist. You really could fly to Ho Chi Minh City and make all the arrangements after arrival, so the only thing you gain by booking ahead is that you might save a little time. However, if your time is more precious than money, a pre-booked package tour could be right for you.

Tours booked outside Vietnam are not a total rip-off given what you get (visa, air tickets, tourist-class accommodation, food, transport, a guide, etc) but then again they're not inexpensive: they range in price from about US$480 for a three-day Saigon 'shopping tour' to over US$1000 for a week-long trip that includes flying all around the country.

Companies in Bangkok selling their own versions of the standard tours often farm out the sale of their offerings to other travel agencies. The price may be pretty much the same if you purchase a tour on Khao San Rd rather than at a travel agency in the West.

In Ho Chi Minh City

There are plenty of local tour agencies. These places can provide cars, book air tickets and extend your visa. Some of them charge the same as Saigon Tourist and Vietnam Tourism, while others are much cheaper. Competition between the private agencies is keen and you can undercut Saigon Tourist's tariffs by 50%.

Almost everyone has good things to say about Kim Café, Getra Tour Company and Ann's Tourist. However, remember the warning at the beginning of this book – 'good places can go bad'. If possible, chat with your fellow travellers before putting down the cash.

A line-up of some agencies in Ho Chi Minh City follows:

Ann's Tourist
   58 Ton That Tung, District 1 (☎ 332564, 334356; fax 323866)
Cantho Tourist
   42 Cao Than St, District 3 (☎ 330675; fax 358943); or contact Lotus Café at 197 Pham Ngu Lao St, District 1.
Cholon Tourist
   (Cong Ty Dich Vu Du Lich Cho Lon) 192-194 Su Van Hanh St, District 5 (☎ 359090; fax 355375)
Dong Thap Tourist
   16/1A Le Hong Phong, District 10 (☎ 355826; fax 298540)
Getra Tour Company
   86 Bui Vien St, District 1 (☎ 353021; fax 298540)
Kim Café
   270-272 De Tham St, District 1 (☎ 359859; fax 298540)
Saigon Tourist
   49 Le Thanh Ton St, District 1 (☎ 298914; fax 224987)
Thanh Thanh Travel Agency
   c/o Thanh Thanh 2 Hotel, 205 Pham Ngu Lao St, District 1 (☎ 360205)
   c/o Café 333, 217 Pham Ngu Lao St, District 1 (☎ 251550)
Vietnam Tourism
   234 Nam Ky Khoi Nghia St, District 3 (☎ 290776; fax 290775)
Vietnam Veteran Tourism
   97 Nguyen Dinh Chieu St, District 3 (☎ 241627; fax 248268)
Youth Tourist Company
   292 Dien Bien Phu St, District 3 (☎ 294580)

WARNING

Remember that all the information in this chapter is subject to rapid change. The airline business in particular is anything but stable – you can expect prices to seesaw, routes to change, new players to enter the field and old ones to depart.

You should get opinions, quotes and advice from as many airlines and travel agencies as possible before parting with your hard-earned cash. The details given in this chapter should be regarded as pointers and are not a substitute for your own careful research.

Getting Around

TO/FROM THE AIRPORT

Ho Chi Minh City's Tan Son Nhat International Airport is seven km from the centre of Saigon. Metered air-conditioned taxis are run by two companies – Airport Taxi and Vina Taxi. The drivers are good about using their meters, which are denominated in US dollars.

The unlicensed and unmetered taxis for hire outside the customs hall will try to grossly overcharge, so bargain hard (a fair price into town is about US$7) or else take a metered taxi. Don't waste your time at the Tan Son Nhat Airport Taxi Booking Desk – the minimum fare is US$25 for a standard taxi, or US$50 for a limousine.

Cyclos (pedicabs) can be hailed outside the gate to the airport, which is a few hundred metres from the terminal building. A ride to central Saigon should cost about US$2. Motorbike 'taxis' hang out near the airport and typically ask US$3 to go to the city centre, though you may be able to bargain something better.

To get to the airport, you can ring up a taxi (see the Taxi section further on for telephone numbers). Some of the cafés in the budget hotel area of Pham Ngu Lao St also do runs to the airport – these places even have sign-up sheets where you can book share taxis for US$2 per person. This, no doubt, will prove considerably cheaper than the limousine services available at the front desk of tourist hotels.

If you take a cyclo or motorbike to Tan Son Nhat, you may have to walk from the airport gate to the terminal. Private cars can bring you into the airport.

BUS

Few foreigners make use of the city buses, though they are safer than cyclos, even if less aesthetically pleasing.

At present, there are only three bus routes though more will undoubtedly be added. No decent bus map is available and bus stops are mostly unmarked, so it's worth summarising the three bus lines, as follows:

Saigon-Cholon – Buses depart Central Saigon from opposite the Saigon Floating Hotel and continue along Tran Hung Dao Blvd to Binh Tay Market in Cholon, then return along the same route. The bus company running this route is an Australian joint-venture – buses have air-conditioning and video movies, and the driver is well dressed! All this for US$0.20. Buy your ticket on board from the female attendant (sharply dressed in a blouse and skirt).

Mien Dong-Mien Tay – Buses depart Mien Dong Bus Station (north-eastern Ho Chi Minh City), pass through Cholon and terminate at Mien Tay Bus Station in the western edge of town. The fare is US$0.40.

Van Thanh-Mien Tay – Buses depart Van Thanh Bus Station (eastern Ho Chi Minh City), pass through Cholon and terminate at Mien Tay Bus Station (western Ho Chi Minh City). The fare is US$0.40.

XE LAM

Xe Lams (tiny three-wheeled vehicles otherwise known as Lambrettas) connect the various long-distance bus stations. There is a useful Xe Lam stop on the north-west corner of Pham Ngu Lao and Nguyen Thai Hoc Sts where you can catch a ride to the Mien Tay Bus Station. This station is where you get buses to the Mekong Delta.

SUBWAY

No, Ho Chi Minh City does not yet have a subway, nor is one under construction. However, a team of foreign consultants has been called in and a feasibility study is under way. It's not likely that the subway will be completed within the lifespan of this book, or even during the next edition. Nevertheless, it's nice to be optimistic. And when the ribbon-cutting ceremony for the Ho Chi Minh City Metro finally occurs, just remember that you read it here first.

CAR

Self-drive cars for hire are not yet available, but – considering the traffic – it's hard to imagine why anybody would want to drive if they didn't have to. On the other hand, it's easy enough to hire a car with driver included. Labour is cheap at US$5 per day, so hiring a local to confront the chaos is only a small part of the rental fee for the vehicle.

A cheap Russian-built rental car can be had for about US$4 per hour, US$25 per day (under eight hours and under 100 km) or US$0.15 to US$0.25 per km. Small Japanese cars can be rented for US$5 per hour, US$35 per day or US$0.35 per km. A minivan can carry up to 12 people and be rented for US$6 per hour, US$40 per day or US$0.40 per km.

Whitewashing Nature
Visitors to Ho Chi Minh City have often wondered why the lower half of all the trees are painted white. Theories posited by tourists have included: (1) the paint protects the trees from termites, (2) the paint protects the trees from Agent Orange, (3) it is some government official's idea of nouveau art and (4) it is an ancient Vietnamese tradition. It turns out that the mystery of the white trees has a much simpler explanation – the trees are painted white so people don't bump into them at night. ■

Cars can be rented from a wide variety of sources. Generally, cafés, hotels and private travel agencies offer the best prices.

New government regulations require that all cars carrying foreigners need a special permit (which simply means that the vehicle owner pays a special tax) and a licensed guide in the car at all times. While this might sound like a noble effort to protect foreigners, the result will certainly be an increase in prices. Bureaucracy is something you pay for.

TAXI

Cabs

Metered taxis occasionally cruise the streets, but it's much easier to find one if you ring up their dispatcher. Generally, you'll only have to wait a few minutes before the vehicle arrives. Vina Taxi (☎ 442170) operates cabs yellow in colour. Airport Taxi (☎ 446666) has white vehicles, and they will drive you anywhere around town, not just to the airport. Flagfall is US$0.75 and cost per km also runs to US$0.75.

Local bus (RS)

Xe Lams (PW)

Motorbike Taxis

A quick and simple way around town is to ride on the
back of a motorbike taxi *(Honda om)*. You can either try
to flag someone down (most drivers can always use
whatever extra cash they can get) or ask a Vietnamese to
find a Honda om for you. The accepted rate is comparable
to what cyclos charge.

MOPED & MOTORBIKE

Rental

If you're brave, you can rent a motorbike and really earn
your 'I Survived Saigon' T-shirt. Travelling by motorbike can be good fun, but it can also be a near-death
experience (or worse). It's not recommended. You can
hire a cyclo driver or some other local person to be your
guide, translator and motorbike driver – this is generally
worth the additional expense (about US$5 per day).

Nevertheless, many travellers like the stimulation of
the self-drive experience. Motorbike rentals are ubiquitous in places where tourists congregate; the Pham Ngu
Lao St area is as good as any to satisfy this need. Ask at
the cafés, hotels, motorcycle shops or else talk to a cyclo
driver for ideas on where to find rentals.

A 50cc motorbike can be rented for US$5 to US$10 per
day. Before renting one, make sure it's rideable. The
renter will probably want security – your passport, visa
or a cash deposit. It's better to use your own lock rather
than the one supplied (renters have been known to have

an accomplice with an extra key 'steal' the bike, thus forcing the rentee to buy a new one).

The legal definition of a moped is any motor-driven two-wheeled vehicle less than 100cc, even if it doesn't have bicycle pedals. Motorcycles are two-wheeled vehicles with engines 100cc and larger. In Vietnam, no driver's licence is needed to drive a moped, while to drive a motorcycle, you will need an international driver's licence endorsed for motorcycle operation. But expats remaining in the country over six months are expected to obtain a Vietnamese driver's licence. The Vietnamese licence will be valid only for the length of your visa!

Technically, the maximum legal size for a motorcycle is 125cc. There are indeed larger bikes around and you will no doubt see them, but to drive one the owner must join a motorcycle association and do voluntary public service (riding in patriotic parades and sporting events, and so on).

The major cities have parking lots *(giu xe)* for bicycles and motorbikes – usually just a roped-off section of sidewalk – which charge US$0.20 to guard your vehicle (bike theft is a major problem).

Locals are required to have liability insurance on their motorbikes, but foreigners are not covered and there is currently no way to arrange this.

The government has been talking about requiring the use of safety helmets. However, most Vietnamese disdain wearing them, in part because of the expense and also because of the tropical heat. You can purchase high-quality safety helmets in Vietnam for US$50, or buy a low-quality 'eggshell' helmet for US$15. As a last resort, you might consider purchasing a slightly battered US Army helmet from the War Surplus Market – the bullet holes provide ventilation.

Purchase

Foreigners lacking a residence visa are not strictly supposed to own a motorbike in Vietnam. However, some people have found that it is possible to buy a bike but register it in the name of a Vietnamese friend or, in some cases, the name of the shop. The big question is what to do with the bike when you are finished with it. You might be able to sell it back (at a discount) to the shop where you bought it.

Japanese-made motorbikes are the best available, but are very expensive. Unless you can get an exceptionally good deal on a used Honda, the best alternative is to buy a Russian-made Minsk 125cc which sells brand new for around US$550. It's quality is mediocre at best and it's a petrol pig, but it is a powerful bike and it's very easy to find spare parts and people who can do repairs (though repair shops frequently overcharge). The two-stroke engine burns oil like mad and the spark plugs frequently become oil-fouled, so always carry a spare spark plug and spark plug wrench. Avoid other Eastern European motorbikes.

CYCLOs

The cyclo or pedicab *(xich lo)*, short for the French *cyclo-pousse*, is the best invention since sliced bread. Cyclos offer a cheap, attractive but slow way to get around sprawling Ho Chi Minh City. Riding in one of these clever contraptions will also give you the moral superiority that comes with knowing you are being kind to the environment – certainly kinder than all those speed-crazed drivers on their whining, wheezing, smoke-spewing motorbikes.

Cyclos can be hailed along major thoroughfares almost any time of the day or night. The drivers are always male, and many of them are former South Vietnamese army soldiers. The ex-soldiers often speak at least basic English while others are quite fluent. Each has a story of war, 're-education', persecution and poverty to tell.

There are a number of major streets on which cyclos are prohibited to ride. As a result, your driver must often take a circuitous route to avoid these trouble spots since the police will not hesitate to fine them. For the same reason, the driver may not be able to drop you off at the exact address you want, though he will bring you to the nearest side street. Many travellers have gotten angry at their cyclo drivers for this, but it is not their fault.

Have your money counted out and ready before getting on a cyclo. It also pays to have the exact money – drivers will sometimes claim they cannot make change for a 5000d note.

Cyclos are cheaper by time rather than distance. A typical price is US$1 per hour. If this works out well, don't be surprised if the driver comes around to your hotel the next morning to see if you want to hire him again.

Since 1995, the government has been requiring cyclo drivers to obtain a licence. The requirements for this including passing an exam on traffic safety laws.

Enjoy cyclos while you can – the government intends to phase them out. In an effort to prevent the cyclo population from expanding, the municipal government no longer registers new cyclos. However, enterprising

Top : Not for hire (RS)
Bottom : Cyclists (ME)

Top : Social Mobility (RE)
Bottom : Old Citroën (RE)

locals have started manufacturing fake licence plates in an effort to thwart the ban on new vehicles. One effect of these 'pirate cyclos' *(xe bo trong)* is that if the driver gives you a bad time and you copy down his licence number to report him to the police, the number may turn out to be a dud.

BICYCLE

A bicycle is a good, slow way to get around the city, so long as you're an experienced cyclist and can manage the chaotic traffic. Bikes can be rented from a number of places: the Prince Hotel (☎ 322657) at 187 Pham Ngu Lao St; from a stand opposite the Rex Hotel; SGT Travel Service (☎ 298914), 49 Le Thanh Ton St; The Youth Centre (☎ 294345), 1 Pham Ngoc Thach St; and Eden Tourist Office (☎ 295417), 114 Nguyen Hue Blvd.

The best place to buy an imported bicycle is at Federal Bike Shop (☎ 332899), which has stores at three locations: 139H Nguyen Trai St, 158B Vo Thi Sau St and 156 Pham Hong Thai St. Cheaper deals may be found at some of the shops around 288 Le Thanh Ton St, on the corner of Cach Mang Thang Tam St. You can also buy bike components: Czech and French frames, Chinese derailleurs, headlamps etc. A decent bicycle with foreign components costs about US$100.

In Cholon, you might try the bicycle shops on Ngo Gia Tu Blvd just south-west of Ly Thai To Blvd (near An Quang Pagoda). In District 4 there are bicycle parts shops along Nguyen Tat Thanh St, just south of the Ho Chi Minh Museum.

For cheap and poorly asssembled domestic bicycles and parts, try the ground floor of Cua Hang Bach Hoa (Tax Department Store) on the corner of Nguyen Hue and Le Loi Blvds. Vikotrade Company, at 35 Le Loi Blvd (across the street from the Rex Hotel), also has locally made components.

For on-the-spot bicycle repairs, look for an upturned army helmet and a hand pump sitting next to the curb. There is a cluster of bicycle-repair shops around 23 Phan Dang Luu Blvd.

Bicycle parking lots are usually just roped-off sections of the sidewalk. For US$0.10 you can leave your bicycle knowing that it will be there when you get back (bicycle theft is a big problem). When you pull up, your bicycle will have a number written on the seat in chalk or stapled to the handlebars. You will be given a reclaim chit (don't lose it!). If you come back and your bicycle is gone, the parking lot is supposedly required to replace it.

WALKING

Exploring the city on foot is an excellent idea, but there is one drawback – the traffic. Foreigners frequently make the mistake of thinking that the best way to cross a busy Vietnamese street is to run quickly across it. Sometimes this works and sometimes it gets you creamed. Locals cross the street slowly – very slowly – giving the motorbike drivers sufficient time to judge their position so they can pass to either side of you. Motorbikes will *not* stop or even slow down, but they *will* try to avoid hitting you. Remember, make no sudden moves.

BOAT

To see Ho Chi Minh City from the Saigon River, you can easily hire a motorised five-metre boat. Warning – there have been quite a few unpleasant incidents with bag snatching and pickpocketing at the docks at the base of Ham Nghi Blvd. It's better to go to the area just south of the Saigon Floating Hotel where you see the ships offering dinner cruises. Around that area, you'll always see someone hanging around looking to charter a boat – ask them to bring the boat to you, rather than you go to the boat (they can easily do this).

The price should be US$5 per hour for a small boat, or US$10 to US$15 for a larger and faster craft. Interesting destinations for short trips include Cholon (along Ben Nghe Channel) and the zoo (along Thi Nghe Channel). Note that both channels are fascinating but filthy – raw sewage is discharged into the water. Many foreigners regard the channels as a major tourist attraction, but the government sees them as a health hazard – there is now a programme to move local residents out and divert the channels into underground sewer pipes.

For longer trips up the Saigon River, it would be worth chartering a fast speedboat from Saigon Tourist. Although these cost US$20 per hour, you'll save money when you consider that a cheap boat takes at least five times longer for the same journey. Splitting the cost between a small group of travellers makes a lot of economic sense, and it's always more fun to travel with others unless you prefer solitude.

Since you hire boats by the hour, some will go particularly slowly because they know the meter is running. You might want to set a time limit from the outset – three hours should be plenty.

Ferries across the Saigon River leave from a dock at the foot of Ham Nghi Blvd. They run every half-hour or so from 4.30 am to 10.30 pm.

Things to See & Do

HIGHLIGHTS

The Vietnam War is a topic that still fascinates foreigners, and many of Ho Chi Minh City's tourist attractions focus on this interest. In central Saigon, the most intriguing sites for war buffs include the War Crimes Museum and Reunification Palace. A day-trip to the Cu Chi tunnels (see the Excursions chapter) is also most rewarding.

If you'd rather pursue the topic of religion, be sure to check out the Giac Lam Pagoda, Jade Emperor Pagoda and Vinh Nghiem Pagoda. A day-long excursion to Tay Ninh is required to visit the incredible Caodai Great Temple. Another worthwhile excursion is to the One Pillar Pagoda.

Buying and selling lies at the heart and soul of Ho Chi Minh City. The best place to get a look at the city's lively commercial side is to visit Ben Thanh Market, Binh Tay Market or Andong Market. These bustling indoor markets are tourist attractions in themselves even if you don't wish to buy anything (see the Shopping chapter).

Boat trips on the Saigon River are always a great way to take refuge from the urban pandemonium. Further afield, beach buffs are sure to appreciate either the glitter of commercialised Vung Tau or the tranquillity of barely developed Long Hai.

MUSEUMS

War Crimes Museum

Once known as the 'Museum of American War Crimes', the name has been changed so as not to offend the sensibilities of American tourists. However, the pamphlet handed out at reception pulls no punches; it's entitled 'Some Pictures of US Imperialists' Aggressive War Crimes in Vietnam'.

Whatever the current name, this has become the most popular museum in the city with Western tourists. Many of the atrocities documented in the museum were well publicised in the West during the war.

In the yard of the museum, US armoured vehicles, artillery pieces, bombs and infantry weapons are on display. There is also a guillotine which the French used to deal with Viet Minh 'troublemakers'. Many of the photographs illustrating US atrocities are from US

sources, including photos of the famous My Lai mass-
acre. There is a model of the notorious tiger cages used
by the South Vietnamese military to house VC prisoners
on Con Son Island. There are also pictures of genetically
deformed babies, their birth defects attributed to the
widespread spraying of Agent Orange by the Americans. In an adjacent room are exhibits detailing
'counter-revolutionary war crimes' committed by sabo-
teurs within Vietnam after the 1975 liberation. The
counter-revolutionaries are portrayed as being allied
with both US and Chinese imperialists.

The main objection to the museum comes, not surprisingly, from American tourists, many of whom complain
that the museum is one-sided. There is a distinct shortage

Top : Helicopter at War Crimes Museum (GB)
Bottom : Reunification Palace (RS)

of information about the many people who disappeared after reunification.

Politically neutral war historians will perhaps be more disturbed by the lack of context and completeness of some of the exhibits. It's surprising, for example, that there are no photos of Thich Quang Duc, the monk who burned himself to death to protest against the war. Or photos of the Kent State students in the USA who were shot while protesting US policies. Hopefully, the museum will be expanded to include a larger slice of the war's history.

Despite these criticisms, there are few museums in the world which drive home so well the point that modern warfare is horribly brutal, and that many of its victims are civilians. Even those who adamantly supported America's position will have a difficult time not being horrified by the photos of innocent children mangled by bombing, napalming and the use of chemicals. There are also scenes of torture – it takes a strong stomach to look at these. You'll also have a rare chance to see some of the experimental weapons used in the Vietnam War which were at one time American military secrets, an example being the 'flechette' (an artillery shell filled with thousands of tiny darts). Certainly, the museum is well worth a visit, if for no other reason than to get a sobering reminder that war is anything but glorious.

The War Crimes Museum (☎ 290325) is housed in the former US Information Service building at 28 Vo Van Tan St (the intersection with Le Qui Don St). Opening hours are from 8 to 11.30 am and 2 to 5 pm daily. Explanations are written in Vietnamese, English and Chinese.

Reunification Palace

It was towards this building – then known as Independence Palace or the Presidential Palace – that the first Communist tanks in Saigon rushed on the morning of 30 April 1975. After crashing through the wrought-iron gates in a dramatic scene recorded by photo-journalist Neil Davis and shown around the world, a soldier ran into the building and up the stairs to unfurl a Viet Cong flag from the 4th-floor balcony. In an ornate 2nd-floor reception chamber, General Minh, who had become head of state only 43 hours before, waited with his improvised cabinet. 'I have been waiting since early this morning to transfer power to you', Minh said to the VC officer who entered the room. 'There is no question of your transferring power', replied the officer, 'you cannot give up what you do not have'.

In 1868 a residence for the French Governor-General of Cochinchina was built on this site. The residence gradually expanded and became known as Norodom Palace. When the French departed, the palace became home for South Vietnamese President Ngo Dinh Diem. So hated was Diem that his own air force bombed the palace in 1962 in an unsuccessful attempt to kill him. Recognising that he had an image problem, the president ordered a new residence to be built on the same site but this time with a sizeable bomb shelter in the basement. The new mansion was designed by Paris-trained Vietnamese architect Ngo Viet Thu – work began in 1962 and was completed in 1966. Diem did not get to see his dream house because he was murdered by his own troops in 1963. The new building was named Independence Palace and was home for South Vietnamese President Nguyen Van Thieu until his hasty departure in 1975. The Communists renamed it Reunification Palace (Hoi Truong Thong Nhat).

The fascinating aspect of the mansion is the eerie feeling you get – walking through the deserted halls – that from here ruled arrogant men wielding immense power who nevertheless became history's losers. The building, once the symbol of the Southern government, is preserved mostly as it was on 30 April 1975, the day that the Republic of Vietnam ceased to exist.

Some recent additions to the building include a statue of Ho Chi Minh and a video viewing room where you can watch the latest version of Vietnamese history in a variety of languages. The national anthem is played at the end of the tape and you are expected to stand up – it would be rude to refuse to do so.

For US$1, you can sit in the former president's chair and have your photo taken. The 3rd floor also boasts a terrace with a heliport – there is still a moribund helicopter parked here, but it costs US$1 admission if you want to walk around on the helipad to take advantage of the photo opportunities. The 4th floor has a dance hall and casino.

Perhaps most interesting of all is the basement with its network of tunnels, telecommunications centre and war room (with the best map of Vietnam you'll ever see pasted to the wall). One tunnel stretches all the way to Gia Long Palace, which is now the Revolutionary Museum.

Reunification Palace is open for visitors from 7.30 to 10 am and 1 to 4 pm daily except when official receptions or meetings are taking place. English and French-speaking guides are on duty during these hours. Each guide is assigned to a particular part of the palace, so you will have numerous guides as you move from room to room. The visitors' office (☎ 290629) and entrance is at 106 Nguyen Du St. The entrance fee for foreigners is US$4 (free for Vietnamese).

Revolutionary Museum

Housed in a neoclassical structure built in 1886 and once known as Gia Long Palace, the Revolutionary Museum (Bao Tang Cach Mang; ☎ 299741) is a singularly beautiful building. The museum displays artefacts from the various periods of the Communist struggle for power in Vietnam. The photographs of anti-colonial activists executed by the French appear out of place in the gilded 19th-century ballrooms, but then again, the contrast helps you get a feel for the immense power and self-confident complacency of colonial France. There are photos of Vietnamese peace demonstrators in Saigon demanding that US troops get out, and a dramatic photo of Thich Quang Duc, the monk who set himself on fire to protest the policies of President Ngo Dinh Diem.

The information plaques are in Vietnamese only, but some of the exhibits include documents in French or English and many others are self-explanatory if you know some basic Vietnamese history. Some of the guides speak English, and will often latch on to you in various rooms or on each floor and provide excellent if unrequested guided tours. There are donation boxes next to the visitors' books in various parts of the museum where you can leave a tip for the guides (US$1 to US$2 is appropriate). Most of the guides do fine work and get paid nothing for it.

The exhibition begins in the first room on the left (as you enter the building), which covers the period from 1859 to 1940. Upstairs, in the room to the left, is a *ghe* (a long, narrow rowboat) with a false bottom in which arms were smuggled. The weight of the contraband caused the boat to sit as low in the water as would any ordinary ghe. Nearby is a small diorama of the Cu Chi tunnels. An adjoining room has examples of infantry weapons used by the VC and various captured South Vietnamese and American medals, hats and plaques. A map shows Communist advances during the dramatic collapse of South Vietnam in early 1975. There are also photographs of the 'liberation' of Saigon.

Deep underneath the building is a network of reinforced concrete bunkers and fortified corridors. The system, branches of which stretch all the way to Reunification Palace, included living areas, a kitchen and a large meeting hall. In 1963, President Diem and his

Top : History Museum (RS)
Middle : Military Museum display (RS)
Bottom : Art Museum piece (RS)

brother hid here immediately before fleeing to a Cholon church where they were captured (and, shortly thereafter, murdered).

In the garden behind the museum is a Soviet tank, an American Huey UH-1 helicopter and an anti-aircraft gun. In the garden fronting Nam Ky Khoi Nghia St is some more military hardware, including the American-built F-5E jet used by a renegade South Vietnamese Air Force pilot to bomb the Presidential Palace (now Reunification Palace) on 8 April 1975.

The Revolutionary Museum is at 65 Ly Tu Trong St (corner of Nam Ky Khoi Nghia St), which is one block south-east of Reunification Palace. It is open from 8 to 11.30 am and 2 to 4.30 pm Tuesday to Sunday. The museum offices are at 114 Nam Ky Khoi Nghia St. Admission is free.

History Museum

The History Museum (Vien Bao Tang Lich Su; ☎ 298146), built in 1929 by the Société des Études Indochinoises and once the National Museum of the Republic of Vietnam, is just inside the main entrance to the zoo, on Nguyen Binh Khiem St. Step inside the door and you're immediately confronted by a big statue of guess who? The museum has an excellent collection of artefacts illustrating the evolution of the cultures of Vietnam, from the Bronze Age Dong Son civilisation (13th century BC to 1st century AD) and the Oc-Eo (Funan) civilisation (1st to 6th centuries AD), to the Chams, Khmers and Vietnamese. There are many valuable relics taken from Cambodia's Angkor Wat.

At the back of the building on the 3rd floor is a research library (☎ 290268; open Monday to Saturday) with numerous books on Indochina from the French period.

Water puppet shows are performed here with advance booking, and cost US$1 per person.

The museum is open from 8 to 11.30 am and 1 to 4 pm, Tuesday to Sunday.

Uncle Ho's Museum for Mementos

This oddly named museum (Khu luu niem Bac Ho; ☎ 291060) is in the old customs house at 1 Nguyen Tat Thanh St, just across Ben Nghe Channel from the quayside end of Ham Nghi Blvd. This place was (and still is) nicknamed the 'Dragon House' (Nha Rong) and was built in 1863. The tie between Ho Chi Minh (1890-1969) and the museum building is tenuous: 21-year-old Ho, having signed on as a stoker and galley-boy on a French freighter, left Vietnam from here in 1911, beginning 30 years of exile in France, the Soviet Union, China and elsewhere.

The museum houses many of Ho's personal effects, including some of his clothing (he was a man of informal dress), sandals, his beloved American-made Zenith radio and other memorabilia. The explanatory signs in the museum are in Vietnamese, but if you know a little about Uncle Ho (Bac Ho), you should be able to follow most of the photographs and exhibits.

The museum is open on Tuesday, Wednesday, Thursday and Saturday from 8 to 11.30 am and 2 to 6 pm; on Sunday, it stays open until 8 pm. The museum is closed on Monday and Friday.

Military Museum

The Military Museum is just across Nguyen Binh Khiem St (corner of Le Duan Blvd) from the main gate of the zoo. US, Chinese and Soviet war matériel is on display, including a Cessna A-37 of the South Vietnamese Air Force and a US-built F-5E Tiger with the 20-mm nose gun still loaded. The tank on display is one of the tanks which broke into the grounds of what is now Reunification Palace on 30 April 1975.

Art Museum

This classic yellow and white building with some modest Chinese influence houses one of the more interesting collections in Vietnam. If you are not interested in the collection, just enter the huge hall with its nice art nouveau windows and floors. The 1st floor seems to have housed revolutionary art in former times. Those pieces are either in storage, thrown out, or you find them in some back rooms close to the toilet. On the first floor now you find officially accepted contemporary art. Most of it is kitsch or desperate attempts to master abstract art, but occasionally something brilliant is displayed here. Most of the recent art is for sale and prices are fair.

The 2nd floor displays the old politically correct art. Some of this stuff is pretty crude – pictures of heroic figures waving red flags, children with rifles, a wounded soldier joining the Communist Party, innumerable tanks and weaponry, grotesque Americans and God-like reverence for Ho Chi Minh. Nevertheless, it's worth seeing because Vietnamese artists managed to be less dull and conformist than their counterparts in eastern Europe. Once you've passed several paintings and scuptures of

Uncle Ho, you will see that those artists who studied before 1975 managed to somehow transfer their own aesthetics into the world of prescribed subjects. Surprisingly, the Vietnamese Communists seem to have only proscribed the subjects but not the style. Most impressive are some drawings of prison riots in 1973. On the floor are some remarkable abstract paintings. Maybe the most striking fact in these politically correct paintings is that all Vietnamese military heroes look a bit more European than Asian.

The 3rd floor displays a good collection of older art, mainly Funan Oc-Eo sculptures. These Oc-Eo pieces strongly resemble the styles from ancient Greece and Egypt. You will also find here the best Cham pieces outside Danang. Also interesting are the many pieces of Indian art, often of an elephant's head. Other pieces clearly originated in Angkor culture.

A café is in the garden in front of the museum and is a preferred spot for elderly gentlemen to exchange stamp collections and sip iced tea.

The Art Museum (Bao Tang My Thuat; ☎ 222577) is at 97A Pho Duc Chinh St in central Saigon. Opening hours are from 7.30 am to 4.30 pm Tuesday to Sunday. Admission is free.

Ton Duc Thang Museum

This small, rarely visited museum (Bao Tang Ton Duc Thang; ☎ 294651) is dedicated to Ton Duc Thang, Ho Chi Minh's successor as president of Vietnam, who was born in Long Xuyen, An Giang Province, in 1888. He died in office in 1980. Photos illustrate his role in the Vietnamese Revolution, including the time he spent imprisoned on Con Dao Island. The explanations are in Vietnamese only.

The museum is along the waterfront at 5 Ton Duc Thang St, half a block north of the Tran Hung Dao statue at the foot of Hai Ba Trung St. It is open Tuesday to Sunday from 8 to 11 am and 2 to 6 pm.

PAGODAS & TEMPLES

Giac Lam Pagoda

First built in 1744, this compound is believed to be the oldest pagoda in Ho Chi Minh City. Because the last reconstruction was in 1900, the architecture, layout and ornamentation have remained almost unaltered by the modernist renovations that have transformed so many religious structures here. A large new pagoda tower was

MAP 2

Plan of Giac Lam Pagoda

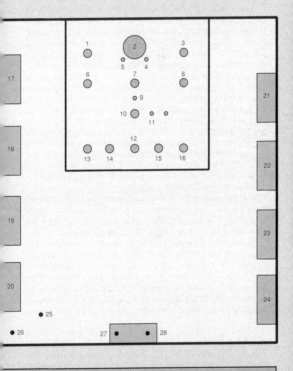

1	Kasyape	11	Ngoc Hoang, the Taoist
2	A Di Da	12	Thich Ca Buddha
3	Anand	13-16	Four Bo Tat
4	Kadip	17-24	Bodhisattvas & Judges of
5	Ana		the Ten Regions of Hell
6	Guardian of Thich Ca	25	'Christmas Tree'
7	Thich Ca Buddha	26	Bell
8	Guardian of Thich Ca	27	Onctieu (Guardian of Hell)
9	Thich Ca Buddha as a child	28	Hophap (Guardian of the
10	Ameda		Buddha)

erected in 1994, so don't mistake it for the main pagoda grounds which are 100 metres to your right as you face the big tower.

To the right of the gate to the pagoda compound are the ornate tombs of venerated monks. The *bo de* (bodhi, or pipal) tree in the front garden was the gift of a monk from Sri Lanka. Next to the tree is a regular feature of Vietnamese Buddhist pagodas, a gleaming white statue of Quan Am (Guanyin in Chinese, the Goddess of Mercy) standing on a lotus blossom, symbol of purity.

The roofline of the main building is decorated both inside and outside with unusual blue and white porcelain plates. Through the main entrance is a reception hall lined with funeral tablets and photos of the deceased. Roughly in the centre of the hall, near an old French chandelier, is a figure of 18-armed Chuan De, another form of the Goddess of Mercy. Note the carved hardwood columns, which bear gilded Vietnamese inscriptions written in *nom* characters, a form of writing in use before the adoption of the Latin-based *quoc ngu* alphabet. The wall to the left is covered with portraits of great monks from previous generations. Monks' names and biographical information about them are recorded on the vertical red tablets in gold nom characters. A box for donations sits nearby. Shoes should be removed when passing from the rough red floor tiles to the smaller, white-black-grey tiles.

On the other side of the wall from the monks' funeral tablets is the main sanctuary, which is filled with countless gilded figures. On the dais in the centre of the back row sits A Di Da (2), the Buddha of the Past (Amitabha). To his right is Kasyape (1) and to his left Anand (3); both are disciples of the Thich Ca Buddha (the historical Buddha Sakyamuni, whose real name was Siddhartha Gautama). Directly in front of A Di Da is a statue of the Thich Ca Buddha (7), flanked by two guardians (6, 8). In front of Thich Ca is the tiny figure of the Thich Ca Buddha as a child (9). As always, he is clothed in a yellow robe.

The fat, laughing fellow, seated with five children climbing all over him, is Ameda (10). To his left is Ngoc Hoang (11), the Taoist Jade Emperor who presides over a world of innumerable supernatural beings. In the front row is a statue of the Thich Ca Buddha (12) with four Bodhisattvas *(bo tat)*, two on each side (13-16). On the altars along the side walls of the sanctuary are various Bodhisattvas and the Judges of the Ten Regions of Hell (17-24). Each of the judges is holding a scroll resembling the handle of a fork.

The red and gold Christmas-tree shaped object (25) is a wooden altar bearing 49 lamps and 49 miniature statues of Bodhisattvas. People pray for sick relatives or ask for happiness by contributing kerosene for use in the lamps. Petitioners' names and those of ill family members are written on slips of paper, which are attached to the branches of the 'tree'.

The frame of the large bronze bell in the corner looks like a university bulletin board because petitioners have attached to it lists of names: the names of people seeking happiness and the names of the sick and the dead, placed there by their relatives. It is believed that when the bell is rung, the sound will resonate to the heavens above and the underground heavens below, carrying with it the attached supplications.

Prayers here consist of chanting to the accompaniment of drums, bells and gongs, and they follow a traditional rite seldom performed these days. Prayers are held daily from 4 to 5 am, 11 am to noon, 4 to 5 and 7 to 9 pm.

Giac Lam Pagoda is about three km from Cholon at 118 Lac Long Quan St in Tan Binh District. Beware: the numbering on Lac Long Quan St is extremely confused, starting over from No 1 several times and at one point jumping to four digits. In many places, odd and even numbers are on the same side of the street.

The best way to get to Giac Lam Pagoda is from Cholon. Take Nguyen Chi Thanh Blvd or 3 Thang 2 Blvd to Le Dai Hanh St. Go north-westward on Le Dai Hanh St and turn right onto Lac Long Quan St. Walk 100 metres to your right when facing the new pagoda tower to reach the gates of the compound. It is open to visitors from 6 am to 9 pm.

Giac Vien Pagoda

Giac Vien Pagoda and Giac Lam Pagoda are similar architecturally. Both pagodas share the same atmosphere of scholarly serenity, though Giac Vien, which is right next to Dam Sen Lake in District 11, is in a more rural setting. Giac Vien Pagoda was founded by Hai Tinh Giac Vien about 200 years ago. It is said that the Emperor Gia Long, who died in 1819, used to worship at Giac Vien. Today, 10 monks live at the pagoda.

Pass through the gate and go several hundred metres down a potholed dirt road, turning left at the 'tee' and right at the fork. You will pass several impressive tombs of monks on the right before arriving at the pagoda itself. Giac Vien Pagoda is open from 7 am to 7 pm, but come before dark as the electricity is often out.

MAP 3

Sanctuary of Giac Vien Pagoda

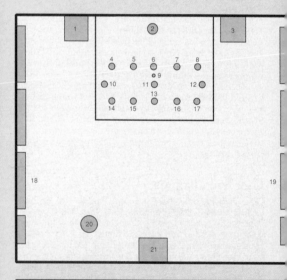

1	Dai The Chi Bo Tat	10	Standing Guardian
2	A Di Da	11	Ameda
3	Quan The Am Bo Tat	12	Standing Guardian
4	Nhien Dang Buddha	13	Thich Ca Buddha
5	Anand	14-17	Four Bo Tat
6	Thich Ca Buddha	18-19	Judges & Bodhisattvas
7	Kasyape	20	'Christmas Tree'
8	Ti Lu Buddha	21	Guardian of the Pagoda
9	Thich Ca as a child		

As you enter the pagoda, the first chamber is lined with funeral tablets. At the back of the second chamber is a statue of the pagoda's founder, Hai Tinh Giac Vien, holding a horse-tail switch. Nearby portraits are of his successors as head monk and disciples. A donation box sits to the left of the statue. Opposite Hai Tinh Giac Vien is a representation of 18-armed Chuan De, who is flanked by two guardians.

The main sanctuary is on the other side of the wall behind Hai Tinh Giac Vien. A Di Da (2), the Buddha of the Past, is at the back of the dais. Directly in front of him is the Thich Ca Buddha (6), or Sakyamuni, flanked by Thich Ca's disciples Anand (5) on the left and Kasyape (7) on the right. To the right of Kasyape is the Ti Lu Buddha (8); to the left of Anand is the Nhien Dang Buddha (4). At the foot of the Thich Ca Buddha is a small figure of Thich Ca as a child. Fat, laughing Ameda (11) is seated with children climbing all over him; far on either side of him stand his guardians (10, 12). In the front row of the dais is Thich Ca (13) with two Bodhisatt-vas on each side (14-17).

In front of the dais is a fantastic brass incense basin with fierce dragon heads emerging from each side. On the altar to the left of the dais is Dai The Chi Bo Tat (1); on the altar to the right is Quan The Am Bo Tat (Avalokiteçvara), the Goddess of Mercy (4). The Guardian of the Pagoda (21) is against the wall opposite the dais. Nearby is a 'Christmas tree' (20) similar to the one in Giac Lam Pagoda. Lining the side walls are the Judges of the Ten Regions of Hell (holding scrolls) and 18 Bodhisattvas (18, 19).

Jade Emperor Pagoda (RS)

The best way to get to Giac Vien Pagoda is to take Nguyen Chi Thanh Blvd or 3 Thang 2 Blvd to Le Dai Hanh St. Turn left (south-west) off Le Dai Han St on to Binh Thoi St and turn right (north) at Lac Long Quan St. The gate leading to the pagoda is at 247 Lac Long Quan St. From Lac Long Quan St there are signs pointing the way to the pagoda.

Prayers are held daily from 4 to 5 and 8 to 10 am, and 2 to 3 , 4 to 5 and 7 to 9 pm.

Jade Emperor Pagoda

This Chinese pagoda (known in Vietnamese as Phuoc Hai Tu and Chua Ngoc Hoang) was built in 1909 by the Cantonese (Quang Dong) Congregation. It's a classic example of fine Chinese architecture. Ethnic-Chinese visitors from overseas (especially Hong Kong and Taiwan) have generously donated funds towards the pagoda's restoration, making this one of the most colourful pagodas in Ho Chi Minh City.

Step inside the building and you'll find it filled with statues of phantasmal divinities and grotesque heroes. The pungent smoke of burning joss sticks fills the air, obscuring exquisite wood carvings decorated with gilded Chinese characters. The roof is covered with elaborate tilework. The statues, which represent characters from both the Buddhist and Taoist traditions, are made of reinforced papier-mâché.

As you enter the main doors of the building Mon Quan (1), the God of the Gate, stands to the right in an elaborately carved wooden case. Opposite him, in a similar case, is Tho Than (Tho Dia), the God of the Land (2). Straight on is an altar on which are placed, from left to right, figures of: Phat Mau Chuan De (5), mother of the five Buddhas of the cardinal directions; Dia Tang Vuong Bo Tat (Ksitigartha), the King of Hell (6); the Di Lac Buddha (Maitreya), the Buddha of the Future (7); Quan The Am Bo Tat (8), the Goddess of Mercy; and a bas-relief portrait of the Thich Ca Buddha (9). Behind the altar, in a glass case, is the Duoc Su Buddha (10), also known as the Nhu Lai Buddha. The figure is said to be made of sandalwood.

To either side of the altar, against the walls, are two especially fierce and menacing figures. On the right (as you face the altar) is a four-metre-high statue of the general who defeated the Green Dragon (3). He is stepping on the vanquished dragon. On the left is the general who defeated the White Tiger (4), which is also getting stepped on.

The Taoist Jade Emperor, Ngoc Hoang (17), presides over the main sanctuary, draped in luxurious robes. He is flanked by the 'Four Big Diamonds' (Tu Dai Kim Cuong), his four guardians (16), so named because they are said to be as hard as diamonds. In front of the Jade Emperor stand six figures, three to each side. On the left is Bac Dau (18), the Taoist God of the Northern Polar Star and God of Longevity, flanked by his two guardians; and on the right is Nam Tao (15), the Taoist God of the Southern Polar Star and God of Happiness, also flanked by two guardians.

In the case to the right of the Jade Emperor is 18-armed Phat Mau Chuan De (13), mother of the five Buddhas of the north, south, east, west and centre. Two faces, affixed to her head behind each ear, look to either side. On the wall to the right of Phat Mau Chuan De, at a height of about four metres, is Dai Minh Vuong Quang (11), who was reincarnated as Sakyamuni, riding on the back of a phoenix. Below are the Tien Nhan (12), literally the 'god-persons'.

In the case to the left of the Jade Emperor sits Ong Bac De (20), a reincarnation of the Jade Emperor, holding a sword. One of his feet is resting on a turtle while the other rests on a snake. On the wall to the left of Ong Bac De, about four metres off the ground, is Thien Loi (22), the God of Lightning, who slays evil people. Below Thien Loi are the military commanders of Ong Bac De (on the lower step) and Thien Loi's guardians (on the upper step). At the top of the two carved pillars that separate the three alcoves are the Goddess of the Moon (on the left) and the God of the Sun (on the right).

Out the door on the left-hand side of the Jade Emperor's chamber is another room. The semi-enclosed area to the right (as you enter) is presided over by Thanh Hoang (24), the Chief of Hell; to the left is his red horse. Of the six figures lining the walls, the two closest to Thanh Hoang are Am Quan (25), the God of Yin (on the left), and Duong Quan (28), the God of Yang (on the right). The other four figures, the Thuong Thien Phat Ac, are gods who dispense punishments for evil acts and rewards for good deeds. Thanh Hoang faces in the direction of the famous Hall of the Ten Hells. The carved wooden panels lining the walls graphically depict the varied torments awaiting evil people in each of the 10 regions of hell. At the top of each panel is one of the Ten Judges of Hell examining a book in which the deeds of the deceased are inscribed.

On the wall opposite Thanh Hoang is a bas-relief wood panel depicting Quan Am Thi Kinh (32), the Guardian Spirit of Mother & Child, standing on a lotus

MAP 4

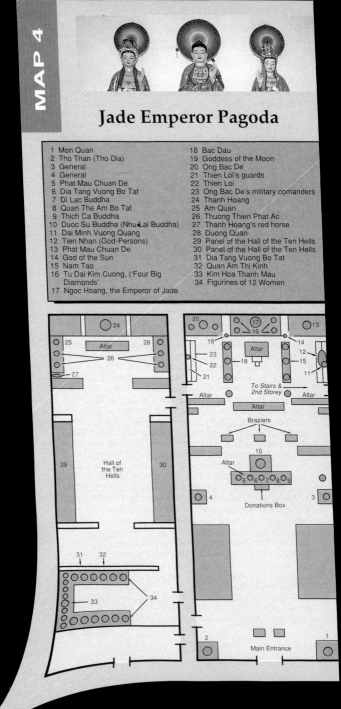

Jade Emperor Pagoda

1 Mon Quan
2 Tho Than (Tho Dia)
3 General
4 General
5 Phat Mau Chuan De
6 Dia Tang Vuong Bo Tat
7 Di Lac Buddha
8 Quan The Am Bo Tat
9 Thich Ca Buddha
10 Duoc Su Buddha (Nhu Lai Buddha)
11 Dai Minh Vuong Quang
12 Tien Nhan (God-Persons)
13 Phat Mau Chuan De
14 God of the Sun
15 Nam Tao
16 Tu Dai Kim Cuong, ('Four Big Diamonds'
17 Ngoc Hoang, the Emperor of Jade

18 Bac Dau
19 Goddess of the Moon
20 Ong Bac De
21 Thien Loi's guards
22 Thien Loi
23 Ong Bac De's military comanders
24 Thanh Hoang
25 Am Quan
26 Thuong Thien Phat Ac
27 Thanh Hoang's red horse
28 Duong Quan
29 Panel of the Hall of the Ten Hells
30 Panel of the Hall of the Ten Hells
31 Dia Tang Vuong Bo Tat
32 Quan Am Thi Kinh
33 Kim Hoa Thanh Mau
34 Figurines of 12 Women

blossom, symbol of purity. Unjustly turned out of her home by her husband, Quan Am Thi Kinh disguised herself as a monk and went to live in a pagoda, where a young woman accused her of fathering her child. She accepted the blame – and the responsibility that went along with it – and again found herself out on the streets, this time with her 'son'. Much later, about to die, she returned to the monastery to confess her secret. When the Emperor of China heard of her story, he declared her the Guardian Spirit of Mother & Child.

It is believed that she has the power to bestow male offspring on those who fervently believe in her. On the panel, Quan Am Thi Kinh is shown holding her 'son'. To her left is Long Nu, a very young Buddha who is her protector. To Quan Am Thi Kinh's right is Thien Tai, her guardian spirit, who knew the real story all along. Above her left shoulder is a bird bearing prayer beads.

To the right of the panel of Quan Am Thi Kinh is a panel depicting Dia Tang Vuong Bo Tat (31), the King of Hell.

On the other side of the wall is a fascinating little room in which the ceramic figures of 12 women, overrun with children and wearing colourful clothes, sit in two rows of six. Each of the women exemplifies a human characteristic, either good or bad (as in the case of the woman drinking alcohol from a jug). Each figure represents one year in the 12-year Chinese calendar. Presiding over the room is Kim Hoa Thanh Mau (33), the Chief of All Women.

To the right of the main chamber, stairs lead up to a 2nd-floor sanctuary and balcony.

The Jade Emperor Pagoda is at 73 Mai Thi Luu St in a part of Ho Chi Minh City known as Da Kao (or Da Cao). To get there, go to 20 Dien Bien Phu St and walk half a block north-westward.

Dai Giac Pagoda

This Vietnamese Buddhist pagoda is built in a style characteristic of pagodas constructed during the 1960s. In the courtyard, under the unfinished 10-level red-pink tower inlaid with porcelain shards, is an artificial cave made of volcanic rocks in which there is a gilded statue of the Goddess of Mercy. In the main sanctuary, the 2.5-metre gilt Buddha has a green neon halo, while below, a smaller white reclining Buddha (in a glass case) has a blue neon halo. Dai Giac Pagoda is at 112 Nguyen Van Troi St, 1.5 km towards the city centre from the gate to the airport.

Vinh Nghiem Pagoda

Inaugurated in 1971, Vinh Nghiem Pagoda is note-worthy for its vast sanctuary and eight-storey tower, each level of which contains a statue of the Buddha. It was built with help from the Japan-Vietnam Friendship Association, which explains the presence of Japanese elements in its architecture. At the base of the tower (which is open only on holidays) is a store selling Buddhist ritual objects. Behind the sanctuary is a three-storey tower, which serves as a repository for carefully labelled ceramic urns containing the ashes of people who have been cremated. The pagoda is in District 3 at 339 Nam Ky Khoi Nghia St and is open from 7.30 to 11.30 am and 2 to 6 pm daily.

Le Van Duyet Temple

This temple is dedicated to Marshal Le Van Duyet, who is buried here with his wife. The Marshal, who lived from 1763 to 1831, was a southern Vietnamese general and viceroy who helped put down the Tay Son Rebellion and reunify Vietnam. When the Nguyen Dynasty came to power in 1802, he was elevated by Emperor Gia Long to the rank of marshal. Le Van Duyet fell into disfavour with Gia Long's successor, Minh Mang, who tried him posthumously and desecrated his grave. Emperor Thieu Tri, who succeeded Minh Mang, restored the tomb, fulfilling a prophecy of its destruction and restoration. Le Van Duyet was considered a great national hero in the South before 1975 but is disliked by the Communists because of his involvement in the expansion of French influence.

Le Van Duyet Temple is three km from the centre of Saigon in the Gia Dinh area at 131 Dinh Tien Hoang St (near where Phan Dang Luu Blvd becomes Bach Dang Blvd).

The temple itself was renovated in 1937 and has a distinctly modern feel to it. Since 1975, the government has done little to keep it from becoming dilapidated. Among the items on display are a portrait of Le Van Duyet, some of his personal effects (including European-style crystal goblets) and other antiques. There are two wonderful life-size horses on either side of the entrance to the third and last chamber, which is kept locked.

During celebrations of Tet and the 30th day of the 7th lunar month (the anniversary of Le Van Duyet's death), the tomb is thronged with pilgrims. Vietnamese used to come here to take oaths of good faith if they could not afford the services of a court of justice. Tropical fish and caged birds are on sale to visitors. The birds, bought by pilgrims and freed to earn merit, are often recaptured and liberated again.

Tran Hung Dao Temple

This small temple is dedicated to Tran Hung Dao, a Vietnamese national hero who in 1287 vanquished an invasion force, said to have numbered 300,000 men, which had been dispatched by the Mongol emperor Kublai Khan. The temple is at 36 Vo Thi Sau St, a block north-east of the telecommunications dishes that are between Dien Bien Phu St and Vo Thi Sau St.

The public park between the antenna dishes and Hai Ba Trung Blvd was built in 1983 on the site of the Massiges Cemetery, burial place of French soldiers and settlers. The remains of French military personnel were exhumed and repatriated to France. Another site no longer in existence is the tomb of the 18th-century French missionary and diplomat Pigneau de Béhaine, Bishop of Adran, which was completely destroyed after reunification.

The temple is open every weekday from 6 to 11 am and 2 to 6 pm.

Xa Loi Pagoda

Xa Loi Vietnamese Buddhist Pagoda, built in 1956, is famed as the repository of a sacred relic of the Buddha. In August 1963, truckloads of armed men under the command of President Ngo Dinh Diem's brother, Ngo Dinh Nhu, attacked Xa Loi Pagoda, which had become a centre of opposition to the Diem government. The pagoda was ransacked and 400 monks and nuns, including the country's 80-year-old Buddhist patriarch, were arrested. This raid and others elsewhere helped solidify opposition among Buddhists to the Diem regime, a crucial factor in the US decision to support the coup against Diem. This pagoda was also the site of several self-immolations by monks protesting against the Diem regime and the war.

Women enter the main hall of Xa Loi Pagoda by the staircase on the right as you come in the gate; men use the stairs on the left. The walls of the sanctuary are adorned with paintings depicting the Buddha's life.

Xa Loi Pagoda is in District 3 at 89 Ba Huyen Thanh Quan St, near Dien Bien Phu St. It is open daily from 7 to 11 am and from 2 to 5 pm. A monk preaches every Sunday morning from 8 to 10 am. On days of the full moon and new moon, special prayers are held from 7 to 9 am and from 7 to 8 pm.

Human Sacrifice

Thich Quang Duc was a monk from Hué who travelled to Saigon and publicly burned himself to death in June 1963 to protest the policies of President Ngo Dinh Diem. A famous photograph of his act was printed on the front pages of newspapers around the world. His death soon inspired a number of other self-immolations.

Many Westerners were shocked less by the suicides than by the reaction of Tran Le Xuan (Madame Nhu, the president's notorious sister-in-law), who happily proclaimed the self-immolations a 'barbecue party' and said, 'Let them burn, and we shall clap our hands'. Her statements greatly added to the already substantial public disgust with Diem's regime; the US press labelled Madame Nhu the 'Iron Butterfly' and 'Dragon Lady'. In November, both President Diem and his brother Ngo Dinh Nhu (Madame Nhu's husband) were assassinated by Diem's own military. Madame Nhu was outside the country at the time (fortunately for her) and was last reported to be living in Rome.

The Thich Quang Duc Memorial (Dai Ky Niem Thuong Toa Thich Quang Duc) is at the intersection of Nguyen Dinh Chieu and Cach Mang Thang Tam Sts, just around the corner from the Xa Loi Pagoda. ∎

Phung Son Tu Pagoda

Phung Son Tu Pagoda (not to be confused with the Phung Son Pagoda), built by the Fujian Congregation in the mid-1940s, is more typical of Ho Chi Minh City's Chinese pagodas than is the Jade Emperor Pagoda. The interior is often hung with huge incense spirals that burn for hours. Worshippers include both ethnic-Chinese and ethnic-Vietnamese. Phung Son Tu Pagoda is dedicated to Ong Bon, Guardian Spirit of Happiness & Virtue, whose statue is behind the main altar in the sanctuary. On the right-hand side of the main hall is the multi-armed Buddhist Goddess of Mercy. This pagoda is only one km from central Saigon at 338 Nguyen Cong Tru St.

Mariamman Hindu Temple

Mariamman Hindu Temple, the only Hindu temple still in use in Ho Chi Minh City, is a little piece of southern India in the centre of Saigon. Though there are only 50 to 60 Hindus in Ho Chi Minh City – all of them Tamils – this temple, known in Vietnamese as Chua Ba Mariamman, is also considered sacred by many ethnic-Vietnamese and ethnic-Chinese. Indeed, it is reputed to have miraculous powers. The temple was built at the end of the 19th century and dedicated to the Hindu goddess Mariamman.

The lion to the left of the entrance used to be carried around Saigon in a street procession every autumn. In the shrine in the middle of the temple are Mariamman flanked by her guardians, Maduraiveeran (to her left) and Pechiamman (to her right). In front of the figure of Mariamman are two lingams (phallic images). Favourite offerings placed nearby include joss sticks, jasmine flowers, lilies and gladioli. The wooden stairs, on the left as you enter the building, lead to the roof, where you'll find two colourful towers covered with innumerable figures of lions, goddesses and guardians.

After reunification, the government took over the temple and turned part of it into a joss stick factory. Another section was occupied by a company producing seafood for export – the seafood was dried in the sun on the roof. The whole temple is to be returned to the local Hindu community.

Mariamman Temple is only three blocks from Ben Thanh Market at 45 Truong Dinh St. It is open from 7 am to 7 pm daily. Take off your shoes before stepping onto the slightly raised platform.

Giac Lam Pagoda (RS)

An Quang Pagoda

The An Quang Pagoda in Cholon gained some notoriety during the Vietnam War as the home of Thich Tri Quang, a politically powerful monk who led protests against the South Vietnamese government in 1963 and 1966. When the war ended, one would have expected the Communists to have treated Thich with gratitude. Instead, he was first placed under house arrest and later thrown into solitary confinement for 16 months. Thich Tri Quang was eventually released and is said to still be living at An Quang Pagoda.

The An Quang Pagoda is on Su Van Hanh St near the intersection with Ba Hat St, District 10.

Tam Son Hoi Quan Pagoda

This Chinese pagoda (Chua Ba Chua in Vietnamese) was built by the Fujian Congregation in the 19th century and retains unmodified most of its original rich ornamentation. The pagoda is dedicated to Me Sanh, the Goddess of Fertility. Both men and women – but more of the latter – come here to pray for children.

To the right of the covered courtyard is the deified general Quan Cong (in Chinese: Guan Gong) with a long black beard; he is flanked by two guardians, the mandarin general Chau Xuong on the left (holding a weapon) and the administrative mandarin Quan Binh on the right. Next to Chau Xuong is Quan Cong's sacred red horse.

Behind the main altar (directly across the courtyard from the entrance) is the goddess Thien Hau, Goddess of the Sea and Protector of Fisherfolk & Sailors. To the right is an ornate case in which Me Sanh (the Goddess of Fertility; in white) sits surrounded by her daughters. In the case to the left of Thien Hau is Ong Bon, Guardian Spirit of Happiness & Virtue. In front of Thien Hau is Quan The Am Bo Tat, the Goddess of Mercy, enclosed in glass.

Across the courtyard from Quan Cong is a small room containing ossuary jars (in which the ashes of the deceased are reposited) and memorials in which the dead are represented by their photographs. Next to this chamber is a small room containing the papier-mâché head of a dragon of the type used by the Fujian Congregation for dragon dancing. There is a photograph of a dragon dance on the wall between Quan Cong's red horse and Me Sanh.

Tam Son Hoi Quan Pagoda is in Cholon at 118 Trieu Quang Phuc St, which is very near 370 Tran Hung Dao B Blvd.

Thien Hau Pagoda

Thien Hau Pagoda (also known as Ba Mieu, Pho Mieu and Chua Ba) was built by the Cantonese Congregation in the early 19th century. This pagoda is one of the most active in Cholon, and the recent extensive renovations are thanks to donations from Overseas Chinese visitors.

The pagoda is dedicated to Thien Hau Thanh Mau (also known as Tuc Goi La Ba), the Chinese Goddess of the Sea. It is said that Thien Hau can travel over the oceans on a mat and ride the clouds to wherever she pleases. Her mobility allows her to save people in trouble on the high seas.

Thien Hau is very popular in Hong Kong (where she's called Tin Hau) and in Taiwan (where her name is Matsu). This might explain why Thien Hau Pagoda is included on so many tour group agendas.

Though there are guardians to either side of the entrance, it is said that the real protectors of the pagoda are the two land turtles which live here. There are intricate ceramic friezes above the roofline of the interior courtyard. Near the huge braziers are two miniature wooden structures in which a small figure of Thien Hau is paraded around each year on the 23rd day of the third lunar month. On the main dais are three figures of Thien Hau, one behind the other, each flanked by two servants or guardians. To the left of the dais is a bed for Thien Hau. To the right is a scale-model boat and on the far right is the Goddess Long Mau, Protector of Mothers & Newborns.

Thien Hau Pagoda is at 710 Nguyen Trai St and is open from 6 am to 5.30 pm.

Nghia An Hoi Quan Pagoda

Built by the Chaozhou Chinese Congregation, this pagoda is noteworthy for its gilded woodwork. There is a carved wooden boat over the entrance and inside, to the left of the doorway, is an enormous representation of Quan Cong's red horse with its groom. To the right of the entrance is an elaborate altar in which a bearded Ong Bon, Guardian Spirit of Happiness & Virtue, stands holding a stick. Behind the main altar are three glass cases. In the centre is Quan Cong; to either side are the general Chau Xuong (on the left) and the administrative mandarin Quan Binh (on the right). To the right of Quan Binh is an especially elaborate case for Thien Hau.

Nghia An Hoi Quan Pagoda is at 678 Nguyen Trai St in Cholon (not far from Thien Hau Pagoda) and is open from 4 am to 6 pm.

Quan Am Pagoda

Founded in 1816 by the Fujian Congregation, the pagoda is named for Quan The Am Bo Tat, the Goddess of Mercy. It's located at 12 Lao Tu St, one block off Chau Van Liem Blvd in Cholon.

This is the most active pagoda in Cholon and the Chinese influence is obvious. The roof is decorated with fantastic scenes, rendered in ceramic, from traditional Chinese plays and stories. The tableaux include ships, houses, people and several ferocious dragons. The front doors are decorated with very old gold and lacquer panels. On the walls of the porch are murals in slight relief picturing scenes of China from the time of Quan Cong. There are elaborate wooden carvings on roof supports above the porch.

Behind the main altar is A Pho, the Holy Mother Celestial Empress, gilded and in rich raiment. In front of her, in a glass case, are three painted statues of Thich Ca Buddha, a standing gold Quan The Am Bo Tat, a seated laughing Ameda and, to the far left, a gold figure of Dia Tang Vuong Bo Tat (the King of Hell).

In the courtyard behind the main sanctuary, in the pink tile altar, is another figure of A Pho. Quan The Am Bo Tat, dressed in white embroidered robes, stands nearby. To the left of the pink altar is her richly ornamented bed. To the right of the pink altar is Quan Cong flanked by his guardians. To the far right, in front of another pink altar, is the black-faced judge Bao Cong.

Phuoc An Hoi Quan Pagoda

Built in 1902 by the Fujian Congregation, Phuoc An Hoi Quan Pagoda is one of the most beautifully ornamented pagodas in Ho Chi Minh City. Of special interest are the many small porcelain figures, the elaborate brass ritual objects, and the fine wood carvings on the altars, walls, columns and hanging lanterns. From outside the building you can see the ceramic scenes, each containing innumerable small figurines, which decorate the roof. Phuoc An Hoi Quan Pagoda is at 184 Hung Vuong Blvd (near the intersection of Thuan Kieu St) in Cholon.

To the left of the entrance is a life-size figure of the sacred horse of Quan Cong. Before leaving on a journey, people make offerings to the horse. They then pet the horse's mane before ringing the bell around its neck. Behind the main altar, with its stone and brass incense braziers, is Quan Cong, to whom the pagoda is dedicated. Behind the altar to the left is Ong Bon and two servants. The altar to the right is occupied by representations of Buddhist (rather than Taoist) personages. In the glass case are a plaster Thich Ca Buddha and two figures of the Goddess of Mercy, one made of porcelain and the other cast in brass.

Ong Bon Pagoda

Ong Bon Pagoda (also known as Chua Ong Bon and Nhi Phu Hoi Quan) was constructed by the Fujian Congregation and is dedicated to Ong Bon, Guardian Spirit of Happiness & Virtue. The wooden altar is intricately carved and gilded. Ong Bon Pagoda is in Cholon at 264

Phuoc An Hoi Quan Pagoda, Cholon (RE)

Hai Thuong Lan Ong Blvd, which runs parallel to Tran Hung Dao B Blvd, and is open from 5 am to 5 pm.

As you enter the pagoda, there is a room to the right of the open-air courtyard. In it, behind the table, is a figure of Quan The Am Bo Tat in a glass case. Above the case is the head of a Thich Ca Buddha.

Directly across the courtyard from the pagoda entrance, against the wall, is Ong Bon, to whom people come to pray for general happiness and relief from financial difficulties. He faces a fine carved wooden altar. On the walls of this chamber are two rather indistinct murals of five tigers (to the left) and two dragons (to the right).

In the area on the other side of the wall with the mural of the dragons is a furnace for burning paper representations of the wealth people wish to bestow on deceased family members. Diagonally opposite is Quan Cong flanked by his guardians Chau Xuong (to his right) and Quan Binh (to his left).

Ha Chuong Hoi Quan Pagoda

Ha Chuong Hoi Quan Pagoda at 802 Nguyen Trai St in Cholon is a typical Fujian pagoda. Like the Thien Hau Pagoda, it is dedicated to Thien Hau Thanh Mau, Goddess of the Sea, who was born in Fujian.

The four carved stone pillars, wrapped in painted dragons, were made in China and brought to Vietnam by boat. There are interesting murals to either side of the main altar. Note the ceramic relief scenes on the roof.

This pagoda becomes extremely active during the Lantern Festival, a Chinese holiday held on the 15th day of the first lunar month (the first full moon of the new lunar year).

Khanh Van Nam Vien Pagoda

Built between 1939 and 1942 by the Cantonese, Khanh Van Nam Vien Pagoda is said to be the only Taoist pagoda in all of Vietnam. This statement needs to be qualified since most Chinese practise a mixture of Taoism and Buddhism, rather than one or the other exclusively. The number of 'true' Taoists in Ho Chi Minh City is said to number only 4000, though you can take this figure with a grain of salt since most of the true Taoists are probably Buddhists too.

A few metres from the door is a statue of Hoang Linh Quan, chief guardian of the pagoda. There is a Yin & Yang symbol on the platform on which the incense braziers sit. Behind the main altar are four figures: Quan

Cong (on the right) and Lu Tung Pan (on the left) represent Taoism; between the two of them is Van Xuong representing Confucianism; and behind Van Xuong is Quan The Am Bo Tat.

In front of these figures is a glass case containing seven gods and one goddess, all of which are made of porcelain. In the altars to either side of the four figures are Hoa De (on the left), a famous doctor during the Han Dynasty, and Huynh Dai Tien (on the right), a disciple of the founder of Taoism, Laotze (Vietnamese: Thai Thuong Lao Quan).

Upstairs is a 150-cm-high statue of Laotze. Behind his head is a halo consisting of a round mirror with fluorescent lighting around the edge.

To the left of Laotze are two stone plaques with instructions for inhalation and exhalation exercises. The 80-year-old chief monk says that he has practised these exercises for the past 17 years and hasn't been sick a day. A schematic drawing represents the human organs as a scene from rural China. The diaphragm, agent of inhalation, is at the bottom. The stomach is represented by a peasant ploughing with a water buffalo. The kidney is marked by four Yin & Yang symbols, the liver is shown as a grove of trees, and the heart is represented by a circle with a peasant standing in it, above which is a constellation. The tall pagoda represents the throat, and the broken rainbow is the mouth. At the top are mountains and a seated figure representing the brain and the imagination, respectively.

The pagoda operates a home at 46/14 Lo Sieu St for 30 elderly people who have no families; next door, also run by the pagoda, is a free medical clinic which offers Chinese herbal medicines. Before reunification, the pagoda ran (also free of charge) the school across the street.

The pagoda is open from 6.30 am to 5.30 pm every day and prayers are held from 8 to 9 am daily. To get there, turn off Nguyen Thi Nho St (which runs perpendicular to Hung Vuong Blvd) between numbers 269B and 271B; the address is 46/5 Lo Sieu St, District 5.

Phung Son Pagoda

Phung Son Pagoda (also known as Phung Son Tu and Chua Go) is extremely rich in statuary made of hammered copper, bronze, wood and ceramics. Some are gilded while others, beautifully carved, are painted. This Vietnamese Buddhist pagoda was built between 1802 and 1820 on the site of structures from the Oc-Eo (Funan) period, which was contemporaneous with the early centuries of Christianity. In 1988, a Soviet archaeological

MAP 5

Plan of Phung Son Pagoda

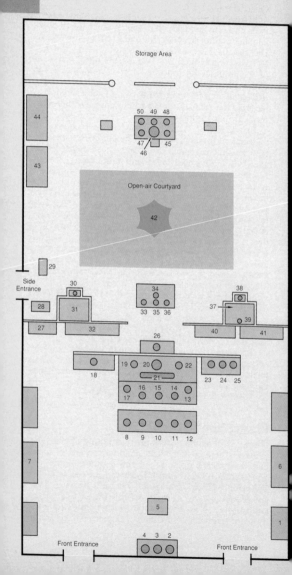

MAP 5 Plan of Phung Son Pagoda

1	Dia Tang Vuong Bo Tat
2	Guardian
3	Guardian of the Pagoda
4	Tieu Dien, a Guardian
5	Donations Box
6-7	Judges of the Ten Regions of Hell
8	Van Thu Bo Tat
9	Quan The Am Bo Tat
10	A Di Da Buddha
11	Dai The Chi Bo Tat
12	Pho Hien Bo Tat
13	Guardian
14	Dai The Chi Bo Tat
15	A Di Da Buddha
16	Quan The Am Bo Tat
17	Guardians
18	Bodhidharma
19	Quan The Am Bo Tat
20	A Di Da Buddha
21	Statuettes of Quan The Am Bo Tat, her guardians & Thich Ca Buddha as a Child
22	Dai The Chi Bo Tat
23	Lang Nu
24	Quan The Am Bo Tat
25	Thien Tai
26-27	Memorial Tablets, Portraits of Ancestor Monks
28	Desk with Old Photos of Monks under Glass
29	Desk with Old Paper Money under Glass
30	Statue of Hue Minh, Founder of the Pagoda
31	Rosewood Platform
32	Memorial Tablets, Portraits of Ancestor Monks
33	Thich Ca Buddha
34	Ameda
35	Bronze Thich Ca Buddha
37	Rosewood Platform
38	Statue of Head Monk Hue Thanh, Successor to Hue Minh
39	Sandalwood Statue of Long Vuong
40-41	Memorial Tablets, Portraits of Ancestor Monks
42	Miniature Mountain made of Volcanic Rocks
43-44	Rosewood Platforms
45	Guardian
46	18-armed Chuan De
47	Guardian
48	Dai The Chi Bo Tat
49	A Di Da Buddha
50	Quan The Am Bo Tat

team carried out a preliminary excavation and found the
foundations of Funanese buildings, but work was
stopped pending authorisation for a full-scale dig.

Phung Son Pagoda is in District 11 at 1408, 3 Thang 2
Blvd, near its intersection with Hung Vuong Blvd.
Prayers are held three times a day from 4 to 5 am, 4 to 5
and 6 to 7 pm. The main entrances are kept locked most
of the time because of problems with theft but the side
entrance (which is to the left as you approach the building) is open from 5 am to 7 pm.

Once upon a time, it was decided that Phung Son
Pagoda should be moved to a different site. The
pagoda's ritual objects – bells, drums, statues – were
loaded onto the back of a white elephant for transport to
the new location, but the elephant slipped because of the
great weight and all the precious objects fell into a
nearby pond. This event was interpreted as an omen that
the pagoda should remain at its original location. All the
articles were retrieved except for the bell, which locals
say was heard ringing whenever there was a full or new
moon, until about a century ago.

The main dais, with its many levels, is dominated by
a gilded A Di Da Buddha (20), the Buddha of the Past,
seated under a canopy flanked by long mobiles resembling human forms without heads. A Di Da is flanked by
Quan The Am Bo Tat (19) on the left and Dai The Chi Bo
Tat (22) on the right. To the left of the main dais is an altar
with a statue of Bodhidharma (18), the founder of Zen
Buddhism who brought Buddhism from India to China.
The statue, which is made of Chinese ceramic, has a face
with Indian features.

As you walk from the main sanctuary to the room
with the open-air courtyard in the middle, you come to
an altar with four statues on it, including a standing
bronze Thich Ca Buddha (35) of Thai origin. To the right
is a rosewood platform (37) used as a table and for
sleeping, and an altar on which there is a glass case
containing a statue made of sandalwood. The statue (39)
is claimed to be Long Vuong (Dragon King) who brings
rain. Around the pagoda building are a number of interesting monks' tombs.

CHURCHES

Notre Dame Cathedral

Built between 1877 and 1883, Notre Dame Cathedral is
set in the heart of town facing down Dong Khoi St. Its
neo-Romanesque form and two 40-metre-high square
towers, tipped with iron spires, dominate the city's

skyline. In front of the cathedral (in the centre of the square bounded by the CPO) is a statue of the Virgin Mary. If the front gates are locked try the door on the side of the building that faces Reunification Palace.

Unusually, this cathedral has no stained-glass windows. The glass was a casualty of fighting during WW II. A number of foreign travellers worship here, and the priests are allowed to add a short sermon in French or English to their longer presentations in Vietnamese. The 9.30 am Sunday mass might be the best one for foreigners to attend.

There are several other interesting French-era churches around Saigon, including one at 289 Hai Ba Trung Blvd.

Cho Quan Church

Built by the French about 100 years ago, this is one of the largest churches in Ho Chi Minh City. This is perhaps the only church in the city where the figure of Jesus on the altar has a neon halo. The steep climb to the belfry will reward you with excellent views.

Coups & Conspiracies

It was in Cha Tam Church that President Ngo Dinh Diem and his brother Ngo Dinh Nhu took refuge on 2 November 1963 after fleeing the Presidential Palace during a coup attempt. When their efforts to contact loyal military officers (of whom there were almost none) failed, Diem and Nhu agreed to surrender unconditionally and revealed where they were hiding.

The coup leaders sent an M-113 armoured personnel carrier to the church to pick them up (Diem seemed disappointed that a limousine befitting his rank had not been dispatched) and the two were taken into custody. But before the vehicle arrived in Saigon, the soldiers in the APC killed Diem and Nhu by shooting them at point-blank range and then repeatedly stabbing their bodies.

When news of the death of the brothers was broadcast on the radio, Saigon exploded into rejoicing. Portraits of the two were torn up and political prisoners, many of whom had been tortured, were set free. The city's nightclubs, closed because of the Ngos' conservative Catholic beliefs, reopened. Three weeks later, US president John F Kennedy was assassinated. Since Kennedy's administration supported the coup against Diem, some conspiracy theorists have speculated that Kennedy was killed by Diem's family in retaliation. Then again, there are theories that Kennedy was murdered by the Russians, the Cubans, left-wing radicals, right-wing radicals, the CIA and the Mafia. ■

The church is in Cholon at 133 Tran Binh Trong St (between Tran Hung Dao Blvd and Nguyen Trai St), and is open daily from 4 to 7 am and 3 to 6 pm and on Sunday from 4 to 9 am and 1.30 to 6 pm. Sunday masses are held in the morning at 5, 6.30 and 8.30 am, and also in the afternoon at 4.30 and 6 pm.

Cha Tam Church

Cha Tam Church, built around the turn of the century, is an attractive white and pastel-yellow structure. The statue in the tower is of François Xavier Tam Assou (1855-1934), a Chinese-born vicar apostolic of Saigon. (A vicar apostolic is a delegate of the pope who administers an ecclesiastical district in a missionary region.) Today, the church has a very active congregation of 3000 ethnic-Vietnamese and 2000 ethnic-Chinese.

Notre Dame Cathedral (RS)

Vietnamese-language masses are held daily from 5.30 to 6 am and on Sundays from 5.30 to 6.30 and 8.30 to 9.30 am and 3.45 to 4.45 pm. Chinese-language masses are held from 5.30 to 6 pm every day and from 7 to 8 am and 5 to 6 pm on Sundays. Cha Tam Church is in Cholon at 25 Hoc Lac St, at the western end of Tran Hung Dao B Blvd.

MOSQUES

Saigon Central Mosque

Built by South Indian Muslims in 1935 on the site of an earlier mosque, the Saigon Central Mosque is an immaculately clean and well-kept island of calm in the middle of bustling central Saigon. In front of the sparkling white and blue structure at 66 Dong Du St, with its four nonfunctional minarets, is a pool for ritual ablutions (washing), required by Islamic law before prayers. As with any mosque, take off your shoes before entering the sanctuary.

The simplicity of the mosque is in marked contrast to the exuberance of Buddhist pagoda decorations and their rows of figures facing elaborate ritual objects. Islamic law strictly forbids using human or animal figures for decoration.

Only half-a-dozen Indian Muslims remain in Saigon; most of the community fled in 1975. As a result, prayers – held five times a day – are sparsely attended except on Fridays, when several dozen worshippers (including many non-Indian Muslims) are present.

There are 12 other mosques serving the 5000 or so Muslims in Ho Chi Minh City. However, the mass emigration deprived the local Muslim community of much of its spiritual leadership, and very few Muslims knowledgeable in their tradition and Arabic, the language of the Koran, remain.

Cholon Mosque

The clean lines and lack of ornamentation of the Cholon Mosque are in stark contrast to nearby Chinese and Vietnamese pagodas. In the courtyard is a pool for ritual ablutions. Note the tile *mihrab* (the niche in the wall indicating the direction of prayer, which is towards Mecca). The mosque was built by Tamil Muslims in 1932. Since 1975, the mosque has served the Malaysian and Indonesian Muslim communities.

Cholon Mosque is at 641 Nguyen Trai St and is open all day Friday and at prayer times on other days.

PARKS

Zoo & Botanical Gardens

The zoo and botanical gardens (Thao Cam Vien) are a pleasant place for a relaxing stroll under giant tropical trees which thrive amidst the lakes, lawns and flower beds. Unfortunately, the zoo facilities are run-down, and the elephants in particular look like they'd be better off dead (many are close to it now). The other animals – which include crocodiles and big cats – seem to have it somewhat better.

The botanical gardens, founded in 1864, were one of the first projects undertaken by the French after they established Cochinchina as a colony. They were once one of the finest such gardens in Asia, but this is certainly no longer true. The emphasis now is on the fun fair, with kiddie rides, fun house, miniature train, house of mirrors, etc.

A rather gruesome form of amusement exists near the entrance to the zoo. There is a ride here where the animals on which people sit are real! There are stuffed bears, deer and large cats, following each other around the revolving platform. Some of them are looking a little tatty, but this no doubt creates employment for local taxidermists. At least these animals are dead (hopefully).

The main gate of the zoo is on Nguyen Binh Khiem St at the intersection of Le Duan Blvd. There is another entrance on Nguyen Thi Minh Khai St near the bridge over Thi Nghe Channel.

The History Museum is next to the main gate. There are occasional water puppet shows performed on a small island in one of the lakes – a small group can arrange a special showing.

Also just inside the main gate is the Temple of King Hung Vuong. The Hung kings are said to have been the first rulers of the Vietnamese nation, having established their rule in the Red River region before being invaded by the Chinese.

The limited food sold here is generally expensive and not too good. Just outside the main gate (along Nguyen Binh Khiem St) there are numerous food stalls selling excellent rice dishes, soup and drinks at reasonable prices.

Cong Vien Van Hoa Park

Next to the old Cercle Sportif, an elite sporting club during the French period, the bench-lined walks of Cong Vien Van Hoa Park are shaded with avenues of enormous tropical trees.

This place still has an active sports club, although now you don't have to be French to visit. There are 11 tennis courts, a swimming pool and a club house which have a grand colonial feel about them. It's worth a look for the pool alone. There are Roman-style baths with a coffee shop overlooking the colonnaded pool.

The tennis courts are available for hire at a reasonable fee. Hourly tickets are on sale for use of the pool and you can buy a bathing costume on the grounds if you don't have one. The antique dressing rooms are quaint but there are no lockers! Other facilities include a gymnasium, table tennis, weight lifting, wrestling mats and ballroom dancing classes.

In the morning, you can often see people here practising the art of *thai cuc quyen* (t'ai chi) or slow motion shadow boxing.

Within the park is a small-scale model of the Cham towers in Nha Trang.

Cong Vien Van Hoa Park is adjacent to Reunification Palace. There are entrances across from 115 Nguyen Du St and on Nguyen Thi Minh Khai St.

Ho Ky Hoa Park

Ho Ky Hoa Park, whose name means Lake & Gardens, is a children's amusement park in District 10 just off 3 Thang 2 Blvd. It is near the Hoa Binh Theatre and behind Vietnam Quoc Tu Pagoda. There are paddleboats, rowboats and sailboats for hire. Fishing is allowed in the lakes and a small swimming pool is open to the public for part of the year. The cafés are open year round and there are also two arcades of Japanese video games. Within the park boundaries is the rather expensive Ky Hoa Hotel. Ho Ky Hoa Park is open from 7 am to 9.30 pm daily and is crowded on Sundays.

OTHER ATTRACTIONS

Hôtel de Ville

Saigon's gingerbread Hôtel de Ville is not a place to stay, despite the name. One of the city's most prominent landmarks, it was built between 1901 and 1908 after years of the sort of architectural controversy peculiar to the French. Situated at the north-western end of Nguyen Hue Blvd and facing towards the river, the white-on-pastel-yellow Hôtel de Ville, with its ornate façade and elegant interior lit with crystal chandeliers, is now the somewhat incongruous home of the Ho Chi Minh City People's Committee. The building is officially called the

Zoo entrance (ME)

People's Committee Building, though few outside the government care to call it that. Whatever it's called, the building is not open to the public and requests by tourists to visit the interior are rudely rebuffed.

Former US Embassies

There are actually two former US embassies in Saigon: the one from whose roof the famous chaotic helicopter evacuation took place as the Communists took over the city in April 1975; and the building used before that one was built.

The older former US Embassy (Dai Su Quan My Truoc 1967) is an ugly fortress-like concrete structure at 39 Ham Nghi Blvd (corner of Ho Tung Mau St). In 1967, the building was bombed by the VC. It now serves as a dormitory for young people studying banking.

The newer structure (Dai Su Quan My Tu 1967-75) –
from which US policy was conducted during the last
eight years of the Republic of Vietnam – is on the corner
of Le Duan Blvd and Mac Dinh Chi St in the middle of
what was (and still is) a neighbourhood of key government buildings. The main building, once the chancery,
is encased in a concrete shield intended to protect it from
bomb blasts as well as rocket and shell fire. There are
round concrete pillboxes, protected with anti-grenade
screens, at each corner of the compound.

The embassy building, which became a symbol of the
overwhelming American presence in South Vietnam,
was finished just in time to almost get taken over in the
1968 Tet offensive. On TV, 50 million Americans watched
chaotic scenes of dazed US soldiers and diplomats firing
at the VC commando team which had attacked the
embassy, leaving the grounds littered with US and
Vietnamese dead. These images were devastating to US
home-front support for the war.

The ignominious end of three decades of US involvement in Vietnam, also shown around the globe on TV,
took place on the roof of the US Embassy chancery
building. As the last defences of Saigon fell to the North
Vietnamese Army and the city's capture became immin-
ent, the Americans, as unprepared for the speed of the
collapse of the South as everyone else (including the
North Vietnamese), were forced to implement emergency evacuation plans. Thousands of Vietnamese
desperate to escape the country (many of them had
worked for the Americans and had been promised to be
evacuated) congregated around the embassy and tried
to get inside; US marine guards forced them back. Over-
head, American helicopters (carrying both Americans

Former US Embassy (GB)

and Vietnamese) shuttled to aircraft carriers waiting offshore. In the pre-dawn darkness of 30 April 1975, with most of the city already in Communist hands, US Ambassador Graham Martin, carrying the embassy's flag, climbed onto the roof of the building and boarded a helicopter. The end.

The compound was for a while occupied by the government-owned Oil Exploration Corporation, but they have now abandoned it. The official word is that the building is being reserved for the Americans to move back in when full diplomatic relations are restored between the USA and Vietnam. Of course, the former embassy will just be a US consulate – a new US Embassy will be built in Hanoi.

Binh Soup Shop

It might seem strange to introduce a restaurant in the sightseeing section of this book rather than the Places to Eat section, but there is more to this shop than just the soup. The Binh Soup Shop was the secret headquarters of the Viet Cong in Saigon. It was from here that the VC planned the attack on the US Embassy and other places in Saigon during the Tet offensive of 1968. One has to wonder how many American soldiers must have eaten here, unaware that the waiters, waitresses and cooks were VC infiltrators.

The Binh Soup Shop is at 7 Ly Chinh Thang St, District 3. By the way, the soup isn't bad.

WALKING TOUR

Ho Chi Minh City's immense sprawl makes it somewhat impractical to see all of it on foot, but a one-day walking tour of District 1 (Saigon) is certainly possible. The biggest problem is just knowing where to start.

Pham Ngu Lao St, a likely place to start, is the hotel and restaurant centre for budget travellers. It has nothing of interest for Western tourists beyond satisfying basic needs such as eating, drinking, socialising and sleeping. But it's a different story for the Vietnamese - Pham Ngu Lao St is where they go to 'look at the hippies'. Yes it's true – Western backpackers have become a tourist attraction much like the hill tribes of the Central Highlands. If you hang out there, remember to smile for the camera when the tour buses roll by.

After a short walk north up Nguyen Thai Hoc St to the New World Hotel (a major landmark), turn right along Le Lai St to the indoor **Ben Thanh Market**. The market is at its bustling best in the morning. You may want to do your actual souvenir buying later in the day, at a time when you can haul the goods straight back to your hotel.

Walk along Le Loi Blvd, and turn left up Nguyen Hue Blvd. At the northern end is the old **Hôtel de Ville**. You'll have to admire it from the outside because it's now home to the local People's Committee – requests to visit the interior are normally abruptly rejected. However, a one-block walk along Le Thanh Ton St will bring you to the **Revolutionary Museum**, where visitors are warmly received.

The popular **War Crimes Museum** is just a few blocks to the north (technically in District 3) along Nam Ky Khoi Nghia St then left on Vo Van Tan St. You'll have to pay attention to your watch because the museum is closed for lunch from 11.30 am to 2 pm.

Nearby is **Reunification Palace**, which most likely you'll have to visit after lunch. It's only open from 7.30 to 10 am and 1 to 4 pm.

Later in the afternoon you can stroll the length of Le Duan Blvd taking a look at the **former US Embassy** on the left. At the end of the boulevard are the **zoo & botanical gardens**, in the grounds of which is the History Museum. Just outside the gate you'll find the Military Museum.

A few blocks to the north along Nguyen Binh Khiem St will bring you to the **Jade Emperor Pagoda**, a colour-ful way to end your tour. By this time you will most likely be tired enough to head for your hotel, take a shower, get a cold drink and prepare yourself for tack-ling the nightlife of Ho Chi Minh City.

ACTIVITIES

Fitness Clubs

Most major hotels in Saigon will allow you to use their facilities (gymnasium, pool, sauna, tennis courts, etc) for the payment of a reasonable daily fee. You do not need to be a guest at the hotel, though the hotel has the right to refuse you (which they might do if the facilities become overcrowded). The fees vary, so you'll need to make local enquiries.

The policy at the New World Hotel is different. Access to the exercise facilities is limited to guests or members of their fitness club. Unfortunately, becoming a club member is not cheap. It involves paying a one-time fee of US$750, plus US$50 per month, and there is still a per-hour fee for use of the tennis courts. The number of memberships is

limited, though this policy (and the fees) could change.
Enquire at the hotel for the latest information.

Golf

The Vietnam International Golf Club is another cash cow
brought to you by Saigon Tourist. It's actually a joint-
venture with a Taiwan-based company – the Taiwanese
were said to be more interested in the appreciating value
of the real estate than the 36-hole golf course. The club
(Cau Lac Bo Golf Quoc Te Viet Nam; ☎ 322084; fax
322083) is at 40-42 Nguyen Trai St, Thu Duc District (Lam
Vien Park), about 15 km east of central Saigon. Member-
ship ranges from US$5000 to US$60,000 but paying
visitors are welcome. It may be worth coming here to use
the driving range (cong trinh xay dung san tap) which
costs US$10, or you can play a full round for US$50.
Other facilities on the site include tennis courts and a
swimming pool.

Song Be Golf Resort is a slick Singapore-Vietnam
joint-venture 20 km north of Saigon. Unfortunately, this
resort is for members only or their guests. This place has
it all – tennis courts, a swimming pool, hotel, restaurant
(surprisingly cheap!), villas, an imported Filipino
jeepney (a customised jeep) and security guards to keep

Hôtel de Ville (RE)

out curious locals. Oh yes, and there's a golf course too. Memberships are priced as follows: social (Vietnamese) US$7000; social (foreigners) US$9000; ordinary (Vietnamese) US$22,000; ordinary (foreigners) US$27,500; corporate A US$33,000; corporate B US$75,000. The villas cannot be purchased, but can be leased for 50 years. For further details, you can ring up the resort (☎ 55800; fax 55516) in Song Be Province, or visit their Ho Chi Minh City office (☎ 231218; fax 231215) at 254B Nguyen Dinh Chieu St, District 3.

Plans are in the works to build a golf course at Gia Dinh Park (Cong Vien Gia Dinh). This is in the northern part of the Phu Nhuan District close to Tan Son Nhat Airport. A tentative opening date of 1997 has been announced, but don't hold your breath. When completed it will certainly be the closest golf course to central Saigon.

Hash House Harriers

This loosely strung organisation meets once a week for a jogging session followed by a drinking session. The meeting time is every Sunday about 2.30 pm at the Saigon Floating Hotel, from where a chartered bus takes you to the beginning of the run. The time and place *can* change. Look for the latest announcements in the Saigon Floating Hotel or else the noticeboard at the Norfolk Hotel, 117 Le Thanh Ton St, District 1. Announcements may also appear in expat pubs around town or in various magazines such the *Vietnam Economic Times* and *What's On in Saigon*.

Roller Skating

There is a roller skating rink across from the Saigon Star Hotel which is at 204 Nguyen Thi Minh Khai St in District 3.

Nha Van Hoa is a small park in Cholon on the south side of Tran Hung Dao Blvd between Ngo Quyen St and Nguyen Tri Phuong Blvd. But it's unusual in that it's a park with nightlife. Features here include an outdoor stage with live music (awful wailing, but they try), an indoor roller skating rink and video game arcade. And there is also a disco of sorts, including a karaoke hall with dance lessons.

Swimming Pools

Ho Chi Minh City's tropical climate makes swimming the ideal way to stay cool and get exercise. The situation here is as mentioned under the preceding Fitness Clubs heading. Upmarket swimming pools can be found at plush tourist hotels. You needn't stay at these hotels to use the facilities, but you must pay an admission fee of US$5 to US$10 per day. Hotels offering access to their pools include the Omni, Palace, Rex and Saigon Floating Hotel. About the only major hotel which does not offer public access to its pool is the New World.

The International Club at 285B Cach Mang Thang Tam Blvd, District 10, also has an excellent swimming pool.

There are a number of public pools where the Vietnamese go, and some of the newer ones are in very good condition. These pools charge by the hour and it works out to be very cheap if you're staying only a short time. One such place is the Olympic-sized Lam Son Pool (☎ 358028), 342 Tran Binh Trong St, District 5 – the weekday charge here is around US$0.50 per hour, which rises to US$0.80 on weekends. For US$1.50 per hour you can visit the pool at the Workers' Club, 55B Nguyen Thi Minh Khai St, District 3.

Waterskiing

Perhaps 'sewage-skiing' would be a more apt term. The Saigon River is pretty murky and there is no telling what sort of contagious diseases you might contract by frolicking in the bubbling broth. Nevertheless, some brave or foolish foreigners have on occasion rented a speedboat from Saigon Tourist (or elsewhere) and headed upstream to Bien Hoa where the water is merely brown rather than black. Probably you'd be better off heading down to the Mekong River for this activity, though that will require at least an overnight trip.

Places to Stay

The current tourist boom has created a shortage of accommodation space in Ho Chi Minh City, with the result that there is a hotel construction boom going on. There is also considerable renovation work going on – old grotty dumps are getting new plumbing, safer electrical wiring and a badly needed facelift. For budget travellers the down side is that renovation comes at a price – it's getting harder and harder to find rooms for under US$10.

Different categories of travellers have staked out their own turf. Budget travellers tend to congregate around Pham Ngu Lao St at the western end of District 1. Travellers with cash to spare prefer the more upmarket hotels concentrated around Dong Khoi St on the eastern side of District 1. French travellers seem to have an affinity for District 3. Cholon attracts plenty of Hong Kongers and Taiwanese, but Western backpackers are rare here despite the availability of cheap accommodation – it seems the herd instinct is too powerful a force to be resisted.

Not all hotels in the city are permitted to receive foreign guests, but those which can will always display a sign in English including the words 'hotel' or 'guest

---

The Fatal Flush

When Saigon surrendered in 1975, North Vietnamese soldiers who grew up in the spartan North were billeted in the emptied high-rise hotels. There is an oft-told story about several such soldiers who managed to scrape together enough money to buy fish and produce at the market. To keep their purchases fresh, they put them in the Western-style toilet, an appliance completely foreign to them. Then, out of curiosity, one of the soldiers flushed the toilet and the fish and vegetables disappeared. Of course, they were furious at having been cheated out of their meal by some sinister plumbing fixture. So they did the logical thing and snuffed the perfidious imperialist booby trap with an AK-47.

While it would be hard to prove that this incident actually took place (or that it happened only once), it's true that a great deal of damage was done to Saigon's hotels after reunification and that toilets were especially targeted. Some of this damage has only recently been repaired. ■

house'. The Vietnamese translation for hotel is *khach san*; a guest house is *nha khach* or *nha nghi*. Very few dormitories *(nha tro)* will accept foreigners.

Official policy is to insist that 'capitalist tourists' pay double what Vietnamese pay, but even so, the prices are still reasonable. Some hotels give a big discount to Overseas Vietnamese, a policy which most foreigners regard as overtly racist.

A few hotels might try to charge the foreigners' price if you are paying for a Vietnamese guide and/or driver who is staying in a separate room. This is not on – they should be charged like any local tourist. Don't accept this nonsense from anyone.

Security is not too good in the cheapest places. Some hotels have a place where you can affix a padlock to the outside of your room's door – if so, bring your own lock and use it. Aside from locking the door to your room, keep your bags in the cabinets or closets which are often provided for this purpose and lock these with a padlock or cable and padlock combination.

For the purposes of this book, **bottom-end** accommodation is defined as costing less than US$25. From US$25 to US$50 would be **mid-range** and anything over that is **top-end**. But it's important to realise that many Vietnamese hotels offer a wide range of prices in the same building. For example, one 'budget hotel' listed here has room prices running from US$12 to US$70. Cheap rooms are almost always on the top floor because few hotels have lifts and most guests paying US$70 are not keen to walk up seven storeys or more.

Riverside Hotel (RE)

Many hotels will insist that you leave your passport or visa with reception so that they can register you with the police. While police registration was indeed required in the past, this is no longer true in Ho Chi Minh City (but *is* true in many backward provinces). What the hotels are doing is simply holding your documents because they want to be sure you don't run off with the towels or TV – police registration has nothing to do with it. While there is nothing wrong with the staff checking your documents, there is really no need for them to take your valuable papers away from you, assuming that you paid for your room in advance. If you resent this, then argue.

PLACES TO STAY – BOTTOM END

District 1

Pham Ngu Lao, De Tham and Bui Vien Sts form the axis of the city's budget traveller's haven. These streets and the adjoining alleys are bespeckled with a treasure trove of cheap accommodation and cafés catering to the low-end market. Unfortunately, a major construction project will begin soon to redevelop the northern side of Pham Ngu Lao St into a luxury tourist area. The construction is estimated to take about four years and will generate a considerable amount of dust and noise. Most likely the budget hotels and restaurants will quickly retreat from Pham Ngu Lao St one block south to Bui Vien St near the intersection with De Tham St.

Except where noted, the following hotels all fall in the area covered by Map 7.

At 193 Pham Ngu Lao St is the huge *Prince Hotel* (Khach San Hoang Tu; ☎ 322657; 66 rooms). Prices range from US$6 to US$11. The cheaper rooms are on the upper floors because there is no lift.

Close by is the decidedly smaller but very pleasant *Hotel 211* (☎ 352353) at 211 Pham Ngu Lao St. Singles/doubles cost US$8/12 with fan, or US$12/16 with air-con.

Also near the Prince Hotel, the first place in this neighbourhood to offer dormitory accommodation was *Thanh Thanh 2 Hotel* (☎ 324027; fax 251550) at 205 Pham Ngu Lao St. Dorm beds start at US$3.50 and regular rooms range up to US$9.

The *Vien Dong Hotel*, 275A Pham Ngu Lao St (☎ 393001; fax 332812; 139 rooms), has budget rooms on the top floor costing US$12. However, on the lower floors, rooms are considerably pricier at US$32 to US$70 (which includes fridge, bathroom and air-con).

Next door at No 265A is the mammoth *Hoang Vu Hotel* (☎ 396522; 161 rooms). It's long been extremely popular with backpackers; singles are US$6 to US$13 and twins US$10 to US$15. Sadly, the building is slated for a major renovation with a corresponding increase in prices. Hopefully, the upper floors will still be kept cheap, as at the Vien Dong.

At 325 Pham Ngu Lao St is the *Thai Binh Hotel* (☎ 399544; 28 rooms). There's no air-con here, but rooms have attached bath and range from US$5 to US$7.

Just around the corner is *My Man Mini-Hotel* (☎ 396544; 10 rooms). Yes, the name is both English and Vietnamese. Rooms with fan are US$10 to US$14, and with air-con they're US$14 to US$18. The address is officially 373/20 Pham Ngu Lao St, but it's actually down a tiny alley just behind the Thai Binh Market.

One block to the north-west of the Thai Binh Market at 83A Bui Thi Xuan St is the *Hoang Yen Mini-Hotel* (☎ 391348; fax 298540; 10 rooms). The owner speaks French but not much English. Singles/twins are US$16 to US$21 and the tariff includes breakfast.

South of Pham Ngu Lao St on Bui Vien St are two very clean private hotels, *Guest House 70* (☎ 330569; eight rooms) and *Guest House 72* (☎ 330321; four rooms). The first charges US$8 to US$14 (add US$2 for air-con), and the latter costs US$7 to US$10. Expect to find many more such places on Bui Vien St by the time you read this.

An alternative to the Pham Ngu Lao area is a string of excellent guest houses on an alley connecting Co Giang and Co Bac Sts. The first hotel to appear here and probably still the best is *Miss Loi's Guest House* (Pham Thi Loi; ☎ 352973), 178/20 Co Giang St. Room prices average US$8 to US$10 for a double. Many of Miss Loi's neighbours are jumping into this business and the area seems destined to develop into another budget travellers' haven.

The *A Chau Hotel* (☎ 331814; eight rooms) is at 92B Le Lai St, one block west of the five-star New World Hotel. Singles/twins with fan cost US$7/10, while air-con twins are US$15.

The *Rang Dong Hotel* (☎ 398264; fax 393318; 127 rooms) at 81 Cach Mang Thang Tam St is new and nice, and fairly reasonably priced for this standard. Room rates range from US$15 to US$45.

Hidden behind the plush Embassy Hotel is the much cheaper *Tao Dan Hotel* (☎ 230299; 94 rooms), 35A Nguyen Trung Truc. Long a favourite with Japanese backpackers, it boasts a wide range of rooms costing from US$12 to US$16 with fan, and US$20 to US$24 with air-con.

A lot of backpackers choose the *Van Canh Hotel* (☎ 294963; 33 rooms) at 184 Calmette St. All rooms have air-conditioning, though the very cheapest rooms are shared bath only. Rates for singles are US$5 to US$13; twins are US$7 to US$15.

Hotel 69 Hai Ba Trung (☎ 291513; 18 rooms) is, as its name suggests, at 69 Hai Ba Trung Blvd. This small, congenial place is conveniently near the centre. The tariff here ranges from US$22 to US$30 (Map 8).

District 5 (Cholon)

All these hotels are on Map 9.

The *Phuong Huong Hotel* (☎ 551888; fax 552228; 70 rooms) is in an eight-storey building at 411 Tran Hung Dao B Blvd. Also known as the Phoenix Hotel, this place is just off Chau Van Liem Blvd in the middle of central Cholon. Rooms with fan/air-con cost US$12/25.

Just up Chau Van Liem Blvd at Nos 111-117 is the *Truong Thanh Hotel* (☎ 556044; 81 rooms). It's definitely a budget place. Rooms with fan are US$5 to US$6, while air-con costs a modest US$13.

Half a block away, at 125 Chau Van Liem Blvd, is the *Thu Do Hotel* (☎ 559102; 70 rooms). It looks very much like a dump, a distinction it shares with the neighbouring Truong Thanh Hotel. Rooms cost a modest US$6 to US$8.

Across the street from the Phuong Huong Hotel, the *Song Kim Hotel* (☎ 559773; 33 rooms) is at 84-86 Chau Van Liem Blvd. It's a grungy and somewhat disreputable establishment with twins for US$5 with fan or US$8 with air-con. Reception is up a flight of stairs. You can do better than this for marginally more money.

The *Trung Mai Hotel* (☎ 552101, 554067; 142 rooms) is a six-storey establishment at 785 Nguyen Trai St, just off Chau Van Liem Blvd. Singles/twins with fan cost US$5/6 while air-con rooms are US$10/11.

The *Tan Da Hotel* (☎ 555711) is at 17-19 Tan Da St, very close to the upmarket Arc En Ciel Hotel. This place is rather tacky. Rooms with fan/air-con cost US$16/21. With air-con and refrigerator it's US$27.

The *Hoa Binh Hotel* (☎ 355133; 35 rooms) is a seven-storey building at 1115 Tran Hung Dao Blvd. Doubles with fan/air-con cost US$7/15.

PLACES TO STAY – MIDDLE

District 1

Close to the five-star New World Hotel is the much cheaper *Palace Saigon Hotel* (☎ 331353; 10 rooms) at No 82 Le Lai St. There are also 16 additional rooms at their annexe (☎ 359421) at 108 Le Lai St. It's a fine place and reasonably good value at US$25 to US$35 for an air-con double (Map 7).

The *Saigon Hotel* (☎ 299734; fax 291466; 100 rooms) is at 47 Dong Du St, across the street from the Saigon Central Mosque. Singles/twins cost from US$36/44 to US$69/79. The deluxe rooms come equipped with satellite TV (Map 8).

The *Thai Binh Duong Hotel* (☎ 322674) at 92 and 107 Ky Con St is a good place with air-con rooms from US$20 to US$25 (Map 7). On the same street at No 105 is the *Phong Phu Hotel* (☎ /fax 222020; 10 rooms) which costs US$25 to US$35 (Map 7).

Nearby at 141 Nguyen Thai Binh St is the *Rose 2 Hotel* (☎ 231573; fax 210070; 12 rooms). As their brochure says, the hotel has 'all comfortable and modern equipments'. All rooms have air-conditioning and cost US$25 (Map 7).

The *Champagne Hotel* (☎ 224922; fax 230776; 38 rooms), 129-133 Ham Nghi Blvd, is also known as the Que Huong Hotel. Singles are US$38 to US$48 and twins go for US$35 to US$45. If you stay three or more nights, you can get a 10% discount. There is a restaurant on the ground floor (Map 7).

The *Orchid Hotel* (☎ 231809; fax 231811) is a relatively small place at 29A Don Dat St. The hotel has its own restaurant, coffee shop and karaoke lounge. Room prices start at US$40 (Map 8).

The *Dong Khoi Hotel* (☎ 294046, 230163; 34 rooms) is at 12 Ngo Duc Ke St (corner with Dong Khoi St). This charming building is notable for its spacious suites with 4.5-metre-high ceilings and French windows. Once a cheapie, the hotel is currently undergoing renovation and most likely the prices will rise as high as the chandeliers (Map 8).

The *Bong Sen Hotel* (☎ 291516; fax 299744; 134 rooms) is affectionately called 'the BS' by travellers. It's at 117-119 Dong Khoi St and offers air-con singles/twins for US$27/36 to US$190, plus 10% surcharge. Formerly called the Miramar Hotel, the Bong Sen is also signposted as the Lotus Hotel, which is a translation of its Vietnamese name. There is a restaurant on the 8th floor (Map8).

The *Huong Sen Hotel* (☎ 291415; fax 290916; 50 rooms) is at 70 Dong Khoi St. It's now an annexe of the nearby Bong Sen Hotel and charges US$35/50 to US$90 (plus 10% service) for singles/twins. The in-house restaurant is on the 6th floor.

The *Hoang Gia Hotel* (☎ 294846; fax 225346; 42 rooms) is at 12D Cach Mang Thang Tam St, just near the traffic circle. Recently refurbished, singles/twins go for US$30/35 and there are a few deluxe rooms for US$45 (Map 7).

Continental Hotel (RS)

The *Majestic Hotel* (Khach San Cuu Long; ☎ 295515; fax 291470; 115 rooms) is located along the Saigon River at 1 Dong Khoi St. Singles/twins with breakfast range from US$35/47 to US$120/140 (Map 8).

The *Palace Hotel* (Khach San Huu Nghi; ☎ 292860; fax 299872; 130 rooms) is at 56-64 Nguyen Hue Blvd. This hotel, whose Vietnamese name means 'friendship', offers superb views from the 14th-floor restaurant and 15th-floor terrace. Singles/twins cost from US$40/55 to US$120/140 with breakfast and tax included. There is a small swimming pool on the 16th floor (Map 8).

The *Tan Loc Hotel* (☎ 230028; fax 298360), 177 Le Thanh Ton St, is a new place offering singles/twins for US$45/58 to US$86/100, plus 10% service charge (Map 8).

The *Riverside Hotel* (☎ 224038; fax 251417; 75 rooms) is at 18 Ton Duc Thang St, very close to the Saigon Floating Hotel. This old colonial building has been renovated and prices have escalated. Singles/twins cost US$45/60 to US$200/230 plus 15% tax (Map 8).

District 3

This district seems to attract a large number of French travellers, possibly because of some remnants of French colonial architecture. The places listed below are on Map 7 except for Guest House Loan.

One place which gets the thumbs up from French travellers is the *Guest House Loan* (☎ 445313; 30 rooms). This place is also known as the No 3 Ly Chinh Thang

Hotel, which is also its address. Prices are US$18 to US$25 and all rooms have air-con and hot water (Map 1).

Just behind the Lao Consulate is the *Huong Tram Hotel* (☎ 296086; fax 298540; 10 rooms) at 24/9 Pham Ngoc Thach St. Singles are US$30 and twins are US$43 to US$53. Breakfast is included in the tariff.

The *Que Huong Hotel* (☎ 294227; fax 290919; 48 rooms) – also known as the Liberty Hotel – is at 167 Hai Ba Trung St. Singles/twins are priced from US$20/30 to US$30/40.

On the north side of Cong Vien Van Hoa Park at 9 Truong Dinh St is the *Bao Yen Hotel* (☎ 299848; 12 rooms). Rooms are a very reasonable US$12 to US$14 and all have air-conditioning.

The *Victory Hotel* (☎ 294989; fax 299604), 14 Vo Van Tan St (one block north of Reunification Palace), charges from US$26 to US$50.

District 5 (Cholon)

All these hotels are on Map 9.

The *Arc En Ciel Hotel* (Khach San Thien Hong; ☎ 554435; fax 550332; 91 rooms) is also known as the Rainbow Hotel. Single/double rooms cost from US$44/55 to US$55/66. Suites cost US$88. The hotel is at 52-56 Tan Da St (corner of Tran Hung Dao B Blvd).

The *Bat Dat Hotel* (☎ 555817, 555843; 117 rooms) at 238-244 Tran Hung Dao B Blvd is near the more well-known Arc En Ciel Hotel. This place was a well-known cheapie before, but it is currently under renovation.

The five-storey *Tokyo Hotel* (Khach San Dong Kinh; ☎ 357558; fax 352505; 96 rooms), 106-108 Tran Tuan Khai St, has all the modern conveniences at nice prices plus friendly staff. Double rooms with air-con, telephone and refrigerator cost US$20 to US$41.

Another near neighbour to the Arc En Ciel is the *Van Hoa Hotel* (☎ 554182; fax 563118), 36 Tan Da St. Rooms are priced at US$30 to US$45.

The *Regent Hotel* (☎ 353548; fax 357094), 700 Tran Hung Dao Blvd, is also called the Hotel 700. The price range here is US$40 to US$68.

The *Cholon Hotel* (☎ 357058; fax 355375; 24 rooms) at 170-174 Su Van Hanh St is superb value. Squeaky-clean singles/twins cost US$22/32 with breakfast part of the package deal.

Right next door is the privately owned *Cholon Tourist Mini-Hotel* (☎ 357100; fax 355375; 11 rooms) at 192-194 Su Van Hanh St. Like its neighbour, the hotel is of a high standard. Singles/twins cost US$22/28.

The *Trung Uong Hotel* (☎ 357952; fax 353432) at 200 Nguyen Tri Phuong Blvd is also known as the Central Hotel. Rates for singles/doubles are US$28/42 to US$36/50.

The *Andong Hotel* (☎ 352001; 45 rooms) is at 9 An Duong Vuong Blvd right at the intersection with Tran Phu Blvd. All rooms feature hot water, telephone, air-con and refrigerator. Doubles cost US$30 to US$38.

District 10

The *Ky Hoa Hotel* (☎ 655036), 12-14 Ba Thang Hai St, is next to the amusement park of the same name. It's rather remote from the centre, but convenient if you like ferris wheels. Rooms in Building A go for US$70 to US$90. Cheaper accommodation in Building B costs from US$45 to US$60 (Map 9).

District 11

About one km north of central Cholon is the *Phu Tho Hotel* (☎ 551309; fax 551255) at 527, 3 Thang 2 Blvd. The price range here is US$40 to US$50, with breakfast thrown in. There is a huge restaurant on the lowest three floors with built-in karaoke facilities (Map 9).

The *Goldstar Hotel* (☎ 551646; fax 551644), 174-176 Le Dai Hanh St, has singles/doubles for US$30/40. All rooms have private bath, refrigerator and air-con, and the upper floors give a bird's-eye view of the race track (Map 9).

Phu Nhuan District

The *Tan Son Nhat Hotel* (☎ 441039; fax 441324; 25 rooms) at 200 Hoang Van Thu Blvd has some truly stunning rooms. This place was built as a guest house for top South Vietnamese government officials. In 1975 the North Vietnamese Army inherited it. There is a small swimming pool out the back. Room rates are moderate at US$25 to US$50 (Map 1).

Tan Binh District

All these hotels are on Map 1.

Almost within walking distance of the airport is the *Mekong Hotel* (☎ 441024; fax 444809), 261 Hoang Van Thu Blvd. Singles/twins in this opulent place are US$35/40, while suites will set you back US$45. It's certainly one of the better deals near the airport.

Just opposite the top-end Chains First Hotel is the decidedly disappointing *De Nhat Hotel* where room rates are US$35 to US$70. From the looks of things, it's not worth it. Right behind Chains First Hotel at 14 Hoang Viet St is the considerably cheaper *Star Hill Hotel* (☎ 443625) which has air-conditioned twins for US$33 to US$44.

Binh Thanh District

At the Binh Quoi Tourist Village eight km north of central Saigon is the *Binh Quoi Bungalows* (☎ 991831, 991833; 50 rooms), perhaps one of the better accommodation deals in Ho Chi Minh City. Built on stilts above the water, the bungalows give you a little taste of traditional river life in the Mekong Delta, but with air-conditioning and tennis courts. The price range here is US$15 to US$35 (Map 1). For details of the village's tourist attractions, see the Excursions chapter.

PLACES TO STAY – TOP END

District 1

Caravelle Hotel (Khach San Doc Lap; ☎ 293704; fax 299902; 112 rooms), 19-23 Lam Son Square. Singles/twins US$51/63 to US$180 (Map 8).

Century Saigon Hotel (☎ 230542, 293168; fax 292732; 109 rooms), 68A Nguyen Hue Ave. Twins US$115 to US$200 plus 10% tax. You can book rooms from Century International offices abroad: Hong Kong (☎ 2598-8888); Australia (☎ (008) 021211; fax (02) 320-4476); USA (☎ (808) 955-9718) (Map 8).

Continental Hotel (☎ 299201; fax 290936; 87 rooms), 132-134 Dong Khoi St. Singles US$85 to US$170, twins US$105 to US$190 (Map 8).

Embassy Hotel (☎ 291430; fax 295019), 35 Nguyen Trung Truc St. Twins US$60 to US$100 (Map 7).

Kimdo Hotel (☎ 225914; fax 225913), Nguyen Hue Blvd (just south of Le Loi Blvd). Singles US$119 to US$449, twins US$134 to US$479, plus 10% tax (Map 8).

Metropole Hotel (☎ 322021; fax 322019; 94 rooms), 148 Tran Hung Dao Blvd. Singles/doubles US$86/95 to US$119/128, suites US$149 (Map 7).

Mondial Hotel (☎ 296291; fax 296324), 109 Dong Khoi St. Singles/twins US$56/86 to US$101/117 (Map 8).

New World Hotel (☎ 228888; fax 243694), 76 Le Lai St. Singles/twins US$175/185, presidential suites US$850 (Map 7).

Norfolk Hotel (☎ 295368; fax 293415), 117 Le Thanh Ton St. Singles/twins US$75/90 to US$150/165, plus 15% tax (Map 8).

Rex Hotel (Khach San Ben Thanh; ☎ 292185; fax 291469; 207 rooms), 141 Nguyen Hue Blvd (cnr Le Loi Blvd). Singles US$80 to US$760, twins US$90 to US$880 (Map 8).

Saigon Floating Hotel (RS)

Saigon Floating Hotel (☎ 290783; fax 290784; 201 rooms),
moored at 1A Me Linh Square. Five-star luxury, twins
US$130 to US$425, plus 15% tax (Map 8).
Saigon Prince (☎ 222999), 63 Nguyen Hue Blvd. Comprehens-
ive facilities including spa, sauna, gym and massage;
however prices not available at the time of writing.

District 3

International Hotel (☎ 290009; fax 290066), 19 Vo Van Tan St.
Twins US$85 to US$165, plus 15% tax (Map 7).
Saigon Lodge Hotel (☎ 230112; fax 251070), 215 Nam Ky Khoi
Nghia St. Singles/twins US$77/121 to US$88/143, pent-
house US$300 (Map 1).
Saigon Star Hotel (☎ 230260; fax 230255), 204 Nguyen Thi Minh
Khai St (on the road to the airport). Twins US$89 to
US$180, plus 15% tax and service charge (Map 7).
Sol Chancery Hotel (☎ 299152; fax 251464), 196 Nguyen Thi
Minh Khai St. Twins US$110 (Map 7).

District 5 (Cholon)

Caesar Hotel (☎ 350677; fax 350106), 34-36 An Duong Vuong St
(inside Andong Market). Twins US$80 to US$150, plus
10% tax (Map 9).
Hanh Long Hotel (☎ 350251; fax 350742), 1027 Tran Hung Dao
Blvd. Twins from US$50 to US$105 (Map 9).
Dong Khanh Hotel (☎ 352410; 81 rooms), 2 Tran Hung Dao B
Blvd. Singles/doubles are US$55/69 to US$129/157 (Map 9).

Phu Nhuan District

Omni Hotel (☎ 449222; fax 449200; 248 rooms), 251 Nguyen
Van Troi St (on the road to the airport). Five-star luxury,
twins US$180 to US$300 (Map 1).

Tan Binh District

Chains First Hotel (☎ 441199; fax 444282; 132 rooms), 18 Hoang
   Viet St. Singles/twins US$65/75 to US$125, plus 10%
   surcharge (Map 1).

RENTAL

Long-term guests can usually negotiate a discount even
at upmarket hotels. It's also possible to arrange to stay
in the homes of local people, but they must register you
with the police. The police can – and often do – arbitrarily deny such registration requests and will force you to
stay in a hotel or guest house licensed to accept foreigners.

Renting a medium-sized house in Ho Chi Minh City
costs about US$20 per month for a Vietnamese family.
Foreigners will be charged roughly US$500 for the same
thing. The authorities are not happy with foreigners
getting off cheaply, and they impose a heavy 'tax' on
places rented to foreigners. And even if your living
arrangements initially receive the approval of the police,
that approval can be arbitrarily revoked at any time (this
is a frequent occurrence).

Places to Eat

One of the delights of visiting Ho Chi Minh City is the amazing cuisine. You'll never have to look very far for food – *nha hang* (restaurants) of one sort or another seem to be in every nook and cranny. If you are willing to sacrifice plush surroundings, you can eat a complete meal for under US$1. However, if you have excess cash burning a hole in your pocket, the upscale restaurants of Ho Chi Minh City can accommodate you.

Most Vietnamese restaurants do not have any prices on the menu at all. You must definitely ask the total price when you place your order, because overcharging is common. Vietnamese diners know this and will always ask, so don't be shy about speaking up. If you don't, be prepared for a shock when the bill finally comes.

FOOD & DRINKS

Wherever you go in Ho Chi Minh City you'll find *pho*. This is noodle soup, and it's delicious. The other staple food is of course *com* (rice), likewise sold on street stalls all over the city.

Nuoc mam (pronounced something like 'nuke mom') is a type of fermented fish sauce – instantly identifiable by its distinctive smell – without which no Vietnamese meal is complete. Most foreigners do not much care for it, but a few become addicted. The sauce is made by fermenting highly salted fish in large ceramic vats for four to 12 months.

If nuoc mam isn't strong enough for you, try *mam tom*, a powerful shrimp sauce which American soldiers sometimes called 'Viet Cong tear gas'.

Salt with chilli and lemon juice is often served as a condiment and most Westerners seem to like it. Soy sauce is also readily available and makes a good, less-smelly substitute for nuoc mam.

For breakfast, rice porridge *(chao trang)*, or some kind of meat sandwich, is popular. Hué-style beef noodle soup is another favourite.

Vietnamese vegetarian cooking *(an chay)* is an integral part of Vietnamese cuisine. However, the majority of Vietnamese do indeed eat meat most of the time. An important exception occurs on the first and 15th days of the lunar month – festival days in which devout Buddhists normally avoid eating meat.

Aside from the wide variety of delicious and exotic foods, the Vietnamese also produce many excellent drinks. Vietnamese coffee is prime stuff, but there is one qualifier – you'll need to dilute it with hot water. The Vietnamese prefer their coffee so strong and so sweet that it will turn your teeth inside out. Ditto for Ovaltine and Milo, which are regarded as desserts rather than drinks.

Unfortunately, tea is not very good in the southern part of Vietnam. The best Vietnamese tea is from the northern part of the country, or else is imported. The Vietnamese never put milk and sugar into their tea, and are amazed when they see foreigners do so.

Bottled mineral water *(nuoc suoi)* is found everywhere and is safe to drink. A Vietnamese speciality is carbonated water with freshly squeezed lemon, sugar and ice *(so-da chanh)*. Coconut milk *(nuoc dua)* served right from a chilled coconut is superb and refreshing. Many 'imported' soft drinks and beers are not imported at all, but made locally by foreign joint-ventures.

Memorise the words *bia hoi* which means 'draft beer'. There are signs advertising it everywhere, and most cafés have it on the menu. Quality varies, but is generally OK and very cheap (averaging US$0.32 per litre!). Places that serve bia hoi usually also have good but cheap food. Vietnamese wine, usually made from rice, is good only for cooking, though if you're looking for a cheap drink, you could do worse.

Finally, if you want to end your meal with a cigarette, there are imported (smuggled) and local brands made by joint-ventures (which are not bad). There are some dirt-cheap homegrown brands like Dien Bien Phu and Dalat which cost around US$0.10 a pack – these have the fragrant aroma of old socks and even the Vietnamese shun them. Recently, there has been a problem with counterfeit 'imported' cigarettes which look like the real thing, but smokers claim they can easily taste the difference.

Some useful Vietnamese food & drink words and phrases are given below.

Breakfast

pancake	*bánh xèo ngọt*
banana pancake	*bánh chuối*
pineapple pancake	*bánh khóm*
papaya pancake	*bánh đu đủ*
orange pancake	*bánh cam*
plain pancake	*bánh không nhân*

bread	*bánh mì*
butter	*bơ*
jam	*mứt*
cheese	*phomai*
honey	*mật ong*
combination sandwich	*săn huýt*
omelette	*trứng chiên*
fried eggs	*trứng ốp la*

Lunch & Dinner

noodles/rice noodles	*mì/hủ tíu*
beef noodle soup	*hủ tíu bò*
chicken noodle soup	*hủ tíu gà*
vegetarian noodle soup	*mì rau/mì chay*
duck & bamboo	
shoot soup	*bún măng*
potatoes	*khoai tây*
french fries	*khoai chiên*
fried potato & tomato	*khoai xào cà chua*
fried potato & butter	*khoai chiên bơ*
fried dishes	*các món xào*
chicken noodles	*mì xào gà/hủ tíu xào gà*
beef noodles	*mì xào bò/hủ tíu xào bò*
mixed fried noodles	*mì xào thập cẩm*
mixed fries	*xào tổng hợp*
chicken	*gà*
roasted chicken	*gà quay/gà rô-ti*
chicken salad	*gà xé phay*
batter fried chicken	*gà tẩm bột rán/chiên*
curried chicken	*gà cà-ri*
fried with lemon sauce	*gà rán/chiên sốt chanh*
fried in mushroom sauce	*gà sốt nấm*
pork	*lợn/he*
skewered-grilled	*chả lợn xiên nướng/*
	chả heo nướng
sweet & sour fried	*lợn xào chua ngọt/*
	heo xào chua ngọt
roast	*heo quay*
grilled	*thịt lợn nướng xả/*
	heo nướng xả
beef	*thịt bò*
beefsteak	*bít tết*
skewered grilled	*bò xiên nướng*
spicy beef	*bò xào sả ớt*

fried with pineapple	*khóm*
fried with garlic	*bò xào tỏi*
grilled with ginger	*bò nướng gừng*
rare with vinegar	*bò nhúng giấm*

hot pot (hot & sour soup)	*lẩu*
beef hot pot	*lẩu bò*
eel hot pot	*lẩu lươn*
fish hot pot	*lẩu cá*
combination hot pot	*lẩu thập cẩm*

spring roll	*nem/chả giò*
meat spring rolls	*chả giò*
vegetarian spring rolls	*chả giò chay*
sour spring rolls	*nem chua*

pigeon	*chim bồ câu*
roasted pigeon	*bồ câu quay*
fried in mushroom sauce	*bồ câu xào nấm sốt*

soup	*súp*
chicken soup	*súp gà*
eel soup	*súp lươn*
combination soup	*súp thập cẩm*
corn soup	*súp bắp*
vegetarian soup	*súp rau*

fish	*cá*
with sugarcane	*chả cá bao mía*
fried in tomato	*cá rán/chiên sốt cà*
sweet & sour fried fish	*cá sốt chua ngọt*
fried fish with lemon	*cá rán, chiên chanh*
fried with mushrooms	*cá xào hành nấm rơm*
steamed with ginger	*cá hấp gừng*
boiled fish	*cá luộc*
grilled fish	*cá nướng*
steamed fish in beer	*cá hấp bia*

shrimp	*tôm*
sweet & sour	*tôm xào chua ngọt*
fried with mushrooms	*tôm xào nấm*
fried with sugarcane	*chạo tôm*
batter fried shrimp	*tôm tẩm bột/*
	tôm hỏa tiễn
steamed in beer	*tôm hấp bia*

crab	*cua*
salted fried crab	*cua rang muối*
crab with chopped meat	*cua nhồi thịt*
steamed crab in beer	*cua hấp bia*

squid	*mực*
fried with pineapple	*khóm*
fried squid	*mực chiên*
fried with mushrooms	*mực xào nấm*
sweet & sour squid	*mực xào chua ngọt*
eel	*lươn*
fried with mince	*lươn cuốn thịt rán/*
simmered eel	*lươn um*
fried with mushrooms	*lươn xào nấm*
snail	*ốc*
spicy snail	*ốc xào sả ớt*
fried with pineapple	*ốc xào dứa, khóm*
fried with tofu, bananas	*ốc xào đậu phu/*
	(đậu hủ) chuối xanh
vegetables	*rau*
fried vegetables	*rau xào*
fried with mushrooms	*rau cải xào nấm*
with fried noodles	*mì, hủ tíu xào rau*
boiled vegetables	*rau luộc*
fried bean sprout	*giá xào*
soup (large bowl)	*canh rau*
salad	*rau sa lát*
sour vegetable	*dưa chua*
vegetarian	*các món chay*
I'm a vegetarian.	*Tôi là người ăn chay.*
tofu	*đậu hủ*
fried with mince	*thịt nhồi đậu hủ*
fried with vegetable	*đậu hủ xào*
fried in tomato sauce	*đậu hủ sốt cà*
rice	*cơm*
steamed rice	*cơm trắng*
mixed fried rice	*cơm chiên*
rice porridge	*cháo*
specialities	*đặc sản*
lobster	*con tôm hùm*
frog	*con ếch*
oyster	*con sò*
bat	*con dơi*
cobra/gecko	*rắn hổ/con tắc kè*
goat	*con dê*
pangolin	*con trúc/tê tê*
porcupine	*con nhím*
python	*con trăn*

small hornless deer	*con nai tơ*
turtle	*con rùa*
venison	*thịt nai*
wild pig	*con heo rừng*

fruit	*trái cây*
apple	*bơm*
apricot	*trái lê*
avocado	*trái bơ*
banana	*trái chuối*
coconut	*trái dừa*
custard apple	*trái măng cầu*
durian	*trái sầu riêng*
grapes	*trái nho*
green dragon fruit	*trái thanh long*
guava	*trái ổi*
jackfruit	*trái mít*
jujube (Chinese date)	*trái táo ta*
persimmon	*trái hồng xiêm*
lemon	*trái chanh*
longan	*trái nhãn*
lychee	*trái vải*
orange/mandarin	*trái cam/trái quýt*
mangosteen	*trái măng cụt*
papaya	*trái đu đủ*
peach	*trái đào*
pineapple	*trái khóm, trái dứa*
plum	*trái mận, trái mơ*
pomelo	*trái bưởi*
rambutan	*trái chôm chôm*
starfruit	*trái khế*
strawberry	*trái dâu*
tangerine	*trái quýt*
three-seed cherry	*trái sê-ri*
water apple	*trái mận*
watermelon	*trái dưa hấu*

other dishes	*các món khác*
fruit salad	*trái cây các loại*
yoghurt	*da-ua*
mixed fruit cocktail	*cóc-tai hoa quả*

condiments	
salt/pepper	*tiêu xay/muối*
sugar	*đường*
ice	*đá*
hot pepper	*ớt trái*
fresh chillis	*ớt*
soy sauce	*nước tương*
fish sauce	*nước mắm*

Drinks

coffee	*cà phê*
hot black coffee	*cà phê đen nóng*
hot milk coffee	*cà phê sữa nóng*
iced black coffee	*cà phê đá*
iced milk coffee	*cà phê sữa đá*
tea	*chè, trà*
hot black tea	*trà nóng*
hot milk black tea	*trà pha sữa*
hot honey black tea	*trà pha mật*
fruit juice	*nước quả/nước trái cây*
hot lemon juice	*chanh nóng*
iced lemon juice	*chanh đá*
hot orange juice	*cam nóng*
iced orange juice	*cam đá*
pure orange juice	*cam vắt*
fruit shakes	*sinh to/trái cây xay*
banana	*nước chuối xay*
milk banana	*nước chuối sữa xay*
papaya	*nước đu đủ xay*
pineapple	*khóm xay*
orange banana	*nước cam, chuối xay*
mixed fruit	*sinh tố tổng hợ/*
	nước thập cẩm xay
mango shake	*nước xoài xay*
mineral water	*nước khoáng/nước suối*
lemon mineral water	*suối chanh*
big spring water	*nước suối chai lớn*
small spring water	*nước suối chai nhỏ*
chocolate - milk	*cacao - sữa*
hot chocolate	*cacao nóng*
iced chocolate	*cacao đá*
hot milk	*sữa nóng*
iced milk	*sữa đá*
tinned soft drinks	*thức uống đóng hộp*
tinned orange juice	*cam hộp*
soda water & lemon	*soda chanh*
soda water with	
lemon & sugar	*soda chanh đường*
beer	*bia*

PLACES TO EAT – BOTTOM END

Noodle soup is available all day long at street stalls and hole-in-the-wall shops everywhere. A large bowl of delicious beef noodles costs US$0.50 to US$1.

Sandwiches with a French look and a very Vietnamese taste are sold by street vendors. Fresh French baguettes are stuffed with something resembling pâté (don't ask) and cucumbers, and seasoned with soy sauce. A sandwich costs between US$0.50 and US$1, depending on what is in it and whether or not you get overcharged. Sandwiches filled with French soft cheese cost a little more.

Markets always have a side selection of food items, often in the ground floor or basement. Be certain that at some point you sample Vietnamese spring rolls (cha gio), an inexpensive Vietnamese speciality found everywhere.

District 1

Food Stalls Some of the best noodle soup on earth can be found in the *Ben Thanh Market*. The food stalls inside the market are clean.

Pham Ngu Lao & De Tham Sts These streets form the axis of Saigon's budget eatery haven. Western backpackers easily outnumber the Vietnamese here, and indeed the locals have trouble figuring out the menus ('banana muesli' does not translate well into Vietnamese).

A major construction project which is about to take place as we go to press will probably have a severe negative impact on Pham Ngu Lao's restaurants. It's our prediction that most of these places will move south to De Tham or Bui Vien Sts, but this remains to be seen.

A long-running hang-out for budget travellers is *Kim Café* (☎ 359859), 272 De Tham St. This is a very good place to meet people, arrange tours and get travel information. *Madras House* (☎ 398122) at 268 De Tham St is right next to Kim Café. This place serves fine Indian vegetarian and non-vegetarian dishes. It's highly recommended.

The *Lotus Café* at 197 Pham Ngu Lao St is possibly the best in the neighbourhood now. The friendly couple who run it prepare excellent Vietnamese and Western food at low prices. The *Saigon Café* at 195 Pham Ngu Lao St (at the corner with De Tham St) is also worthy of a plug. *Café 333* (☎ 251550) at 217 Pham Ngu Lao St is yet another favourite of the backpacker set. *Sawadee* at 252

De Tham St does excellent Thai food. *My Thanh Restaurant* (☎ 357580) at 40 Bui Vien St is just around the corner from De Tham St. This place does splendid Chinese food. You can eat at their outdoor tables or go upstairs where there are air-conditioned rooms.

Vegetarian The *Tin Nghia Vegetarian Restaurant* is run by strict Buddhists. This small, simple little establishment is at 9 Tran Hung Dao Blvd about 200 metres from Ben Thanh Market. It is open from 7 am to 8 pm daily, but closes between 2 and 4 pm so the staff can take a rest. The prices here are incredibly cheap.

Just off the main drag down a small side street (it's clearly signposted), the *Zen Vegetarian Restaurant*, 175 Pham Ngu Lao St, is away from the traffic and has an excellent, good-value menu. There's a wide range of Vietnamese dishes (clearly described in English on the menu) as well as European standards and delicious fruit juices. It's a simple, friendly place and you can eat well for a dollar or two.

Self-Catering Simple meals can easily be assembled from fruits, vegetables, French bread, croissants, cheese and other delectables sold everywhere.

Perhaps the best bakery outside of Cholon is *Nhu Lan Bakery* at 66 Ham Nghi Blvd. You can buy oven-fresh bread here from morning till night.

By far the best place to go for Western groceries is the *Minimart* (☎ 298189, ext 44) on the 2nd floor of the Saigon Intershop, which is at 101 Nam Ky Khoi Nghia St (just off Le Loi Blvd). If this ultimate symbol of Western capitalism looks like it was transported lock, stock and barrel from Singapore, that's because it was. The Minimart is open from 9 am to 6 pm daily.

Besides the Minimart, there are several other options though none quite as good. One is the supermarket next to the Saigon Hotel (opposite the mosque) at 35 Dong Du St. There is also a supermarket at 41 Hai Ba Trung St. The government-owned *Agrimexco Supermarket* is at 85 Dong Khoi St.

There are at least two places in Saigon calling themselves *7 Eleven*, both of which are impostors. The better of the two is at 16 Nguyen Hue Blvd and carries imported foods (no Slurpies though). There is a real popcorn machine here, possibly the first in Vietnam.

Le Chalet Suisse (☎ 293856) at 211A Dong Khoi St, is a small Swiss meat market on the ground floor. A bar and restaurant are upstairs.

Top : Dried shrimp (RE)
Middle : Eggs (RE)
Bottom : Rice puddings (RE)

Ice Cream The best ice cream (kem) in Ho Chi Minh City is served at the two shops called *Kem Bach Dang*, which are on Le Loi Blvd on either side of Nguyen Thi Minh Khai St. Kem Bach Dang 1 is at 26 Le Loi Blvd and the other is at No 28. Both are under the same management and serve ice cream, hot and cold drinks and cakes for very reasonable prices. A US$1.50 speciality is ice cream served in a baby coconut with candied fruit on top (kem trai dua).

District 5 (Cholon)

Food Stalls There are clusters of food stalls in the *Andong Market* where you can score cheap noodle and rice dishes. Everything is fresh and excellent.

Market stall (ME)

Vegetarian In Cholon, *Tiem Com Chay Thien Phat Duyen* is a small Chinese vegetarian restaurant about one km east of Chau Van Liem Blvd at 509 Nguyen Trai St. There are two Chinese vegetarian places, both called *Phat Huu Duyen*, at 513 Nguyen Trai St and 116 Nguyen Tri Phuong St.

Tiem Com Chay Phat Huu Duyen, also Chinese, is at 952 Tran Hung Dao Blvd (corner of An Binh St, where Tran Hung Dao B Blvd begins); it is open from 7 am to 10 pm but is very expensive (by Vietnamese standards). Across An Binh St at 3 Tran Hung Dao B Blvd is another Chinese place, *Tiem Com Chay Van Phat Duyen*, which is open from 7 am to 9 pm. You can also check out the vegetarian restaurants at 45 Tran Hung Dao B Blvd and 523 Nguyen Trai St.

Self-Catering The *Superstore* (☎ 357176) at 10-20 Tran Hung Dao Blvd is in reality a small supermarket. It's just next to the Dong Khanh Hotel in Cholon. You can pick up all manner of goods here from frozen yoghurt to cheese puffs and peanut butter.

District 6

Food Stalls *Binh Tay Market* has a large collection of cheap food stalls serving up all sorts of tasty noodle and rice dishes.

PLACES TO EAT – MIDDLE

District 1

Dong Khoi St The *Givral Restaurant* (☎ 242750) at 169 Dong Khoi St (across the street from the Continental Hotel) has an excellent selection of cakes, home-made ice cream and yoghurt. Aside from the junkfood, there's French, Chinese, Vietnamese and Russian cuisine on offer.

Augustin, 10 Nguyen Thiep St, just off Dong Khoi St, is a small, good-quality French bistro. There are all the traditional favourites, from onion soup on. Entrees range from $2.50 to $4, main courses from $3.50 to $7 (for the top-end seafood dishes).

Buffalo Blues (☎ 222874), 72 Nguyen Du St, at the cathedral or northern end of Dong Khoi St, is a refuge for homesick expats. It's a bar/restaurant with good-quality live music, decent counter meals (including excellent shepherd's pie) and English beer on tap.

The *Liberty Restaurant* (☎ 299820), 80 Dong Khoi St, is a joint-venture with Ben Thanh Tourist (Saigon District 1 municipal government). It has a small but cheap and excellent Vietnamese menu, plus expensive Chinese and Western food. There is live music upstairs in the evening provided by a Vietnamese band.

The *Brodard Café* (☎ 223966), also known as Nha Hang Dong Khoi, is an oldie but goodie. Despite ongoing renovations, the decor is still vintage 1960s. This place is known for French food. Brodard is at 131 Dong Khoi St (corner of Nguyen Thiep St).

The *Lemon Grass Restaurant* (☎ 298006) at 63 Dong Khoi St is a personal favourite, *the* place for power dining. You'd be hard pressed to find anything bad on the menu, so if you can't decide what to order just pick something at random. Two women in traditional clothing play musical instruments and serenade while you eat.

Homesick Korean travellers looking for a little *kimchi* and camaraderie come to the *Korean Food Restaurant* (☎ 223166) at 213B Dong Khoi St. The other competitor in this market is the *Seoul Restaurant* at 34 Ngo Duc Ke St.

Maxim's Dinner Theatre (☎ 296676) at 15 Dong Khoi St is very much what the name implies: a restaurant with live musical performances. The menu includes Chinese and French food. If you look Western they give you the French menu, but ask for the Chinese menu which is cheaper and more interesting. There is a very dark nightclub upstairs (free entry) with a live band playing '60s tunes. Maxim's is open from 11 am to 11 pm, but expect it to be empty until around dinnertime.

Gartenstadt (☎ 223623) at 34 Dong Khoi St is run by a German woman and a Swiss cook who dish up non-Vietnamese delicacies such as Pils vom Fass and Nürnberger Bratwürste. Figure on US$5 or more for a complete meal.

Vietnam House (☎ 291623) is at 93-95 Dong Khoi St on the corner of Mac Thi Buoi St. It's possibly the nicest combined bar and restaurant in Saigon. The cuisine is Vietnamese style, and a standard dinner or lunch is US$8. In the 2nd-floor dining room, a traditional four-piece Vietnamese ensemble plays during dinner, starting at 7.30 pm. The best part is the bar and lounge on the 1st floor. There is a young female pianist playing here from 5.30 pm until late at night. Beer costs US$1.50 and is served up in a frozen glass, with peanuts and shrimp crackers on the side. The restaurant is open from 10 am until midnight.

The *Paloma Café* (☎ 295813) at 26 Dong Khoi St is a stylish place with wooden tables, white tablecloths, polished silverware, aggressive air-conditioning and

Local speciality (ME)

waiters who need to be tipped. Judging from the crowd that packs in every night, they must be doing something right. This place stays open until nearly midnight.

Elsewhere in District 1 *Annie's Pizza* (☎ 392577) is at 59 Cach Mang Thang Tam St, a few blocks north of the Pham Ngu Lao backpackers' ghetto. You can walk it from Pham Ngu Lao St, but if you don't want to bother then just ring up – the pizza is the best in town and they do home deliveries! Also available are toasted ham and cheese sandwiches and imported Aussie meat pies.

The excellent *Sapa Bar & Restaurant* at 8A8 Don Dat St is two blocks east of the Municipal Theatre. Run by a Swiss expat and his Vietnamese wife, you'll find everything here from schnitzel to snake (special order for the latter). Good music, beer and friendly staff all contribute to the pleasant atmosphere.

Following Dong Khoi St up to its northern extremes, you pass the CPO and Notre Dame Cathedral, then cross Han Thuyen St and Le Duan Blvd. This hike brings you to an alley called Nguyen Van Chiem where you find *Manhattan*. This place has the best hamburgers in Vietnam (reasonably priced at less than US$1), and the menu also features pizza and fried chicken. The official address here is 1 Nguyen Van Chiem St. There is also a smaller branch at 165 Pham Ngu Lao St.

California Chicken is at 67 Hai Ba Trung Blvd at Le Loi Blvd (south-east corner). This restaurant features American-style greasy fast food, hamburgers, cheeseburgers, fried chicken, pizzas, milkshakes, ice cream, Cokes and so on. It's the Vietnamese, not the foreigners, who pack this place out.

For spicy, hot Chinese food, try the *China Szechuan Restaurant* (☎ 241248) at 55 Nguyen Hue St.

A new eating precinct is quickly developing to the east of Hai Ba Trung Blvd, particularly along Le Thanh Ton and Thi Sach Sts. Patronised by locals, tourists and expats, the area is quieter and considerably more laid-back than bright and bustling Dong Khoi St. There are a

Delicatessen (RE)

number of open-air café/bars along Thi Sach St that are crowded with Vietnamese family groups, and on Le Thanh Ton St, a number of moderately priced restaurants (by Western standards) representing world cuisine from French to Indian and Mexican.

Ashoka (☎ 231372), 17A Le Thanh Ton St, is a remarkably good-quality, genuine Indian restaurant with a tandoor oven. Although there are few apparent links between Indian and Vietnamese cooking, the Vietnamese waitresses look quite at home in the traditional Indian *kameez*, which isn't all that different to the ao dai. They serve all the standard dishes and there are a good number of vegetarian possibilities. Expect to pay around US$10 per person.

Le P'tit Bistrot de Saigon (☎ 230219), 58 Le Thanh Ton St, is a small but excellent French restaurant with friendly staff. Without wine, a feast could cost US$10. This restaurant is just up the street from the H"tel de Ville, where Le Than Ton St intersects with Hai Ba Trung St. Some French travellers also feel right at home at *Ami Restaurant* (☎ 242198), 170 Pasteur St.

One place which does home deliveries and catering is *Jimmy's* (☎ 223661) at 57 Nguyen Du St. The cuisine here is Vietnamese and American.

La Coussoussière (☎ 299148), 24 Nguyen Thi Minh Khai St, is a great place to eat even if most patrons can't pronounce the restaurant's name. This is Saigon's first Arabic eatery and the only place in the city where you can sample couscous.

Tex-Mex Bar & Restaurant (☎ 223017, 295950) is distinguished by being the only Mexican restaurant in Ho Chi Minh City. It can be found at 24 Le Thanh Ton St. There's everything you'd expect including a relaxed atmosphere, a band, a pool table and chili con carne.

The *Montana Café* (☎ 295067) at 40E Ngo Duc Ke St is a large café open all day. The sandwiches are superb.

A good source of Italian cakes, tarts, ice cream and the like is *Café Ciao* (☎ 251203) at 72 Nguyen Hue Blvd. The Vietnamese food is also fine, and it's open for breakfast, lunch and dinner.

Dinner Cruises Wining and dining while floating around the Saigon River is not the worst way to spend an evening. The floating restaurants are all government-owned and are docked just opposite the Riverside Hotel. Most of the floating restaurants open at 6 pm, depart the pier at 8 pm and return at 10 pm. Prices vary upwards from US$12 for à-la-carte dinner, though you could spend significantly more if you go heavy on the booze. Tickets for the cruise can be bought at the pier and you can call for information (☎ 225401). Most of the boats feature live music and dancing.

District 3

The *Saigon Lodge Hotel* (☎ 230112), 215 Nam Ky Khoi Nghia St, is on the way to the airport and features all-you-can-eat buffet meals. The buffet lunch costs US$3.50 while dinner is US$4.50. This makes it one of the best bargains in town. Aside from the buffet, another speciality here is Malaysian food.

Down a side street just opposite the French Consulate, *Nha Hang* (☎ 225909), 11 Nguyen Vai Chien St (133 Hai Ba Trung Blvd), is renowned for its seafood. There's a pleasant outdoor eating area, and although it all looks a little frayed around the edges, it's moderately priced, and attracts a large, mixed crowd of mobile-phone-toting expats and local business people.

The *180 Restaurant* (☎ 251673) at 180 Nguyen Van Thu St deserves a plug for its fine steak dinners.

Restaurant A, The Russian Restaurant (☎ 359190) is the only place in Saigon that dishes up borscht and blintzes. The food is so good here that it's hard to believe it can be so bad in Moscow. Furthermore, you don't have to queue up to get a meal. The owner is a Russian-Vietnamese woman and the cook really is from Russia. You can find this unique restaurant at 361/8 Nguyen Dinh Chieu St.

Fried silkworms, fish spawn and other exotic treats are on the menu at a little restaurant at 79 Nguyen Dinh Chieu St.

District 5 (Cholon)

District 5 boasts many fine restaurants, though the classier ones are more expensive than in central Saigon. A far bigger problem than price is the lack of comfortable chairs. Even many of the upmarket places give you no choice but to sit on stools with no back support. This is hard to reconcile – do Cholonese have stronger than normal backbones, or is it a plot by the local acupuncturists to drum up business? After all, even the budget cafés on Pham Ngu Lao St have plastic chairs with backs on them. Nevertheless, if you search diligently, you should find some place to eat that won't leave you in traction the next day.

If you want to pig out on pastries, Cholon is certainly the best place in Vietnam to do it. One fine bakery after another can be found along Tran Hung Dao B Blvd. Perhaps the best of the lot (but they all look good) is

Croissants de Paris (☎ 566635) at No 27B. Aside from being a bakery, it's also a coffee shop and a teahouse. The seats here are adequate for prolonged sitting.

If you haven't ruined your appetite with pastries, check out some of the Chinese food restaurants. The *Arc En Ciel Hotel* at 52-56 Tan Da St (corner of Tran Hung Dao B Blvd) has a good restaurant on the top floor (also with comfortable seats).

The *Jade-Orchid Restaurant* (☎ 552227) is also known as Nha Hang Ngoc Lan Dinh. This place features good food, a noisy band and uncomfortable seats. If your back can take it, the Chinese food is wonderful. The official address is 466 Tran Hung Dao B Blvd.

A rare combination in Cholon is an inexpensive restaurant with seats which you can sit on for a reasonable length of time. One which falls into this category is *Trung Mai Restaurant* (☎ 562890) at 801 Nguyen Trai St (just west of Chau Van Liem Blvd).

Binh Thanh District

There is a waterfront restaurant at the *Binh Quoi Tourist Village*, eight km from central Saigon in the Binh Thanh district. You can have dinner à la carte for under US$10 or buy a package deal which includes dinner, a water puppet show and river cruise costing US$20 for the whole evening.

The *Tancang* (New Port) *Restaurant* is on the Saigon River right by the Saigon Bridge. This place is only busy in the evening. You can get to the restaurant by motorbike, taxi or boat. Prices are mid-range and the food is excellent.

PLACES TO EAT – TOP END

District 1

Restaurants *Nha Hang Tan Nam* (☎ 223407) is at 59-61 Dong Khoi St. This very upmarket establishment boasts a fine garden restaurant in the rear courtyard. If you like to eat in plush surroundings, it would be hard to do better.

A fine French restaurant is *L'Etoile* (☎ 297939) at 180 Hai Ba Trung St. An absolutely outstanding meal will run to something like US$15.

Located on the corner of Cao Ba Quat (the eastern continuation of Le Loi Blvd, past the Municipal Theatre) and Thi Sach Sts, *Camargue* (☎ 243148) is in a restored villa and has an attractive open-air terrace. Favoured by well-off businesspeople, it's an attractive, atmospheric

Top : Vietnamese food (GB)
Bottom : Basket of fruit (HS)

spot with good-quality food. The menu has a variety of Western-style dishes. It's at the expensive end of the spectrum, and you could easily spend $15 to $20.

Hotel Restaurants Many hotel restaurants offer Vietnamese and Western food at prices varying from reasonable to ridiculous. Check the price list first to avoid indigestion later.

The restaurant at the *Norfolk Hotel*, 117 Le Thanh Ton St, is a popular expat hang-out. The superb breakfast for US$5 is recommended if you like plush surroundings and a chance to catch CNN or BBC World News on a large-screen TV. Lunch and dinner can easily cost considerably more.

Chez Guido Ristorante (☎ 299255) is an Italian pizza restaurant on the ground floor of the Continental Hotel. This is a joint-venture between Saigon Tourist and a gentleman from Italy by the name of Guido.

The *Continental Palace Restaurant* (☎ 299255) is in the basement underneath the Continental Hotel. Vietnamese and Chinese cuisine can be enjoyed to the accompaniment of classical music. It's open from 6 to 10 pm.

The Saigon Floating Hotel has two restaurants. *The Oriental Court* does Asian cuisine. *The Marina Café* serves some excellent European food from US$5 to US$15 – the all-you-can-eat salad buffet at US$5.50 really is a superb treat.

The *Rex Royal Court Restaurant* is on the 2nd floor of the Rex Hotel. Sadly, this place was once good but is now on the decline. Don't bother coming in shorts: such attire is considered inappropriate in a tropical climate and you'll be shown the door. The Rex's rooftop bar is less formal so you can get away with being a slob, but it's also expensive and serves bland food. On the ground floor is *Nihon Basi* (☎ 292186), a Japanese restaurant which charges Japanese prices.

The Dai Nam Hotel (☎ 242555), 79 Tran Hung Dao St, features the *Marco Polo Restaurant*. The chef dishes up pizza, pasta and the like from 11 am until 11.30 pm.

The New World Hotel at 76 Le Lai St is home to no less than six different restaurants. Popular ones include the *Dynasty Restaurant* (Chinese food – expensive), *Hoa Mi Restaurant* (Vietnamese food – excellent and cheap) and the *Coffee Shop* (Western food). The Coffee Shop is actually quite a bargain – the outstanding all-you-can-eat luncheon buffet (noon to 2.30 pm) costs US$10.

The Mondial Hotel at 109 Dong Khoi St offers sweeping views from its *Skyview Restaurant*. The cuisine is primarily Vietnamese.

District 3

The International Hotel, 19 Vo Van Tan St, is the venue for the *Fook Yuen Cantonese Restaurant*. This place dishes up dim sum from 7 am to 3 pm, then reopens for set meals from 5.30 to 10 pm.

Phu Nhuan District

You can get your fill of snake, turtle, deer antlers and other exotic dishes at *Tri Ky Restaurant*, 82 Tran Huy Lieu St. Tran Huy Lieu St runs between Hoang Van Thu Blvd and Nguyen Van Troi St, the two major roads leading to Tan Son Nhat Airport.

The very upscale Omni Hotel at 251 Nguyen Van Troi St (on the road to the airport) offers good food to those who can afford the ticket. This is where you can find the *Rom Thai Restaurant* (☎ 449222 ext 168) which does both Vietnamese and Thai food.

The *Gourmet Shop* inside the Omni Hotel, 251 Nguyen Van Troi St, is a treasure trove of rare items like cranberry sauce, French cheese, Sri Lankan tea and frozen cherry cheesecake.

Adjacent to the Omni Hotel is the significantly less expensive Melody Hotel at 151 Nguyen Van Trai St. Here you can try the *Spices Restaurant* (☎ 441719) which does Malaysian cuisine. Operating hours are 8 am until 11 pm.

Entertainment

Wartime Saigon was always known for its riotous nightlife. Liberation in 1975 brought other forms of entertainment, including 're-education'. This put a real dampener on evening activities.

The good news is that the pubs and discos have recently staged a mild comeback. The bad news is the midnight curfew. During the war, one Saigon DJ said 'You can boogie till you puke', and that's still true as long as you puke before midnight. After that, you can look forward to STAR TV.

SUNDAY NIGHT LIVE

Central Saigon is *the* place to be on Sunday and holiday nights. The streets are jam-packed with young locals in couples and groups, cruising the town on bicycles and motorbikes, out to see and be seen. The mass of slowly moving humanity is so thick on Dong Khoi St that you may have to wait until dawn to get across the road. It is utter chaos at intersections, where 10 or more lanes of two-wheeled vehicles intersect without the benefit of traffic lights, safety helmets or sanity.

Near the Municipal Theatre, fashionably dressed young people take a break from cruising around to watch the endless procession, lining up along the street next to their cycles. The air is electric with the glances of lovers and animated conversations among friends. It is a sight not to be missed.

DISCOS

There is dancing with a live band at the *Rex Hotel*, 141 Nguyen Hue Blvd, nightly from 7.30 to 11 pm. *Cheers* is the disco inside the Vien Dong Hotel at 257 Pham Ngu Lao St. This very popular place has both a Filipino band and taped music. Interestingly, when the band starts to play, everyone sits down to watch and listen – they get up to dance when the music tapes are played! Well, this is Vietnam. Besides the more open public dancing area, there are also plush private sitting rooms for the rich business types. Admission to Cheers costs US$8 and things get rolling from 8 pm onwards.

The *VIP Club* (☎ 229860, 231187), 2D Pham Ngoc Thach St, is a bar and disco with video game machines

Cruising on Dong Khoi St (HS)

and billiard tables. There is also a karaoke room. This is considered by many to be the No 1 disco with the expat crowd. Admission costs US$4, but there is an obligation to buy three drinks at US$1 minimum each (soft drinks). Currently, this place is only allowing admission to foreigners and Overseas Vietnamese, though this could change. The *Starlight Nightclub* is on the 11th floor of the Century Saigon Hotel (☎ 231818 ext 46) at 68A Nguyen Hue Blvd, District 1. Here you'll find music of the '60s, '70s and '80s. It's open nightly from 7 pm until 2 am.

At the Saigon Floating Hotel you'll find the *Down Under Disco*. Males must pay a cover charge of US$20, but females are permitted to enter for free. The excellent band (Filipinos, not Vietnamese) really knows how to rock 'n' roll. The *Palace Hotel* at 56 Nguyen Hue Blvd, District 1, has a nightclub open from 8 to 11 pm. Ditto for the *Caravelle Hotel* at 19 Lam Son Square, District 1. The *Superstar Disco Nightclub* (☎ 440242) is at 431/A/2 Hoang Van Thu St in the Tan Binh District. This is one of those brightly lit fancy clubs with staff able to speak a variety of languages such as English, Chinese, Korean, Japanese and Thai, not to mention Vietnamese. There is also a karaoke here. The club opens at 8 pm.

The *Venus Club* is in the Saigon Star Hotel, 204 Nguyen Thi Minh Khai St, District 3. It's notable for its disco and karaoke rooms. The *Orient Club* (☎ 222547) at 104 Hai Ba Trung, District 1, is another disco. You can find a disco-karaoke combination at the *Queen Bee* (☎ 229860) at 104 Nguyen Hue Blvd, District 1. Close to the Dong Khoi Hotel (but not in it) is *Pub International* (☎ 295427), 32 Ngo Duc Ke St, District 1. The disco is upstairs.

It's a bit of a long trek out to *Shangri-La* (☎ 556831) at 1196 Ba Thang Hai St, District 11. It turns out to be a respectable discotheque and karaoke. There is also a health club here (gymnasium etc) which will perhaps help you get in shape for the nighttime carousing.

Ballroom Disco

Vietnam is one of the few places left where a major component of the nightlife is still ballroom dancing. Of course, these *soirées dansantes* have become more and more like mutated discos in recent years, and the guests are likely to be affluent young people dressed in jeans and the latest designer bootlegs, but the principle is the same.

One place to find ballroom disco is at *Nha Van Hoa Lao Dong* which is in Cong Vien Van Hoa Park (north side – enter from Nguyen Thi Minh Khai St, just west of Huyen Tran Cong Chua St). Admission costs US$1 and it's open from 8 to 10 pm, Thursday, Saturday and Sunday. It's a similar scene at *Ko Lac Bo* on the waterfront side of Ben Chuong St (just south of Ham Nghi Blvd) on the Saigon River.

PUBS

During the Vietnam War, pubs staffed with legions of prostitutes were a major form of R&R ('rest & recreation') for American soldiers. After reunification, the pubs were shut down and the prostitutes were encouraged to find other employment, like stoop labour in the rice paddies.

The pubs are back, and whatever prostitution exists must now remain low key to protect Saigon's 'family image'. Though the city's pubs still tend to be male-oriented businesses, more and more places are also tame enough for a single woman to feel comfortable. Amenities in the better places include air-conditioning, decent pub grub and taped background music.

In the Pham Ngu Lao area is the *Easy Rider Pub* (☎ 359338) at 193 Nguyen Thai Hoc St. This place opens at 11 am. Aside from the drinks, the house cuisine is American and French.

Not far away is *Bar Rolling Stones* at 177 Pham Ngu Lao St. This pub is known for its *loud* music.

Nguyen Chat at 161 Pham Ngu Lao St is a Vietnamese place where you can sample local draft beer (bia hoi) for US$0.40 per litre. There are also plenty of cheap snacks here.

Buffalo Blues (☎ 222874), 72 Nguyen Du St, District 1, is a jazz bar with live music, billiards, darts and backgammon. It boasts the city's longest happy hour (2 to 8 pm) and dishes up fine meals.

Mogambo Café (☎ 251311), 20 Thi Sach St (at Hai Ba Trung Blvd), is noted for its Polynesian decor. This place is a pub, café and guest house.

Hien & Bob's Place (☎ 230661), 43 Hai Ba Trung Blvd (at Dong Du St), District 1, advertises the coldest beer in town and American-style sandwiches. The interesting thing about this place is that Bob Shibley first came to Vietnam in 1969 as an American soldier. He is the first US veteran to have returned to open up a pub. Hien is his Vietnamese wife.

At 24 Mac Thi Buoi St is the legendary *Hard Rock Café*. The music here is mellower than the name suggests, but it's certainly a popular spot. Next to the Hard Rock Café but even more sedate is the *VSOP Club* (☎ 290520) at 56 Mac Thi Buoi St. This place touts its 'tropical cocktails' and 'famous cognacs'. Other refreshments on offer include brandy, coffee, cakes and sandwiches.

Saigon Headlines (☎ 225014), 7 Lam Son Square, District 1, is a slick jazz bar and restaurant at the back of the Saigon Concert Hall. It serves the best Marguerita on the rocks this side of Hong Kong. The atmosphere is relaxed but chic and there is an excellent band. Open from 10 am until 2 am.

Built right into one side of the Municipal Theatre is the *Q Bar* (☎ 291299), a trendy place with murals on the walls and tables outside by a little garden. Expats tend to congregate here and swap yarns.

The slogan of the *River Bar* (☎ 293734) at 5-7 Ho Huan Nghiep St is 'a beat of Brazil, a beat of Africa, a lot of passion'. Good interior decorating (including rattan furniture) adds to the atmosphere at this popular watering hole.

Apocalypse Now, at the southern, riverside end of Thi Sach St, is extremely popular with the young Western crowd. On a good night it spills out on the street – and if ever a crowd could be said to spill, this is it. It's very noisy, very hectic and it can be great fun.

The *Press Club* at the corner of Hai Ba Trung and Le Duan Blvds is run by the Ho Chi Minh City Journalists' Association. It appeals to both expats and Vietnamese, and you don't need to be a journalist to go there.

The *Hammock Bar* is the only floating bar in Vietnam. Moored in the Saigon River at Bach Dang Quay (the terminus of Ham Nghi Blvd), the boat can accommodate over 100 people on its two decks.

Stephanie's (☎ 258471), 14 Don Dat St, District 1, is a large bar with billiard tables upstairs.

Tiger Tavern (☎ 222738) at 227 Dong Khoi St seems to be an outlet for Singapore's most famous brew, Tiger Beer. Personally, I found this place a bit pricey and not too friendly, but expats do gather here. The pub is open daily from 11 am until midnight. The pub advertises live entertainment nightly from 6.30 to 9.30 pm featuring various performers (pianist, jazz band, etc).

KARAOKE

For those who haven't experienced karaoke, it's simply a system where you are supposed to sing along with a video. The words to the song are flashed on the bottom of the screen (a number of languages are possible) and participants are supplied with a microphone. Really fancy karaoke bars have superb audio systems and big-screen video, but no matter how good the equipment, it's not going to sound any better than the ability of the singer. And with a few exceptions, it usually sounds awful. While it has not proven quite so popular with Westerners, karaoke has taken over Asia.

To find karaoke, look for signs advertising 'KTV' ('Karaoke TV', Asia's answer to MTV). In Ho Chi Minh City, the neighbourhood to head for is Cholon. The speciality here is karaoke accompanied by great food and all you can drink. You can choose to sing your heart out in a little private booth, or visit one of the places where you can go up on stage and get your first big break in show business (or make a fool of yourself trying). The larger places put on really big dinner show extravaganzas at about 100 decibels – bring earplugs or you'll need a hearing aid the next morning.

The *Volvo Disco & Karaoke* is a Chinese-oriented disco-karaoke inside the Arc En Ciel Hotel at 52-56 Tan Da St in Cholon. This disco is a joint-venture between Saigon Tourist and Golden Desire Company of Hong Kong.

Nha Hang Le Uyen (☎ 553358), 131 Chau Van Liem St, is one of Cholon's spiffy restaurant-karaoke combinations. It's on the north side of the Thu Do Hotel. This place serves only Western food, and rents karaoke cubicles for US$8 per hour.

A stone's throw away on the south side of the Thu Do Hotel is *Tan Le Uyen* (☎ 557620), 123 Chau Van Liem St. This is another place that delivers food to your karaoke

Karaoke bar (RS)

cubicle. The cost here is US$5 per hour, plus the food (which is excellent).

Tan Dong Thang (☎ 556864), 570 Nguyen Trai St, is a karaoke club where you get your own private cubicle. You can order food and drinks, but it's more of a bar than a restaurant. This place is upstairs and you have to enter through a garage.

Bach Hy (☎ 553434), 51-53 Chau Van Liem St, is one of those huge places that does it all – karaoke, live band, dancing and a restaurant featuring uncomfortable stools instead of chairs. Seafood is a speciality – select your own fish out of the tank and it will be caught, executed, fried and delivered to your table in no time.

Dai Bac (☎ 550542) means 'Taipei', so don't be surprised if you see a lot of Taiwanese tourists congregating here. It's at 706 Nguyen Trai St. This place also doubles as a disco.

If Taipei seems too exotic, you may want to try *Dai La Thien* (☎ 557327) which means 'Toronto'. This is a combination of restaurant, karaoke, dance hall and video parlour all rolled into one. It has plenty of good food and noise. It's at 177/31 Hai Thuong Lan Ong Blvd, near Phung Hung St (south-east corner in an alley). This place is owned by Cholon Tourist, the Chinese nemesis of Saigon Tourist.

The *Tokyo Hotel* at 106-108 Tran Tuan Khai St in Cholon has a dance hall and karaoke combination.

The Omni Hotel (☎ 449222 ext 105) at 251 Nguyen Van Troi St in the Phu Nhuan District (near the airport) has the *Stars Karaoke Lounge*. You can expect to find top-notch sound equipment, VIP rooms, hostesses dressed in the latest fashions and prices to match.

Other upmarket hotels cater to the karaoke market but you can expect the price of admission to be steep. An example is the Saigon Floating Hotel, noted for its *Kimono Karaoke Lounge*.

Next to the Saigon Floating Hotel is the *Floating Karaoke* (☎ 230042) at 10B Bach Dang port. This place is both a karaoke bar and a restaurant, complete with public and private cubicles and microphones to wail into.

COFFEE SHOPS

Coffee shops can be found everywhere and anywhere in Ho Chi Minh City. These should not be confused with cafés (which serve complete meals). Coffee shops don't do meals, but most usually have snacks. Key features of Vietnamese coffee shops are superbly comfortable lawn chairs (which always face towards the street) and plenty of *loud* music. The chairs are wonderful, but the music usually consists of Vietnamese pop songs which seldom appeal to non-Vietnamese tourists. More and more coffee shops are being set up with karaoke sound systems which allow you to create your own noise.

Nevertheless, you might find these coffee shops quite enjoyable if you're deaf or if you visit during an electrical outage. They are also a good place to take refuge from a sudden downpour.

Chi Lang Coffee Shop (☎ 242936) deserves special mention. This outdoor drinking establishment is in a park-like garden on Dong Khoi St between Ly Tu Trong and Le Thanh Ton Sts. You can sit in the park, listen to music, drink a cold beer or coffee and relax away an afternoon or evening. No food is served.

POP & ROCK

To really taste Ho Chi Minh City's youth culture, you have to catch one of the pop music shows. It matters little where you go since it's very much the same at numerous venues all over the city. The music is almost entirely Western bubble-gum pop hits from the '60s and '70s. An essential difference from Western-style performances is that each vocalist (accompanied by a house band) gets to perform one or two songs each. The singers seem to have a uniform of sorts – a sequins and satin outfit with a perma-press hairdo. The best bands (if there are any) always play at the end of the concerts, forcing you to sit through the rest. If you're lucky, you might get to see a very rare performance by a foreign band (a Russian heavy-metal band called Vomit has been threatening to make a Saigon tour).

There's an outdoor venue on Ly Tu Trong St between Nam Ky Khoi Nghia and Pasteur Sts. There is no admission fee – you just pay for your drinks. Shows are nightly at 8 pm. Two nights a week they do traditional Vietnamese music with folk instruments which are largely drowned out by the waves of mushy synthesized sound. The other five nights are modern and pop, which sounds very similar to the traditional music.

An outdoor amphitheatre called *Trong Dong* is in the south-west part of Cong Vien Van Hoa Park (corner of Cach Mang Thang Tam and Nguyen Du Sts); admission costs US$1.The official address is 8 Cach Mang Thang Tam St. There is an unnamed place with similar music at 126 Cach Mang Thang Tam St.

Not as good is the *Sontra Coffee Concert*, nightly from 8 to 10 pm. This is the trashy park just south of the New World Hotel on Le Lai St. Admission is free. For a higher class version of the same stuff, go to the *Hoa Binh Theatre* in District 10. The main exception here to the uninspiring fare is the vocalist Baoy Yen. This woman is one of the few Saigonese who can really rock 'n' roll. On her songs you will hear real electric guitar – rock-starved travellers in Vietnam should try to catch her show, though the fix is short-lived (two songs).

A couple of heavy-metal bands also vying for attention include Da Vang (they sing in English) and Ba Con Meo (they sing in both English and Vietnamese).

TRADITIONAL MUSIC

Both traditional Vietnamese and Western classical music are performed publicly at the *Conservatory of Music* (Nhac Vien Thanh Pho Ho Chi Minh; ☎ 396646), which is near Reunification Palace at 112 Nguyen Du St. Concerts are held at 7.30 pm each Monday and Friday evening during the two annual concert seasons, from March to May and from October to December. Tickets cost about US$0.25.

Students aged seven to 16 attend the Conservatory, which performs all the functions of a public school in addition to providing instruction in music. The music teachers here were trained abroad.

CINEMAS

Most maps of Ho Chi Minh City have cinemas *(rap* in Vietnamese) marked with a special symbol. Western movies, either subtitled or dubbed, vie with cheapie Vietnamese kung fu flicks and cheesy love stories.

Vietnamese censors take a dim view of nudity and sex – murder and mayhem are OK. The government likes to produce movies about the successful wars against French colonialism and American imperialism, as well as the life and times of Ho Chi Minh. Gripping stuff.

There are several cinemas downtown, including the *Rex Cinema* (☎ 292185) at 141 Nguyen Hue Blvd (next door to the Rex Hotel); another on Le Loi Blvd a block towards Ben Thanh Market from the Rex Hotel; and a third, *Rap Mang Non*, on Dong Khoi St, 100 metres up from the Municipal Theatre. *Rap Dong Khoi* is at 163 Dong Khoi St.

Video Parlours

A variation on the theme are unauthorised video parlours. Vietnam's opening to the outside world is creating massive headaches for the country's censors. Despite their best efforts, customs agents haven't been able to hold back the flood tide of video tapes which are smuggled into Vietnam. The pirating of video tapes has become big business and the tapes are sold or rented all over the country. Kungfu movies from Hong Kong and

Municipal Theatre (RS)

pornography from the West and Japan are much in demand. Ditto for the latest MTV tapes. Such spiritual pollution is bad enough, but a thornier problem for the culture police are videos about the Vietnam War. Illegal but popular war movies include *Rambo, Apocalypse Now, Full Metal Jacket, Platoon, The Deer Hunter, Good Morning Vietnam, Born on the 4th of July, Air America* and *Heaven and Earth*.

Obviously, most Vietnamese cannot afford video equipment, but that hardly matters. Budding entrepreneurs have set up instant mini-theatres consisting of a video cassette recorder (VCR), a few chairs and curtains to keep out nonpaying onlookers. The admission price is very low, on the order of US$0.20. Some of these video parlours provide food and beverage services.

THEATRE

Municipal Theatre

The *Municipal Theatre* (Nha Hat Thanh Pho; ☎ 291249, 291584) is on Dong Khoi St between the Caravelle and Continental hotels. It was built in 1899 for use as a theatre but later served as the heavily fortified home of the South Vietnamese National Assembly.

Each week, the theatre offers a different programme, which may be gymnastics, nightclub music or traditional Vietnamese theatre. There are performances at 8 pm nightly. Refreshments are sold during intermission; public toilets are in the basement.

Hoa Binh Theatre

The huge and elegant *Hoa Binh Theatre* complex (Nha Hat Hoa Binh, or the Peace Theatre) in District 10 often has several performances taking place simultaneously in its various halls. The largest hall seats 2400 people in air-conditioned comfort. The complex is at 14, 3 Thang 2 Blvd (next to the Vietnam Quoc Tu Pagoda). The ticket office (☎ 655199) is open from 7.30 am until the end of the evening show.

Performances begin at 7.30 pm, but some are held only once or twice a week. Shows range from traditional and modern Vietnamese plays to Western pop music and circus acts. On Sunday mornings, there are marionette shows for children at 9 am in the 400-seat hall.

Films are screened all day every day beginning at 8.30 am. Most of the films – from former Socialist countries, France, Hong Kong and the USA (Disney productions are a favourite) – are live-dubbed (someone reads a translation of the script over the PA system), leaving the original soundtrack at least partly audible. A weekly schedule of screenings is posted outside the building next to the ticket counter.

The disco on the ground floor is open Tuesday to Sunday from 8 to 11 pm. Admission is US$1.25.

Water Puppetry

There is only one place where you can see water puppet shows in Ho Chi Minh City and that is in the History Museum, within the grounds of the zoo. See under Parks in the Things to See & Do chapter for more information on the Zoo & Botanical Gardens area.

CULTURE CLUBS

These are really geared towards the domestic audience, but you might have some interest in seeing what sort of culture the government produces for the masses. Some venues for Vietnamese cultural entertainment include the *Youth House of Culture* at 4 Pham Ngoc Thach St; the *Children's House of Culture* at 4 Tu Xuong St; and the *Workers' Club* at 55B Xo Viet Nghe Tinh St.

SPECTATOR SPORTS

Venues

Ho Chi Minh City's stadium (Dai Phat Thanh) is in District 1 at the corner of Dinh Tien Hoang and Nguyen Thi Minh Khai Sts (one block west of the zoo).

Street Sports

The Vietnamese are incredibly skilled at badminton (shuttlecock). Other favourites include volleyball and ping-pong. It can be amazing to watch badminton even if you don't play. Competitions take place regularly in front of a church called Nha Thoi in District 6.

Horse Racing

When South Vietnam was liberated in 1975, one of Hanoi's policies was to ban debauched capitalistic pastimes such as gambling. Horse race tracks – mostly found in the Saigon area – were shut down. This forced Vietnam's compulsive gamblers to go underground – even today, you find illegal cock fights in the back alleys of Cholon near the river.

Liberalisation and the government's need for hard cash has caused a rethink of official policy towards gambling. The *Saigon Race Track* (Cau Lac Bo TDTT; ☎ 551205), which dates back to around 1900, was permitted to reopen in 1989.

Much of the credit for the reopening goes to Philip Chow, a Chinese-Vietnamese businessman who fled to Hong Kong as a youth but returned to Vietnam in 1987 after the government promised to launch capitalist-style reforms. After getting the race track up and running through his own hard work, Mr Chow was rewarded for his efforts by being sacked from his position. Government officials, sensing the opportunity to line their own pockets, saw no reason to keep an entrepreneur on the payroll.

Like the state lottery, the race track is extremely lucrative. But grumbling about just where the money is going has been coupled with widespread allegations about the drugging of horses. The minimum legal age for jockeys is 14 years; most look like they are about 10.

The overwhelming majority of gamblers are Vietnamese though there is no rule prohibiting foreigners. The maximum legal bet is currently US$2. High rollers can win a million dong (about US$92). Races are held Saturday and Sunday afternoons starting at 1 pm. Plans to introduce off-track betting have so far not materialised. However, illegal bookmaking (bets can be placed in gold!) offers one form of competition to the government-owned monopoly.

The Saigon Race Track is in District 11 at 2 Le Dai Hanh St.

TV Sports

Football (soccer) is number one with spectators. The World Cup Championships are not shown on Vietnamese TV stations, but are broadcast on satellite TV (and copied onto pirated video tapes the very same day and rapidly distributed).

Tennis has considerable snob appeal – trendy Vietnamese like to catch the games on TV. The upper crust likes to play, but there is a shortage of public tennis courts and few people have rackets.

Shopping

To the Western mind, one of the odd things about shopping in Ho Chi Minh City is the tendency for vendors of the same product to congregate all in one spot. For example, it's not uncommon for 50 or more shops and stalls selling TVs to all cram together on one street, while there is a dearth of such shops elsewhere. This situation is found in other parts of Asia: there are streets devoted to music CDs, watches, jewellery, glasses, stationery, cloth, clothing, cameras, etc. The shops offer little to choose between them – prices, quality and selection are nearly identical in all these adjacent business establishments. At least in theory, cutthroat competition like this should create a buyers' market. In practice, Vietnamese shopkeepers wouldn't be in business if they were not making a profit.

As a general principle, try to find a shop that 1) does not cater particularly to tourists, and 2) puts price tags on all its items. In touristy areas, items sold with no visible price tags must be bargained for – expect the vendor to start the bidding at two to five times the real price.

Duty-Free Shopping

Like elsewhere in the world, the duty-free shop at Tan Son Nhat Airport offers the usual array of pricey souvenirs which cost much less if you buy them elsewhere. This having been said, browsing the duty-free shops offers an outlet for boredom while waiting for your delayed or cancelled flight.

All the standard Western consumer lines are available, such as perfumes, whiskey, pens, ties and so on. There are also, however, somewhat more exotic items for purchase, such as Korean ginseng and Taiwanese bee pollen (the latter reputedly an aphrodisiac).

If you've got a nicotine habit, stock up on duty-free Dunhills or 555s. Please observe the signs in the airport that say 'No Smoking', and note the ashtrays directly below the signs.

There is something for everyone, including the children. Reasonably nonviolent is the 'Tumble Action All-Terrain Vehicle' (batteries not included). 'Star Robot' looks like a mean dude, but for real mayhem try the 'F14 Tomcat Jet Fighter' (ammunition not included). My personal favourite is the electric 'Crazy Axe' – it has a built-in speaker that screams when you bury it in somebody's skull. ■

SHOPPING AREAS

Street Markets

You can buy everything at these places: mousetraps, electric mosquito zappers, video cassette players, clothing, washing detergent, lacquerware, condoms, pirated cassettes, posters of celebrities like Ho Chi Minh, Michael Jackson and Mickey Mouse, smuggled bottles of Johnny Walker, Chinese-made 'Swiss' Army knives and just about anything else to satisfy your material needs. About half the items have marked prices, otherwise the tariff is subject to negotiation.

Indoor Markets

Ho Chi Minh City has a number of vast indoor markets selling all manner of goods. They are some of the best places to pick up the conical hats and ao dais for which Vietnam is famous.

Ben Thanh Market Ben Thanh Market (Cho Ben Thanh) and the surrounding streets are one of the city's liveliest, most bustling market areas. Everything commonly eaten, worn or used by local residents is available here: vegetables, fruits, meat, spices, biscuits, sweets, tobacco, clothing, conical hats, travel bags, backpacks, household items, hardware and so forth. The tourism market has not been overlooked, so you can even find lacquerware and other handicraft items. The legendary

Market scene (PW)

slogan of US country stores applies equally well here: 'If we don't have it, you don't need it'. Nearby, food stalls sell inexpensive meals, and a surprisingly large number of vendors here understand basic English.

Ben Thanh Market is 700 metres south-west of the Rex Hotel at the intersection of Le Loi Blvd, Ham Nghi Blvd, Tran Hung Dao Blvd and Le Lai St. Known to the French as the Halles Centrales, it was built in 1914 of reinforced concrete and covers an area of 11 sq km; the central cupola is 28 metres in diameter. The main entrance, with its belfry and clock, has become a symbol of Saigon.

Opposite the belfry, in the centre of the traffic roundabout, is an equestrian statue of Tran Nguyen Hai, the first person in Vietnam to use courier pigeons. At the base, on a pillar, is a small white bust of Quach Thi Trang, a Buddhist woman killed during anti-government protests in 1963.

Binh Tay Market Binh Tay Market (Cho Binh Tay) is Cholon's main marketplace. Actually, it's technically not in Cholon proper, but about one block away in District 6 (Cholon is District 5). Much of the business here is wholesale. Binh Tay Market is on Hau Giang Blvd. It is about one km west of Chau Van Liem Blvd.

Andong Market Cholon's other indoor market, Andong, is very close to the intersection of Tran Phu and An Duong Vuong Blvds. This market is four storeys tall and is packed with shops. The upmarket Caesar Hotel (a foreign joint-venture) is built right into the ground floor of the marketplace. The 1st floor has heaps of clothing – the latest pumps from Paris, Shiseido make-up from Tokyo, counterfeit designer jeans from the sweatshop next door – and everything else imaginable. The basement is a gourmet's delight of small restaurants – a perfect place to pig out on a shoestring.

Old Market Despite the name, this is not a place to find antiques. Rather, the Old Market is where you can most easily buy imported (black market?) foods, wines, etc. There is a problem using the Vietnamese name for this market (Cho Cu), because written or pronounced without the tones it means 'penis'. Your cyclo driver will no doubt be much amused if you say that this is what you're looking for. Perhaps directions would be better – the Old Market is on the north side of Ham Nghi Blvd between Ton That Dam and Ho Tung Mau Sts.

De Tham St

In the Pham Ngu Lao budget hotel zone is De Tham St, which has recently acquired a string of downmarket shops geared towards backpackers. Prices are reasonable, rapacious bargaining is rare, the staff speak English and there is a wide selection of interesting items. Nevertheless, you may find what you need somewhat cheaper if you are willing to hunt around the back alleys and markets of Ho Chi Minh City where the rents are lower.

Tax Department Store

The Tax Department Store (Cua Hang Bach Hoa), the biggest department store in Ho Chi Minh City, is on the corner of Le Loi and Nguyen Hue Blvds. Built as the Grands Magasins Charner six decades ago, this three-storey emporium, which for years was run by the government and had a pathetic selection of goods, has been 'privatised', and floor space is now rented to individual shop-owners. Items for sale include consumer electronics, blank and pirated cassette tapes, locally produced bicycles and parts, domestic alcoholic beverages, stationery, little globes of the world labelled in Vietnamese, sports equipment, cheap jewellery and synthetic clothing.

Tourist Shops

Dong Khoi St and Nguyen Hue Blvd are thick with shops geared towards the tourist traffic. Not surprisingly, you can expect high prices, and bargaining is *de rigueur*. By way of compensation, there is at least a fairly wide selection of goods here.

You'll also find overpriced souvenir shops inside all the major tourist hotels but most of these places won't bargain.

WHAT TO BUY

Arts & Crafts

In the last few years the Saigon tourist kitsch-junk market has really come into its own. Without any effort at all, you'll be able to find that special something for your loved ones at home – perhaps a battery-powered stuffed koala bear that sings 'Waltzing Matilda' or a lacquered alligator with a light bulb in its mouth.

Other handicrafts which make attractive souvenirs include lacquerware, items with mother-of-pearl inlay, ceramics (including enormous elephants), colourful embroidered items (hangings, tablecloths, pillow cases, pyjamas and robes), greeting cards with silk paintings on the front, wood-block prints, oil paintings, watercolours, blinds made of hanging bamboo beads (many travellers like the replica of the *Mona Lisa*), reed mats (rushes are called *lac*), Chinese-style carpets, jewellery and leatherwork.

In the budget zone near Pham Ngu Lao St, check out the shop in the back of Getra Tour Company at 86 Bui Vien St. It's also productive to look at some of the stalls inside the Ben Thanh Market.

Dong Khoi St is the centre for handicrafts, though the shop-owners can be rapacious. Remember that the 'antiques' are almost certainly fakes, which is OK as long as you don't pay 'antique prices'.

One of the larger stores in this business is Culturimex (☎ 292574, 292896) at 50 Dong Khoi St, which sells ceramics, wood carvings, hand-painted greeting cards, copies of antiquities and other items you'd expect to find in a shop with a name like Culturimex.

Tu Do Art Gallery (☎ 231785), 142 Dong Khoi St, pushes oil and lacquer paintings.

The Saigon Lacquerwares Factory (☎ 294183), at 139 Hai Ba Trung Blvd, is the sort of place to which busloads of tourists are brought to do their souvenir shopping. The selection of lacquerware, ceramics, etc is large but prices are high.

Just opposite the Omni Hotel (on the way to the airport) is Lamson Art Gallery (☎ 441361) at 106 Nguyen Van Troi St, Phu Nhuan District. This place sells exquisite but relatively expensive lacquerware, rattan, ceramics, wood carvings and more. You can watch the artisans create their masterpieces and it's certainly worth stopping by to have a look.

Oil paintings, watercolours and paintings on silk can be bought at Phuong Tranh Art Arcade, 151 Dong Du St (opposite the Caravelle Hotel). There is another art gallery, Thang Long, at 70 Nguyen Hue Blvd (next to the Century Saigon Hotel).

The Ho Chi Minh City Association of Fine Arts (☎ 230025), 218 Nguyen Thi Minh Khai St, District 1, is where aspiring young artists display their latest works. Typical prices for paintings are in the US$30 to US$50 range, but the artists may ask 10 times that.

Books

You won't find many places to buy books. Such book-shops as there are tend to stock material of the technical and instructional variety, printed by the government for the edification of the people.

Top : Cloth stall (HS)
Middle : Snake market (RS)
Bottom : Flower market (PW)

Hieu Sach Xuan Thu (☎ 224670) at 185 Dong Khoi St, District 1, is the best of the government-run bookstores. You should at least manage to find a good dictionary or some maps here, as well as some more general books in English and French.

Tiem Sach Bookstore, 20 Ho Huan Nghiep St, has a massive selection of mostly used English and French titles. The owner is an elderly ex-journalist. The shop is open daily from 8.30 am to 10 pm and also functions as an ice cream parlour.

The best area to look for general map, book and stationery stuff is along the north side of Le Loi Blvd between the Rex Hotel and Nam Ky Khoi Nghia St (near the Kem Bach Dang ice cream parlours). There are many small privately run shops and one large government bookstore here.

Clothing

At the budget end of the scale, T-shirts are available from vendors along Nguyen Hue Blvd in the centre, or De Tham St in the Pham Ngu Lao area. Expect to pay about US$2 for a printed T-shirt, or US$3 to US$5 for an embroidered one.

Vietsilk (☎ 291148), whose shop is at 21 Dong Khoi St, sells ready-made garments as well as embroidery and drawings on silk.

Women's ao dais (pronounced 'ow-yai'), the flowing silk blouse slit up the sides and worn over pantaloons, are tailored at shops in and around Ben Thanh Market or the Saigon Intershop area. Behind Ben Thanh Market these can be found at a store called Italy, 11 Thu Khoa Huan St.

Thai Fashion at 92H Le Thanh Ton St, District 1, has ready-made women's fashions. You might want to check out nearby Down Under Fashions at 229 Le Thanh Ton St, District 1. Ditto for The He Moi at 87 Pasteur St, District 1.

Custom-made suits for men can be tailored at Cuu Long (☎ 296831), 175 Dong Khoi St.

There are numerous tailors' shops in Cholon and several in central Saigon; the Rex and Century Saigon hotels each have in-house tailors.

Sandals are a practical item in the tropical heat. At around US$4, they certainly are worth the money. Finding large sizes to fit Western feet can be a problem, though. Make sure they are very comfortable before you purchase them – some tend to be poorly made and will give you blisters.

Coffee

Vietnamese coffee is prime stuff and is amazingly cheap if you know where to buy it. The best grades are from Buon Ma Thuot in the Central Highlands and the beans are roasted in butter. Obviously, price varies according to quality and also with the seasons. You can buy whole beans or have them ground into powder at no extra charge.

The city's major markets are where you can find the best prices and widest selection. Ben Thanh Market sells top-grade caffeine, coffee drippers and coffee grinders.

Electronics

The street market which runs along Huynh Thuc Khang and Ton That Dam Sts sells everything. The area used to be known as the Electronics Black Market until early 1989, when it was legalised. It's now generally called the Huynh Thuc Khang Street Market or else the Electronics Street Market, though it doesn't have an official name.

Gems

Vietnam produces some good gems, but there are plenty of fakes and flawed gems around. This doesn't mean that you shouldn't buy something if you think it's beautiful, but don't think that you'll find a cut diamond or polished ruby for a fraction of what you'd pay at home. Some travellers have actually thought that they could buy gems in Vietnam and sell these at home for a profit. Such business requires considerable expertise and good connections in the mining industry.

Old Cars

Assuming you are an automobile collector and have sufficient funds to support such an expensive habit, Ho Chi Minh City is a worthwhile place to check out. During the war, Saigon had a large population of resident US technical advisors, businesspeople, journalists, diplomats, CIA agents, etc, many of whom bought imported American and European cars for personal use. When South Vietnam suddenly collapsed in 1975, the Americans had to flee abruptly, abandoning their vehicles in the process.

Ironically, Vietnam's poverty means that automobile owners must take good care of their vehicles since replacements are expensive. So if you're in the market for a 1965 Ford Mustang, an Austin-Healey convertible or an old De Soto, this is the place to look. Automobiles easily exceed the 20-kg luggage weight limit imposed by Vietnam Airlines, so you'll have to make arrangements to ship the vehicle home by sea freight, unless you want to attempt a land crossing into Cambodia.

Rubber Stamps & Seals

No bureaucracy, Communist or otherwise, can exist without the official stamps and seals that provide the *raison d'être* for legions of clerks. This need is catered to by the numerous shops strung out along the street just north of the New World Hotel (opposite side of the street and just west of Ben Thanh Market). Other things that can be custom-made here include personalised signs, keyrings, nameplates and so on.

Most Vietnamese also own carved seals (called 'name chops') bearing their name, an old tradition borrowed from China. You can have one made too, but ask a local to help translate your name into Vietnamese. You might want to get your seal carved in Cholon using Chinese characters, since those are certainly more artistic (though less practical) than the Romanised script now used by the Vietnamese.

Stamps & Coins

As you enter the CPO, immediately to your right is a counter selling stationery, pens, etc; it also has some decent stamp collections. Also as you face the entrance from the outside, to your right are a few stalls which have stamp collections as well as other goods such as foreign coins and banknotes. You can even find old stuff from the former South Vietnamese regime. Prices are variable: about US$2 will get you a decent set of late-model stamps already mounted in a book, but the older and rarer collections cost more.

Perhaps the best place to look is Cotevina, the government corporation which issues Vietnamese stamps. There is a branch (☎ 22326, 91637) at 18 Dinh Tien Hoang St, District 1. The range is from 1960s stamps up to late-issued ones.

Many bookshops and antique shops along Dong Khoi St sell overpriced French Indochinese coins and banknotes and packets of Vietnamese stamps.

War Surplus

If you need a chic pair of combat boots and rusty dog tags, the place to go is Dan Sinh Market at 104 Nguyen Cong Tru St (next to Phung Son Tu Pagoda). The front part of the market is filled with stalls selling automobiles and motorbikes, but directly behind the pagoda building you can find reproductions of what appears to be second-hand military gear.

Stall after stall sells everything from gas masks and field stretchers to rain gear and mosquito nets. You can also find canteens, duffel bags, ponchos and boots. Anyone planning on spending time in Bosnia or New York City should consider picking up a second-hand flak jacket (demand has slumped since the Vietnam War ended, and the prices are now very competitive). On the other hand, exorbitant overcharging of foreigners looking for a poignant souvenir is common.

The 'Zippo' lighters seem to be the hottest-selling item. You can pay extra to get one that's been beat up to look like a war relic, or just buy a new shiny one for less money.

One thing you should think twice about purchasing are weapons and ammunition *even if fake*. You may have several opportunities to buy old bullets and dud mortar shells. Most of these items are either fake or deactivated, but metal scavengers from the countryside occasionally turn up in the markets with real bullets that are still useable. Real or not, it's illegal to carry ammunition on airlines and many countries will arrest you if any such goods are found in your luggage. Customs agents in Singapore are particularly strict and thorough, and travellers carrying souvenir ammunition and weapons have been arrested there.

Excursions

There are times when you simply need to get away from the whining motorcycles, throngs of people and heavy-duty commercialism that give Ho Chi Minh City its robust character. Amazingly, refugees from this urban chaos don't even have to go far to find serenity and sanity. There are plenty of one-day journeys that will bring you to rural places seemingly untouched by the heart-attack pace of city living. The only problem is that public transport to most of them is virtually nonexistent. A hired car, shared with others, is the best option.

Some of the cafés on or near Pham Ngu Lao St run combined full-day tours to the Cu Chi tunnels and Caodai Temple, often for as little as US$5. Organised tours are also available from travel agencies and hotels.

CU CHI TUNNELS

The town of Cu Chi is now a district of greater Ho Chi Minh City with a population of 200,000. At first glance, there is little evidence here to indicate the heavy fighting, bombing and destruction that went on in Cu Chi during the Vietnam War. To see what went on, you have to dig deeper – underground.

The tunnel network of Cu Chi became legendary during the 1960s for its role in facilitating Viet Cong control of a large rural area only 30 to 40 km from Saigon. At its height, the tunnel system stretched from the South Vietnamese capital to the Cambodian border; in the district of Cu Chi alone, there were over 250 km of tunnels. The network, parts of which were several storeys deep, included innumerable trapdoors, specially constructed living areas, storage facilities, weapons factories, field hospitals, command centres and kitchens.

The tunnels made possible coordination between VC-controlled enclaves isolated from each other by South Vietnamese and American land and air operations. They also allowed the guerrillas to mount surprise attacks wherever the tunnels went – even within the perimeters of the US military base at Dong Du – and to disappear into hidden trapdoors without a trace. After ground operations against the tunnels claimed large numbers of casualties and proved ineffective, the Americans resorted to carpet bombing, eventually turning Cu Chi's 420 sq km into a moonscape.

Today, Cu Chi has become a pilgrimage site for school children, Party cadres and foreign tourists. Parts of this remarkable tunnel network – enlarged and upgraded versions of the real thing – are open to the public. The unadulterated tunnels, though not actually closed to tourists, are hard to get to and are rarely visited. There are numerous war cemeteries all around Cu Chi, though tour groups don't usually stop at these except on special request.

Presently, two of the tunnel sites are open to visitors. One is near Ben Binh and the other is at Ben Duoc.

Ben Binh Tunnels

This small, renovated section of the tunnel system is near the village of Ben Binh. In one of the classrooms of the visitors' centre, a large map shows the extent of the network (the area shown is in the north-western corner of Map 6).

The section of the tunnel system presently open to visitors is a few hundred metres south of the visitors' centre. The tunnels are about 1.2 metres high and 80 cm across. A knocked-out M-48 tank and a bomb crater are near the exit, which is in a reafforested eucalyptus grove.

Entry to the tunnel site, which is now controlled by Saigon Tourist, costs US$2 for foreigners but is free for Vietnamese nationals.

Ben Duoc Tunnels

These are not the genuine tunnels, but a fully fledged reconstruction for the benefit of tourists. The emphasis here is more on the funfair, and tourists are given the chance to imagine what it was like to be a guerrilla. At this site there is even the opportunity to fire an M-16, AK-47 or Russian carbine rifle. This costs US$1 per bullet, but may be the only opportunity you'll ever get. It's recommended that you wear hearing protection. Saigon Tourist has talked of dressing the place up with heroic statues of Viet Cong guerrillas.

Admission to the tunnels at Ben Duoc costs US$3.

Cu Chi War History Museum

This museum is not actually at the tunnel sites, but rather just off the main highway in the central area of the town of Cu Chi. Sad to say, the Cu Chi War History Museum (Nha Truyen Thong Huyen Cu Chi) is rather disappointing and gets few visitors. It's a small museum where almost all explanations are in Vietnamese.

Cu Chi tunnels (RI)

The exhibits have a severe propaganda bias. There is a collection of some gruesome photos showing severely wounded or dead civilians after being attacked by American bombs or burned with napalm. A painting on the wall shows American soldiers armed with rifles being attacked by Vietnamese peasants armed only with sticks. A sign near the photos formerly read (in Vietnamese) 'American conquest and crimes', but this was changed in 1995 to read 'Enemy conquest and crimes'. Apparently, some effort is being made to tone down the rhetoric in anticipation of receiving more American visitors.

One wall of the museum contains a long list of names, all Viet Cong guerrillas killed in the Cu Chi area. An adjacent room of the museum displays recent photos of prosperous farms and factories, an effort to show the benefits of Vietnam's socialist revolution. There is also an odd collection of pottery and lacquerware with no explanations attached. In the lobby near the entrance is a statue of Ho Chi Minh with his right arm raised, waving hello.

Admission costs US$1 for foreigners.

Getting There & Away

Cu Chi is a district which covers a large area, parts of which are as close as 30 km to Saigon. The Cu Chi War History Museum is the closest place to the city, but the actual tunnels that exist now are about 65 km from central Saigon by highway. However, there is a backroad which cuts the commute down to 35 km, though it means driving on bumpy dirt roads.

Cu Chi War History Museum (RS)

Bus Buses from Ho Chi Minh City to Tay Ninh leave from the Tay Ninh Bus Station (Ben Xe Tay Ninh) in Tan Binh District and Mien Tay Bus Station in An Lac. All buses to Tay Ninh pass though Cu Chi town, but getting from the town of Cu Chi to the tunnels by public transport is difficult.

Car Hiring a car in Saigon and just driving out to Cu Chi is not all that expensive, especially if the cost is split by several people. A visit to the Cu Chi tunnel complex can easily be combined with a stop at the headquarters of the Caodai sect in Tay Ninh. A car for an all-day excursion to both should cost about US$40.

TAY NINH

Tay Ninh serves as the headquarters of one of Vietnam's most interesting indigenous religions, Caodaism.

The Tay Ninh region was also, during the period of tension between Cambodia and Vietnam in the late 1970s, the scene of raids by the Khmer Rouge, during which horrific atrocities were committed against the civilian population. Several cemeteries around Tay Ninh are stark reminders of these grisly atrocities.

Caodai Holy See

The Caodai Great Temple at the sect's Holy See is one of the most striking structures in Vietnam. Built between 1933 and 1955, it is a rococo extravaganza combining the architectural idiosyncrasies of a French church, a Chinese pagoda, the Tiger Balm Gardens and Madame Tussaud's Wax Museum. As in all Caodai temples, above the altar there is the 'divine eye', which became the religion's official symbol after the sect's founder Ngo Minh Chieu saw it in a vision (see box). Americans often comment that it looks like the symbol found on the back of a US$1 bill.

All Caodai lands were confiscated by the new Communist government and four members of the sect were

The Caodai Religion

Caodaism was an attempt to create the ideal religion through the fusion of the secular and religious philosophies of the East and West. The result is a colourful and eclectic potpourri of the religious philosophies known in Vietnam during the early 20th century – Buddhism, Confucianism, Taoism, Christianity and Islam – together with native Vietnamese animism and Western humanism.

Caodaism was founded by the mystic Ngo Minh Chieu (born 1878), a civil servant who was widely read in Eastern and Western religious works. He became active in seances, at which his presence was said to greatly improve the quality of communication with the spirits. Around 1919 he began to receive a series of revelations in which the tenets of Caodai doctrine were set forth. Most of the sacred literature of Caodaism consists of messages communicated to Caodai leaders during seances held between 1925 and 1929. Since 1927, only the official seances held at Tay Ninh have been considered reliable and divinely ordained by the Caodai hierarchy.

Spirits who have been in touch with the Caodai include deceased Caodai leaders, patriots, heroes, philosophers, poets, political leaders and warriors. Westerners include Joan of Arc, René Descartes, William Shakespeare (who hasn't been heard from since 1935), Louis Pasteur and Vladimir Lenin. One very frequent contact, Victor Hugo, was posthumously named the chief spirit of foreign missionary works.

Within a year of its founding, the group had 26,000 followers. By the mid-1950s, one in eight southern Vietnamese was a Caodai. The sect established a virtually independent feudal state in Tay Ninh Province and retained enormous influence in local affairs until the Communist victory in 1975. ∎

executed in 1979. But in 1985 the Holy See and some 400 temples were returned to Caodai control. Though Caodaism is strongest in Tay Ninh Province and the Mekong Delta, temples can be found throughout southern and central Vietnam. Today, perhaps 2% of Vietnamese are followers of Caodaism.

Caodai temples observe four daily ceremonies, which are held at 6 am, noon, 6 pm and midnight. Visitors from Ho Chi Minh City usually try to arrive on time to witness the noon ceremony.

Information

Tourist Office Tay Ninh Tourist (☎ 22376) is presently in the Hoa Binh Hotel on 30/4 St. However, the office is supposed to move just across the street when a new building is completed, though there is no word yet on just when that might be. The staff here have plans to introduce tours to nearby Dau Tieng Reservoir, complete with boat trips and optional waterskiing.

Long Hoa Market

Long Hoa Market is several km south of the Caodai Holy See complex and open every day from 5 am to about 6 pm. Before reunification, the Caodai sect had the right to collect taxes from the merchants here.

Places to Stay

The main place in town is the *Hoa Binh Hotel* (☎ 22376, 22383; 57 rooms) on 30/4 St. Rooms with fan only are US$6, but most rooms are air-con and are priced from US$8 to US$18. The hotel is five km from the Caodai Temple.

The other alternative is the *Anh Dao Hotel* on 30/4 St, 500 metres west of the Hoa Binh Hotel. There are 14 double rooms here priced from US$8 to US$16.

Places to Eat

Nha Hang Diem Thuy (☎ 27318) on 30/4 St is a great restaurant with low prices. Giant crayfish *(tom can)* are one of their specialities.

One km north of the Tay Ninh market near the river is the *Hoang Yen Restaurant*, considered by locals to be the best in town. Right on the river next to the bridge is the government-owned *Festival Restaurant* which has great ambience, though the food is not spectacular.

Top : Window in Caodai Great Temple (RS)
Middle : Monks at Caodai Great Temple (DS)
Bottom : Caodai Great Temple (RS)

Getting There & Away

Buses from Ho Chi Minh City to Tay Ninh leave from the Tay Ninh Bus Station in Tan Binh District and Mien Tay Bus Station in An Lac. Tay Ninh is 96 km from Ho Chi Minh City on National Highway 22.

NUI BA DEN

Nui Ba Den (Black Lady Mountain), 15 km north-east of Tay Ninh town, rises 850 metres above the surrounding countryside. Over the centuries, Nui Ba Den has served as a shrine for various peoples of the area, including the Khmer, Chams, Vietnamese and Chinese. There are several cave-temples on the mountain.

Nui Ba Den was used as a staging ground by both the Viet Minh and the Viet Cong and was the scene of fierce fighting during the French and American wars. At one time, there was a US Army fire base and relay station at the summit of the mountain, which was set up after being defoliated and heavily bombed by American aircraft.

Nui Ba Den (Black Lady Mountain) (RS)

The name Black Lady Mountain is derived from the legend of Huong, a young woman who married her true love despite the advances of a wealthy mandarin. While her husband was away doing military service, she would visit a magical statue of Buddha at the summit of the mountain. One day, Huong was attacked by kidnappers, but preferring death to dishonour threw herself off a cliff. She reappeared in the visions of a monk living on the mountain, who told her story.

The hike from the base of the mountain to the main temple complex and back takes about 1½ hours. Although steep in parts, it's not a difficult walk. At the base of the mountain, you'll have to fend off the usual crowd of very persistent kids selling tourist junk, lottery tickets and chewing gum – they'll pursue you up the mountain but you can easily outpace them if you wear running shoes and don't carry a heavy bag. Things are much more relaxed around the temple complex where there are only a few stands selling snacks and drinks and the vendors are not pushy.

If you need more exercise, a walk to the summit of the peak and back takes about six hours.

Visiting during a holiday or festival is a bad idea. Aside from the crowds, at such times the main gate is closed. This forces vehicles to park two km away from the trailhead, which means you've got an additional four-km walk added to the return trip. This extra walking eats up a good deal of extra time, making it difficult to complete the trip if you're coming from Saigon and returning the same night.

Places to Stay

About 500 metres past the main entrance gate are eight A-frame bungalows, where double rooms can be rented for US$6 to US$10.

ONE PILLAR PAGODA

The official name of this interesting place is Nam Thien Nhat Tru, but everyone calls it the One Pillar Pagoda of Thu Duc (Chua Mot Cot Thu Duc).

The pagoda is modelled after Hanoi's One Pillar Pagoda, though the two structures do not look identical. Hanoi's original pagoda was built in the 9th century, but was destroyed by the French and rebuilt by the Vietnamese in 1954. Ho Chi Minh City's version was constructed in 1958.

When Vietnam was partitioned in 1954, Buddhist monks and Catholic priests wisely fled south so that they could avoid persecution and continue practising their religion. One monk from Hanoi who came south in 1954 was Thich Tri Dung. Shortly after arrival in Saigon, Thich petitioned the South Vietnamese government for permission to construct a replica of Hanoi's famous One Pillar Pagoda. President Diem, a Catholic with little tolerance for Buddhist clergy, denied him permission; nevertheless, Thich and his supporters raised the funds and built the pagoda. Ordered to tear down the temple, the monks refused even though threatened with imprisonment for not complying. The government's dispute with the monks reached a stand-off, a stalemate that lasted until 1963.

In the current political atmosphere, Vietnamese history books say that this pagoda later served as a base for Viet Cong guerrillas disguised as clergy. Certainly, at this pagoda and others, VC cadres did pose as poor peasants willing to donate their labour to Buddhism. This provided them with a convenient cover in Saigon, where they conducted secret activities (holding political indoctrination meetings, smuggling weapons, planting bombs, etc) at night. However, since most monks then (and now) were divorced from politics, it's doubtful that they had any idea just to what extent they were being used by the VC, and it's unlikely they offered their protection wittingly.

During the war, the One Pillar Pagoda of Thu Duc was in possession of an extremely valuable plaque, said to weigh 612 kg. After liberation, the government took it for 'safe-keeping' and brought it to Hanoi. However, none of the monks alive today could say just where it is. There is speculation that the government sold it to overseas collectors, but this cannot be confirmed.

The One Pillar Pagoda (☎ 960780) is in the Thu Duc District, about 15 km east of central Saigon. The official address is 1/91 Nguyen Du St. Tours to the pagoda are rare, so most likely you'll have to visit by rented motorbike or car.

BINH QUOI TOURIST VILLAGE

Built on a small peninsula in the Saigon River, the Binh Quoi Tourist Village (Lang Du Lich Binh Quoi; ☎ 991831) is a slick tourist trap operated by Saigon Tourist.

The 'village' is essentially a park featuring boat rides, water puppet shows, a restaurant, swimming pool, tennis courts, camping ground, guest house, bungalows and amusements for the kiddies. The park puts in a plug for Vietnam's ethnic minorities by staging traditional-

Top left : Statue at One Pillar Pagoda (RS)
Top right : Statue at One Pillar Pagoda (RS)
Bottom : One Pillar Pagoda (RS)

style minority weddings accompanied by music. There are some alligators kept in an enclosure for viewing, but so far no alligator-wrestling shows. River cruises can be fun – the smaller cruise boats have 16 seats and the larger ones have 100 seats. You can also get middle-range accommodation here (see the Places to Stay chapter for details).

Next to the water puppet theatre, you can make bookings for the local nightlife. A sign in English advertises all sorts of fun-filled evening activities, as follows: 'Saigon Tourist bring you Magical Evenings. Sunset cruise, traditional show, dinner under the stars. Daily: Cruise & dinner show US$20 (5.30 to 9 pm); cultural show alone US$5 (7 to 8 pm)'.

Binh Quoi Tourist Village is eight km north from central Saigon in the Binh Thanh District. The official address is 1147 Xo Viet Nghe Tinh St. You can get there by cyclo, motorbike or taxi. A much slower alternative is to charter a boat from the Floating Hotel area.

Water puppet theatre, Binh Quoi Tourist Village (RS)

ORCHID FARMS

There are a number of orchid farms (Vuon Cay Kieng) in suburban Ho Chi Minh City, but most are concentrated in the Thu Duc District. These places raise more than orchids. The Artex Saigon Orchid Farm is the largest of all, with 50,000 plants representing 1000 varieties. It is primarily a commercial concern but visitors are welcome to stop by to relax in the luxurious garden.

The farm uses revenues from the sale of orchid flowers for its operating budget but makes its real profit selling orchid plants, which take six years to mature and are thus very expensive. In addition to varieties imported from overseas, the farm has a collection of orchids native to Vietnam. Ask to see the orange-yellow *Cattleya* orchid variety called Richard Nixon; they have another variety named for Joseph Stalin. The nurseries are at their most beautiful just before Tet when demand for all sorts of flowers and house plants reaches its peak. After Tet, the place is bare.

The Artex Saigon Orchid Farm is 15 km from Saigon in Thu Duc District, a rural part of Ho Chi Minh City, on the way to Bien Hoa. The official address is 5/81 Xa Lo Vong Dai, but this highway is better known as 'Xa Lo Dai Han', the 'Korean Highway', because it was built during the war by Koreans. At 'Km 14' on Xa Lo Dai Han there is a two-storey police post. Turn left (if heading out of Saigon toward Bien Hoa), continue 300 metres, and turn left again.

BIEN HOA

Bien Hoa is on the east bank of the Dong Hai River, 32 km north-east of Ho Chi Minh City. It's now the capital of Dong Nai Province.

Bien Hoa has the distinction of being the place to claim the very first US casualties in the Vietnam War – in July 1959, two American soldiers were killed here during a VC raid.

Pagodas & Temples

Buu Son Temple The most famous religious site in Bien Hoa is Buu Son Temple, which houses a Cham statue of Vishnu dating from the 15th century. The four-armed figure, carved in granite, was erected on the orders of a Cham prince who conquered the region. When the area reverted to Khmer control, the statue was hidden in a tree trunk where it remained until rediscovered in the 18th century by Vietnamese farmers, who built a temple for it. Buu Son Temple is in Binh Thuoc village, 1.5 km from town and 150 metres from the river bank.

Thanh Long Pagoda Ornately decorated Thanh Long Pagoda is in Binh Thuoc village about 300 metres from the Bien Hoa railway station.

Dai Giac Pagoda Dai Giac Pagoda is near Bien Hoa on an island not far from the railroad bridge. It is claimed to be at least 150 years old.

Buu Phong Pagoda Buu Phong Pagoda, with its numerous granite statues, stands on top of a hill of blue granite seven km from Bien Hoa. The pagoda was built on the site of an earlier Cham or Khmer temple on the orders of Emperor Gia Long.

Getting There & Away

There is a four-lane highway from Ho Chi Minh City to Bien Hoa, a distance of 32 km.

BUU LONG MOUNTAIN

Various tourist pamphlets and even Saigon residents will tell you that Buu Long Mountain is the 'Halong Bay of the south'. Seeing how Halong Bay is northern Vietnam's top scenic drawcard, you might be forgiven for thinking that Buu Long Mountain must be nothing short of stunningly beautiful. In fact it's quite the opposite, and Halong Bay people might consider filing a defamation lawsuit against whoever invented the epithet.

Nevertheless, if you're bored and want to enjoy some perverse sort of comic relief, it does no harm to visit Buu Long Mountain. The summit towers a big 60 metres above the car park. During the five-minute walk to the top, you need to fight off a constant parade of beggars and vendors who will follow half a metre behind you the entire way. Your followers might try to steer you off-course to visit the 'English-speaking monk' who will charge you a fee for speaking English to him.

The top of the mountain is marked by a pagoda. From this vantage point, you can look down and clearly see Dragon Lake (Long An). The shoreline is dressed up with a few pavilions and decorative souvenir stands. To reach the lake, you have to descend the mountain and pass through another gate where you pay an additional admission fee. And for a small extra charge, you can paddle a boat around the slimy green waters in pursuit of the dragon which is said to live at the bottom of the lake. Although dragons are hard to spot, the boat ride offers an excellent way to escape the lottery-ticket and postcard vendors.

Buu Long Mountain is 32 km from central Saigon. It's two km off the main highway after crossing the bridge that marks the border between Ho Chi Minh City and Dong Nai Province. The admission fee is US$0.30, plus there is an extra charge for bringing in a camera. Considering how little there is to see here, you might as well leave the camera at home. There are a few refreshment shops here where you can buy cold drinks and warm noodles.

TRI AN FALLS

The Tri An Falls are a cascade on the Be River (Song Be), eight metres high and 30 metres wide. They are especially awesome in the late autumn, when the river's flow is at its greatest. The Tri An Falls are in Song Be Province, 36 km from Bien Hoa and 68 km from Saigon (via Thu Dau Mot).

Further upstream from Tri An Falls is Tri An Reservoir (Ho Tri An), a large artificial lake completed in the early 1980s with Soviet assistance. However, the dam, which supplies the lion's share of Ho Chi Minh City's electric power, is off limits to tourists for security reasons.

LANGA LAKE

Highway 20 spans this reservoir, which is crossed by a new bridge. There are many floating houses here, all built since 1991 when the area was opened to locals. The

Langa Lake (RS)

whole point behind living in a floating house is to harvest the fish underneath. It's a very scenic spot for photography, though the local children have become very pushy beggars because foreigners have been feeding them candy.

It's easy to hire small boats for cruises on the lake. There is also the possibility of hiking from the far side of the lake (reachable only by boat) into Nam Cat Tien National Park.

CAN GIO

The name Can Gio denotes both a small village (sometimes called Duyen Hai) by the sea and the Can Gio District of Ho Chi Minh City. Can Gio District is the largest in Ho Chi Minh City and consists entirely of swampy delta islands at the mouth of the Nha Be River.

As you would expect in a river delta, the beach consists of hard-packed mud rather than the fluffy white sand that sun worshippers crave. Furthermore, the beach sits in an exposed position and is lashed by strong winds. For these reasons, Can Gio gets few visitors and the beach remains entirely undeveloped.

Caodai Temple, Can Gio (RS)

Before you scratch Can Gio off your list of places to visit, it's worth knowing that the island does have a wild beauty of its own. Unlike the rest of Ho Chi Minh City, overpopulation is hardly a problem here. The lack of human inhabitants is chiefly because the island lacks any fresh water supply.

The land here is only about two metres above sea level and the island is basically one big mangrove swamp. The salty mud makes most forms of agriculture impossible, but aquaculture is another matter. The most profitable business here is shrimp farming. Also, the hard-packed mud beach teems with clams and other sea life which island residents dig up to sell or eat themselves. There is also a small salt industry – sea water is diverted into shallow ponds and is left to evaporate until a white layer of salt can be harvested. Can Gio also has a small port where fishing boats can dock, but the shallow water prevents any large ships from dropping anchor.

From about 1945 through 1954, Can Gio was controlled by General Bay Vien, an independent warlord, gangster and member of the notorious Binh Xuyen crime syndicate, who also controlled a casino in Cholon. He was persuaded by former South Vietnamese President Ngo Dinh Diem to join forces with the government. Not long thereafter, Bay Vien was murdered by an unknown assailant. Diem also went on to defeat the private armies of the Hoa Hao and Caodai religious sects.

Can Gio Market

Can Gio does have a large market, made conspicuous by some rather powerful odours. Seafood and salt are definitely the local specialities. The vegetables, rice and fruit are all imported by boat from Saigon.

Caodai Temple

Though much smaller than the Caodai Great Temple at Tay Ninh, Can Gio can boast a Caodai Temple of its own. The temple is near the market and is easy to find.

War Memorial & Cemetery

Adjacent to the shrimp hatchery is a large and conspicuous cemetery and war memorial (Nghia Trang Liet Si Rung Sac). Like all such sites in Vietnam, the praise for bravery and patriotism goes entirely to the winning side and there is nothing said about the losers. Indeed, all of the former war cemeteries containing remains of South

Vietnamese soldiers were bulldozed after liberation, a fact which still causes much bitterness.

The War Memorial & Cemetery is two km from Can Gio Market.

Shrimp Hatchery

COFIDEC (Coastal Fishery Development Corporation, or Cty Phat Trien Kinh Te Duyen Hai in Vietnamese) is a large company which has sewn up much of the shrimp-breeding industry in Can Gio. This is a joint-venture with the Philippines and appears to be very well organised. Two types of shrimp – black tiger and white shrimp – are bred here. One building houses a small plant where the shrimp are cleaned, packed and frozen before being shipped off to Saigon.

COFIDEC has its operational headquarters close to the War Memorial in Can Gio, but the shrimp-breeding ponds stretch out for several km along the beachfront.

The staff at COFIDEC are friendly and not opposed to your poking around a bit, but please don't interfere with their operations. Foreigners will only continue to be welcomed here if they tread lightly. This is private property, and the management could easily lock up for good and put up 'no trespassing' signs if travellers don't behave themselves. Some of the staff speak English, and if you approach them positively they may be willing to show you around and explain their operation.

Beach

The southern side of the island faces the sea, creating a beachfront nearly 10 km long. Unfortunately, a good deal of it is inaccessible because it's been fenced off by shrimp farmers and clam diggers. Nevertheless, there is a point about four km west of the Can Gio Market where a dirt road turns off the main highway to Saigon and leads to the beach. The road can be distinguished by some telephone poles and wires alongside it. At the beach, you'll find a small collection of buildings belonging to COFIDEC and a forlorn shack selling food and drinks.

The surface of the beach is as hard as concrete, and it is possible to drive a motorbike on it. However, this is not recommended as it damages the local ecology. While the beach may seem dead at first glance, it swarms with life just below the surface, as the breathing holes in the mud suggest. You can hear the crunch of tiny clam shells as you stroll along the surface. The water here is extremely shallow and you can walk far from shore, but

War Memorial & Cemetery, Can Gio (RS)

take care – you can be sure that there is a good deal of inhospitable and well-armed sea life in these shallow waters. Stingrays, stonefish and sea urchins are just some of the xenophobic marine residents who can and will retaliate if you step on them.

The hills of the Vung Tau peninsula are easily visible on a clear day. You should also be able to see the offshore oil-drilling platforms.

Places to Stay

The only hotel in Can Gio is a four-room dump. Despite this, the *Duyen Hai Hotel* (☎ 740246) is usually full and you need to call ahead for a reservation if you intend to stay. Vietnamese pay US$2, foreigners are asked for US$10 which is probably negotiable down to US$5.

The hotel does have a fresh water tank, which means you don't have to bathe with sea water. The water is brought in from Saigon by ship. Toilets are a long walk from the main building and consist of a makeshift platform suspended over a canal by bamboo stilts. This canal is one of several where the locals harvest clams. The hotel is about four km from the main beach area.

Places to Eat

There are a few stalls around the market near the fishing port, but one look at the level of sanitation can eliminate your appetite without the need to eat anything at all.

That having been said, Can Gio boasts one remarkably good restaurant with an extensive menu. In fact, it's so good that Saigonese in the know come to Can Gio for no other reason than to eat here. The place you want is the *Duyen Hai Restaurant*, which is a stone's throw from the Duyen Hai Hotel. Unlike the hotel, the restaurant is good value.

There is one solitary food and drink stall next to the beach. Basically, all they have on the menu is Coca-Cola and instant noodles, but it beats starving. It might be prudent to bring some bottled water with you on the odd chance that this food stall is closed.

Getting There & Away

Car & Motorbike Can Gio is about 60 km from central Saigon, and the fastest way to make the journey is by motorbike. Travel time is approximately three hours.

Cars can also make the journey, but this is much slower. The reason is that you need to make two ferry crossings. The large ferries which can accommodate cars are infrequent, averaging about one every 1½ hours. By contrast, small boats make these crossings every few minutes, shuttling passengers and motorbikes. These small boats are so cheap that you could even charter one if need be.

The first ferry crossing is 15 km from Saigon at Cat Lai, a former US Navy base. Small ferry boats cost about US$0.20 for a motorbike and two passengers. Cars must wait for the large ferry which runs about once every 30 minutes, and there is usually a long queue of vehicles.

The second ferry, which is less frequent, is 35 km from Saigon and connects the two tiny villages of Dan Xay (closer to Saigon) and Hao Vo (on Can Gio Island). Motorbike riders can take a small ferry which costs around US$0.35 and runs about once every 10 to 15 minutes. The car ferry is much less frequent, but there is a posted schedule – departure times are as follows:

Dan Xay		Hao Vo	
am	5	am	5.15
	7		7.15
	8.30		8.45
	10		10.15
	11.30		11.45
pm	1	pm	1.15
	2.30		2.45
	4		4.15
	5.30		5.45
	7		–

The road is paved up to the first ferry at Cat Lai – after that, it's a dirt surface but gets regular maintenance and is in good nick. Once you get past the first ferry, there is very little traffic and both sides of the road are lined with lush mangrove forests.

Boat There is one boat daily between Can Gio and Saigon. From either direction, the boat departs at approximately 5 to 6 am and takes six hours for the journey.

There is also a small boat between Can Gio and Vung Tau. Departure from Can Gio is at 5 am, arriving in Vung Tau at 8 am. The boat departs Vung Tau about noon, arriving in Can Gio three hours later. Occasionally, there is a later boat leaving Can Gio around 2 pm, but you need to enquire because it doesn't run daily.

In Can Gio, you catch boats at the shipyards which are built on an inlet two km west of the Can Gio Market. In Saigon, you get the boat at Thu Thiem, the pier on the opposite shore of the Saigon River from the Floating Hotel. In Vung Tau, you catch the boats from the beach-front market area opposite the Grand Hotel.

VUNG TAU

Vung Tau, known under the French as Cap Saint Jacques (named by Portuguese mariners in honour of their patron saint), is a beach resort on the South China Sea, 128 km south-east of Saigon. Vung Tau's beaches are not Vietnam's nicest by any stretch of the imagination, but they are easily reached from Ho Chi Minh City and have thus been a favourite of the Saigonese since French colonists first began coming here around 1890. Seaside areas near Vung Tau are dotted with the villas of the pre-1975 elite, now converted to guest houses and villas for the post-1975 elite.

In addition to sunning on the seashore and sipping sodas in nearby cafés, visitors to this city of 100,000 can cycle around or climb up the Vung Tau peninsula's two mountains. There are also a number of interesting religious sites around town, including several pagodas and a huge standing figure of Jesus blessing the South China Sea.

Vung Tau was once the headquarters of Vietsovpetro, a joint Soviet-Vietnamese company that operates oil rigs about 60 km offshore. The rigs are still there and the occasional Russian can be seen about town, but the old Soviet technology has fallen out of favour. New oil-drilling sites in the South China Sea are being explored with Western help. There is also an active fishing fleet based in Vung Tau.

Vung Tau became briefly known to the world in 1973, when the last American combat troops in Vietnam departed from here by ship. However, thousands of American 'civilians' (including diplomats and CIA agents) remained in Vietnam for another two years – their moment on the world's centre stage came in 1975 during the rooftop helicopter evacuation from the US Embassy in Saigon.

Vung Tau long ago established its name in the 'sex tour' industry. Recent crackdown-cleanup campaigns are supposed to have eliminated this business, though the all-male groups of 'business travellers' seem as numerous as ever.

A warning – watch out for kids around the kiosks along Front Beach. They will try to pick your pockets or snatch a bag if given half a chance.

Vung Tau is heavily commercialised and the water pollution seems to be getting worse. Despite this and a few other negative points, you'd still have a hard time not enjoying the place – plenty of sand, sun, hiking opportunities, good food, draft beer and even a few budding discos. It's a party town and – for traffic-weary Saigonese – a welcome change of pace.

Orientation

The triangular Vung Tau peninsula juts into the South China Sea near the mouth of the Saigon River. There are four main beach areas. On the central-west portion of the peninsula is Front Beach (Bai Truoc), the most commercialised but reasonably scenic. The south-west area is Bai Dua Beach, which is too rocky for swimming but OK to look at; Back Beach (Bai Sau), on the eastern side of the peninsula, is the largest beach but the least scenic; and Bai Dau Beach, in the north-west area, is the most laid-back and scenic, but has very little sand.

Vung Tau (GB)

Information

Tourist Offices Ba Ria-Vung Tau Tourism (☎ 47467; fax 59860) is the official provincial tourism authority for Ba Ria-Vung Tau Province. The office is at 40/5 Thu Khoa Huan St. This outfit should not be confused with Vung Tau Tourism (Cong Ty Du Lich Vung Tau; ☎ 52314) at 18 Thuy Van St.

Oil Service Company & Tourism (Cong Ty Du Lich Phuc Vu Dau Khi Viet Nam; ☎ 52405; fax 52834) – better known by it's acronym OSC – owns 10 hotels in Vung Tau and is involved in a wide range of tourist-related businesses. The office is at 2 Le Loi Blvd.

Money Vietcombank (Ngan Hang Ngoai Thuong Viet Nam; ☎ 59874) is at 27-29 Tran Hung Dao Blvd.

Post Office The CPO (☎ 52377, 52689, 52141) is at 4 Ha Long St at the southern end of Front Beach.

Immigration Police The Immigration Police operate out of the police station on Truong Cong Dinh St, near the intersection with Ly Thuong Kiet St.

Beaches

Back Beach The main bathing area on the peninsula is Back Beach (Bai Sau, also known as Thuy Van Beach), an eight-km-long stretch of sun, sand and tourists. It's got the cleanest water, a benefit of the heavy surf (which can also be dangerous). Unfortunately, it's also the ugliest stretch of beach in Vung Tau, largely thanks to

Hon Ba Temple (GB)

crass commercialisation. The northern section of Back Beach is a little better because the palm trees have been left standing, but elsewhere it's basically concrete, car parks and cafés.

Front Beach Front Beach (Bai Truoc, also called Thuy Duong Beach) borders the centre of town. The trees make it reasonably attractive, though the beach itself has become eroded, rocky and polluted. Shaded Quang Trung St, lined with kiosks, runs along Front Beach. Early in the morning, local fishing boats moor here to unload the night's catch and clean the nets.

Bai Dau Bai Dau, a quiet coconut-palm-lined beach, is probably the most scenic spot in the Vung Tau area because it hasn't been overdeveloped (yet). The only real problem with Bai Dau is that there isn't a lot of sand – it's a rocky beach with only a few small sandy coves where you can go bathing. Nevertheless, Bai Dau's many cheap guest houses are attractive for low-budget travellers.

Bai Dau is three km from the city centre along Tran Phu St. The best way to get there is by bicycle or motor-bike – there is no public transport and the road is too rough and hilly to be negotiated by cyclos.

Bai Dua Bai Dua (Roches Noires Beach) is a small, rocky beach about two km south of the town centre on Ha Long St. This is a great place to watch the sun setting over the South China Sea.

Temples

Hon Ba Temple Hon Ba Temple (Chua Hon Ba) is on a tiny island just south of Back Beach. It can be reached on foot at low tide.

Niet Ban Tinh Xa Niet Ban Tinh Xa, one of the largest Buddhist temples in Vietnam, is on the western side of Small Mountain. Built in 1971, it is famous for its 5000-kg bronze bell, a huge reclining Buddha and intricate mosaic work.

Thich Ca Phat Dai Park

Thich Ca Phat Dai, a must-see site for domestic tourists, is a hillside park of monumental Buddhist statuary built in the early 1960s.

The park is on the eastern side of Large Mountain at 25 Tran Phu St. To get there from the town centre, take Le Loi Blvd north almost to the end and turn left onto Tran Phu St.

Lighthouse

The 360° view of the entire hammerhead-shaped peninsula from the lighthouse *(hai dang)* is truly spectacular. The lighthouse was built in 1910 and sits atop Small Mountain.

The narrow paved road up Small Mountain to the lighthouse intersects Ha Long St 150 metres south-west of the CPO.

Giant Jesus

An enormous Rio de Janeiro-style figure of Jesus (Thanh Gioc) with arms outstretched gazes across the South China Sea from the southern end of Small Mountain.

The Giant Jesus, 30 metres high, was constructed in 1974 on the site of a lighthouse built by the French a century before. The statue can be reached on foot by a path that heads up the hill from a point just south of Back Beach.

Bach Dinh

Bach Dinh, the White Villa (Villa Blanche), is a former royal residence set amidst frangipanis and bougainvilleas on a lushly forested hillside overlooking the sea.

Bach Dinh was built in 1909 as a retreat for French governor Paul Doumer. It later became a summer palace for Vietnamese royalty. King Thanh Thai was kept here for a while before being shipped off to hard labour on the French island of Réunion. In the late 1960s to the early '70s, the building was a part-time playground for President Thieu.

The main entrance to the park surrounding Bach Dinh is just north of Front Beach at 12 Tran Phu St. It is open from 6 am to 9 pm. The admission price is US$1.20 for foreigners. There is an additional 'camera fee' of US$0.20, while the 'video fee' is US$1.20.

Boat-Building Yards

New wooden fishing craft are built at a location which, oddly enough, is over a km from the nearest water. The boat yards are on Nam Ky Khoi Nghia St, 500 metres south of Vung Tau Bus Station.

Golf Course

A Taiwanese joint-venture is constructing a golf course in Vung Tau. It is not known when it will be open.

Small Mountain Circuit

The six-km circuit around Small Mountain (Nui Nho; elevation 197 metres), known to the French as le tour de la Petite Corniche, begins at the CPO and continues on Ha Long St along the rocky coastline. A road leads up the hill to the lighthouse, 150 metres south of the CPO.

Ha Long St passes Ngoc Bich Pagoda (which is built in the style of Hanoi's famous One Pillar Pagoda), Bai Dua Beach and a number of villas before reaching the tip of the Vung Tau peninsula.

Phan Boi Chau St goes from the southern end of Back Beach into town along the eastern base of Small Mountain, passing century-old Linh Son Temple which contains a Buddha of pre-Angkor Khmer origin.

Large Mountain Circuit

The 10-km circuit around Large Mountain (Nui Lon; elevation 520 metres) passes seaside villas and Bai Dau Beach. On the eastern side of Large Mountain, which faces tidal marshes and the giant cranes of the Vietsovpetro docks, is Thich Ca Phat Dai statuary park.

Places to Stay

The Vung Tau peninsula has a large number of hotels, but these can get booked out during weekends and holidays.

Front Beach This part of town is definitely moving upmarket. If you want a cheap place to stay, first take a look at Bai Dau. Some suggestions on Front Beach include the following (Map 10):

Canadian Hotel (☎ 59852; fax 59851), 48 Quang Trung St. Classy rooms cost US$45 to US$90.

Grand Hotel (☎ 52469; fax 59878; 60 rooms), 26 Quang Trung St, just opposite the beachfront. Singles with fan and private bath are US$15, while singles/doubles with air-con are US$20/30 and US$30/40.

Ha Long Hotel (☎ 52175), 45 Thong Nhat St. At one time very cheap, but currently under renovation.

Hai Au Hotel (☎ 52178; 64 rooms), 100 Ha Long St on the southern end of Front Beach near the CPO. Excellent rooms cost from US$35 to US$55 (see Map 9).

Hai Yen Hotel (☎ 52571; 23 rooms), 8 Le Loi Blvd. Doubles range from US$25 to US$40.

Lu Son Hotel (☎ 52576; 65 rooms), 27 Le Loi Blvd (far from the beach). Air-con doubles cost US$15.

Pacific Hotel (☎ 52279; 53 rooms), 4 Le Loi Blvd (cnr Ly Tu Trong St). Rooms from US$23 to US$33.

Palace (Hoa Binh) Hotel (☎ 52265; fax 59878; 105 rooms), on Nguyen Trai St, 100 metres off Quang Trung St. Rooms cost between US$35 and US$70.

Petro House Hotel (☎ 52462; 57 rooms), 89 Tran Hung Dao Blvd. New hotel with rooms from US$25.

Rang Dong Hotel (☎ 52133; 84 rooms), 5 Duy Tan St just off Le Loi Blvd. Doubles cost US$10 to US$20.

Rex Hotel (☎ 52135; fax 59862), 1 Duy Tan St, no relation to the Rex in Saigon. Rooms cost US$30 to US$45, but surly staff ruin the place.

Sea Breeze (Hanh Phoc) Hotel (☎ 52392; fax 59856; 36 rooms), 11 Nguyen Trai St. Rooms cost US$40 to US$60.

Song Hong Hotel (☎ 52137; 39 rooms), 12 Hoang Dieu St (cnr Truong Vinh Ky St). Doubles US$16 to US$30.

Song Huong Hotel (☎ 52491; 33 rooms), 10 Truong Vinh Ky St. Singles/doubles are US$30/45.

Back Beach Perhaps the most beautiful place to stay in otherwise ugly Back Beach is the *Thang Muoi Hotel* (☎ 52665, 52645; 93 rooms) at 4-6 Thuy Van St. This old hotel featuring single-storey buildings is set on quiet, spacious grounds with trees. Doubles cost between US$11 and US$23. Other places worth checking out include (Map 9):

Beautiful Hotel (Khach San My Le; ☎ 53174; fax 53177; 100 rooms), 100 Thuy Van St. Rooms cost US$32 to US$55.

Phuong Dong Hotel (☎ 52593; 45 rooms), 2 Thuy Van St. Rooms cost US$30 to US$40.

Saigon Hotel, 72 Thuy Van St. Rooms are good value at US$10 to US$35.

Thuy Duong Hotel (☎ 52635; nine rooms), north end of Thuy Van St. It's also called the *Weeping Willow Hotel*. Room rates are US$25 to US$50.

Thuy Van Hotel (93 rooms), north end of Thuy Van St. Rates are US$18 to US$32.

Bai Dau There are dozens of guest houses (*nha nghi*) in former private villas along Bai Dau. This is the cheapest neighbourhood in Vung Tau because of its isolated location. Most of the guest houses have rooms with fans and communal bathrooms and cost US$10 or less, but several places have added air-con and private baths.

Nha Nghi 29, 29 Tran Phu St (on the seafront). Rooms with air-con cost US$20.

Nha Nghi 128, 128 Tran Phu St. Rooms for four cost US$7, but it's rather dilapidated.

Nha Nghi DK 142 has relatively high-standard air-con rooms with private bath for US$25.

Nha Nghi Doan 28, 126 Tran Phu St. Doubles cost US$25.

Nha Nghi My Tho, 47 Tran Phu St. Rooms with fan and beach view cost US$7 to US$10. Banquet-style dinners for US$3.

Thuy Tien Hotel, 96 Tran Phu St, is absurdly overpriced at US$100 for rooms which are worth about US$10. This dump is now the most expensive hotel in Vung Tau!

Bai Dua Among the villas-turned-guest houses at Bai Dua are *Nha Nghi 50 Ha Long* at 50 Ha Long St, *Nha Nghi Dro* at 88B Ha Long St and, at 48 Ha Long St, *Nha Nghi 48 Ha Long*, which charges foreigners US$20 for a triple with air-con. Their cheapest double goes for US$15.

Places to Eat

For excellent seafood, try *Huong Bien Restaurant*, which is along Front Beach at 47 Quang Trung St. There are several places to eat nearby and quite a few more along Tran Hung Dao Blvd. Hotels with excellent restaurants include the *Palace*, *Pacific* and the *Grand*.

At the southern end of Back Beach is the excellent *Thuy Trieu Restaurant*, which does a mean salad and splendid seafood, yet charges low prices. The largest restaurant along Back Beach is the *Thang Muoi Restaurant* (☎ 52515) at 7-9 Thuy Van St.

Entertainment

Apocalypse Now is indeed related to its infamous cousin in Ho Chi Minh City. This raging bar and café is at 438 Truong Cong Dinh St.

Another favourite with foreigners and locals alike is the disco at the back of the *Canadian Hotel*. It is an excellent hi-tech place with a US$3.50 cover charge. Drinks are about US$1.50.

The *Grand Hotel* has a disco and karaoke lounge which operate from 7 pm until midnight.

Getting There & Away

Air Since 1995 Vietnam Airlines has been operating international flights between Vung Tau and Singapore. The planes are small 40-seater jets and the round-trip airfare is US$280.

Bus The most convenient minibuses to Vung Tau depart from in front of the Saigon Hotel on Dong Du St near the Saigon Central Mosque. Departures are approximately once every 15 minutes between 6 am and 6 pm. The 128-km trip takes two hours and costs US$2. To return to Ho Chi Minh City from Vung Tau, you catch these minibuses at the petrol station or Sea Breeze Hotel.

Buses to Vung Tau also leave from the Mien Dong Bus Station and the Van Thanh Bus Station.

Vung Tau Bus Station (Ben Xe Khach Vung Tau) is about 1.5 km from the city centre at 52 Nam Ky Khoi Nghia St. To get there from Front Beach, take either Bacu St or Truong Cong Dinh St to Le Hong Phong St. Turn right and then turn right again onto Nam Ky Khoi Nghia St. There are non-express buses from here to Baria, Bien Hoa, Saigon, Long Khanh, Mytho and Tay Ninh. An express bus to Ho Chi Minh City leaves at 6 and 9 am and 3 pm.

Boat It is possible to get to Vung Tau from Can Gio. See the Can Gio section earlier in this chapter for details.

Getting Around

The best way to get around the Vung Tau peninsula is by bicycle. These are available for hire from some hotels for around US$1 per day.

LONG HAI

Commercialised tourism has turned Vung Tau into something of a circus, and many travellers crave a less-developed seaside retreat. As a result, travellers are increasingly heading to Long Hai, 30 km north-east of Vung Tau. The western end of the beach here is where fishing boats moor, and therefore not too clean. However, the east end is quite all right, with a reasonable amount of white sand and palm trees.

Most Westerners seem to agree that the one unpleasant feature of Long Hai is the evening noise. Forget about sitting on your hotel's porch listening to the waves roll in. That sinister plot by hearing-aid manufacturers – karaoke – has taken Long Hai by storm. Your eardrums will be pounded all evening until about 11 pm, and some of the real enthusiasts fire up in the morning too. There is no use complaining about this – it comes with the territory. If you're deaf, you should love Long Hai. If you're not, you will be by the time you leave.

Places to Stay

There are currently only three hotels in Long Hai, but this is expected to change quickly. Currently, the largest hotel on offer is the *Long Hai Hotel* (☎ 68010; 25 rooms). It's difficult to recommend this place – rooms cost US$20 to US$25, the beach next to the hotel is dirty and the 'massage service' looks kinky.

On the opposite end of the beach is the *Palace Hotel*. It resembles the Long Hai Hotel in both price and facilities.

The preferred place to stay is the *Military Guest House* (Doan An Duong 298; ☎ 68002; 28 rooms) at the east end of the beach. The main building has 17 rooms priced from US$8 to US$20. There are also two beach houses (recommended) where rooms cost only US$5.

Getting There & Away

As usual, there isn't any public transport. Rent a motorbike in Vung Tau or Saigon and drive yourself. If you can afford to rent a car and round up a group to share the cost, so much the better.

The Military Guest House in Long Hai has a boat which can be rented (US$30 per hour) which holds five people and can make the run to Vung Tau. This same guest house also has its own minibus for hire.

No doubt enterprising locals will eventually start offering minibus service to Long Hai. Ask around the cafés in Saigon or Vung Tau for the latest transport news.

Low tide at Long Hai (RS)

HO COC BEACH

A short drive to the east of Long Hai is the remote but beautiful Ho Coc Beach. It's still a very undeveloped area, though this will no doubt change. The *Ho Coc Guest House* consists of one bungalow with five rooms. It's the only place to stay at Ho Coc and you might have it to yourself. To get there, you'll need a car or a motorbike because no public transport is available.

BINH CHAU HOT SPRINGS

About 50 km north-east of Long Hai is Binh Chau Hot Springs (Suoi Nuoc Nong Binh Chau). There is a small resort here, but tacky commercialisation is blessedly absent. The resort is in a compound six km from the village of Binh Chau, and foreigners have to pay an admission fee of US$0.20.

Massage and acupuncture are available (check the needles). Locals may also offer to take you on a hunting expedition (for a fee) to help exterminate what little wildlife remains in the area. From the look of things, they've already done a good job – the only wildlife around seems to be the swarms of noisy cicadas buzzing away in the trees.

The resort consists of a hotel and adjoining restaurant. To see the actual hot springs, you have to walk down a wooden path. Be sure that you don't stray from the paths, as the earthen crust is thin here and you could conceivably fall through into an underground pool of scalding water. The hottest spring here reaches 82°C, which is warm enough to boil eggs. Indeed, you'll find a small spring where bamboo baskets have been laid aside for just this purpose. If you don't happen to have any eggs in your pockets, enquire back at the hotel's restaurant.

Places to Stay

If you want to spend the night, the only choice on offer is the *Binh Chau Hotel*. There are 16 rooms in the main hotel building costing US$10 to US$15. The hotel also has bungalows for rent costing just US$8; the toilet is outside.

MYTHO

Mytho, the capital of Tien Giang Province, is a quiet place 90 minutes by car from Ho Chi Minh City. The town is in the lush Mekong Delta region.

Dong Tam Snake Farm

There is a snake farm at Dong Tam, which is about 10 km west from Mytho towards Vinh Long. Most of the snakes raised here are pythons and cobras. The snakes are raised for a variety of purposes: for eating, for their skins and for the purpose of producing snake antivenins. The king cobras are raised only for exhibit – they are extremely aggressive and are even capable of spitting poison – do not get too close to their cages. The regular cobras are kept in an open pit and will generally ignore you if you ignore them, but will strike if provoked. On

Playing a board game, Mytho (GB)

the other hand, the pythons are docile enough to be taken out of their cages and 'played with' if you dare, but the larger ones are capable of strangling a human.

Dong Tam also has a collection of mutant turtles and fish on exhibit. The cause of their genetic deformities dates almost certainly from the war against the USA, when forested parts of the Mekong Delta were intensively sprayed with Agent Orange. Other creatures kept on exhibit here include deer, monkeys, bears, crocodiles, owls, canaries and various other birds.

The Snake Farm is operated by the Vietnamese military for profit. It's definitely open to the public and taking photos is even encouraged. At your request, the staff will be all too happy to drape you with a large python to create that perfect photo for the loved ones back home.

The technology for raising the animals is somewhat basic, as are the housing facilities for the reptiles. It's certainly a sharp contrast to Bangkok's slick Snake Institute. Nevertheless, Dong Tam Snake Farm is an interesting place to visit. Admission costs US$1.

Vinh Trang Pagoda

Vinh Trang Pagoda is a beautiful and well-maintained sanctuary. The charitable monks here provide a home to orphans and handicapped and other needy children.

The pagoda is about one km from the city centre at 60A Nguyen Trung Truc St. To get there, take the bridge across the river (at Nguyen Trai St) and continue for about a km. The entrance to the sanctuary is on the right-hand side of the building as you approach it from the ornate gate.

Riverboat Trips

It is possible to take short cruises on the Mekong River and visit some of the nearby islands. Unfortunately, the government of Tien Giang Province monopolises this business and charges ridiculous prices for short journeys. It's bad value, but you cannot hire a local private boat – doing so will most likely get you and the boat owner arrested. The locals, of course, know this and are unlikely to take the risk.

Glossary

ao dai – national dress of Vietnamese women and (rarely) men

bang – congregation (in the Chinese community)

bo doi – North Vietnamese troops who occupied Ho Chi Minh City in 1975

buu dien – post office

Caodai – indigenous Vietnamese religious sect

Champa – Hindu kingdom dating from the late 2nd century AD

Chams – the people of Champa

cho – market

Cochinchina – the southern part of Vietnam during the French colonial era

cyclo – pedicab or bicycle rickshaw (from French)

doi moi – economic renovation, restructuring

flechette – experimental American weapon, an artillery shell containing thousands of darts

Funan – see Oc-Eo

ghe – long, narrow rowboat

Hoa – ethnic-Chinese

Honda om – motorbike taxi

huyen – rural district

Indochina – Vietnam, Cambodia and Laos. The name derives from the influence of Indian and Chinese cultures on the region

khach san – hotel

Khmer – ethnic Cambodians

Liberation – the 1975 takeover of the South by the North; what most foreigners call 'reunification'

napalm – jellied petrol (gasoline) dropped and lit from aircraft, with devastating effect

nha hang – restaurant

nha khach – hotel or guest house

nha nghi – guest house

nha thuoc – pharmacy

nha tro – dormitory

NLF – National Liberation Front; official name for the Viet Cong

nuoc mam – fish sauce, served with almost every meal in Vietnam

NVA – North Vietnamese Army

Oc-Eo – Indianised kingdom (also called Funan) in southern Vietnam between 1st and 6th centuries

pagoda – traditionally, an eight-sided Buddhist tower, but in Vietnam the word is commonly used to denote a temple

quan – urban district
quoc ngu – Latin-based phonetic alphabet in which Vietnamese is written
rap – cinema
roi nuoc – water puppetry
Tet – the Vietnamese lunar new year
VC – Viet Cong or Vietnamese Communists
Viet Kieu – Overseas Vietnamese
Viet Minh – League for the Independence of Vietnam, a nationalistic movement which fought the Japanese and French but later became fully Communist-dominated
xe lam – three-wheeled motorised vehicle, Lambretta

Index

Map references are in **bold** type.

Maps

Top : Children's outing (PW)
Bottom : Child street vendor (RS)

Wedding celebrations (PW)

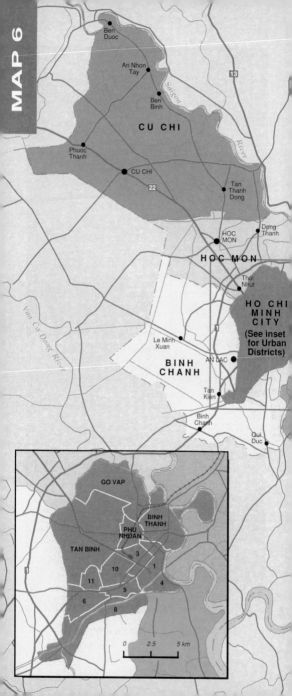

Ho Chi Minh City
(Urban & Rural Districts)

Tri An Lake

0   10   20 km

1

51

Long Binh

THU DUC   Tan Phu

THU DUC

Thanh My Loi

Dong Nai River

Tan Thuan Dong

NHA BE

NHA BE

Nhon Duc

Hiep Phuoc   An Thoi Dong   Tam Thon Hiep

CAN GIO

Ly Nhom

CAN GIO

Long Hoa

SOUTH CHINA SEA

MAP 8

Central Saigon

0   250   500 m

Map 7 Central Ho Chi Minh (Saigon)

PLACES TO STAY

1	Huong Tram Hotel
2	Que Huong (Liberty) Hotel
12	Victory Hotel
14	International Hotel
15	Sol Chancery Hotel
17	Embassy Hotel
18	Tao Dan Hotel
21	Bao Yen Hotel
22	Saigon Star Hotel
25	Rang Dong Hotel
28	Hoang Gia Hotel
33	New World Hotel
34	Palace Saigon Hotel
35	A Chau Hotel
38	Hoang Yen Mini-Hotel
40	My Man Mini-Hotel
41	Thai Binh Hotel
42	Vien Dong Hotel
44	Guest House 70 & 72
45	Hoang Vu Hotel
49	Prince (Hoang Tu) Hotel
56	Van Canh Hotel
59	Champagne (Que Huong) Hotel
67	Rose 2 Hotel
68	Thai Binh Duong Hotel
69	Phong Phu Hotel
71	Metropole Hotel
72	Miss Loi's Guest House

PLACES TO EAT

3	La Couscoussière Restaurant
7	Ashoka
8	Tex Mex Bar & Restaurant
9	Buffalo Blues
10	Thanh Nien
26	Annie's Pizza
46	Lotus & Saigon Cafés
47	Kim Café & Madras House
48	Zen
57	Tin Nghia Vegetarian Restaurant

OTHER

4	French Consulate
5	Former US Embassy (1967-1975)
6	Zoo & Botanical Gardens
11	Manhattan & VIP Club
13	War Crimes Museum
16	Reunification Palace
19	Swimming Pool
20	Nha Van Hoa Lao Dong (Ballroom Disco)
23	Xa Loi Pagoda
24	Thich Quang Duc Memorial

Buddha at One Pillar Pagoda (RS)

Map 8 Dong Khoi Area

PLACES TO STAY

5	Orchid Hotel
16	Tan Loc Hotel
18	Norfolk Hotel
24	Rex Hotel
30	Continental Hotel
33	Caravelle Hotel
36	Hotel 69 Hai Ba Trung
41	Saigon Hotel & Vung Tau Minibus Stop
44	Saigon Floating Hotel
47	Riverside Hotel
48	Dong Khoi Hotel
52	Bong Sen Hotel & Mondial Hotel
55	Century Saigon Hotel
57	Kimdo Hotel
58	Palace Hotel
60	Majestic Hotel

PLACES TO EAT

3	Jimmy's Restaurant
4	Le P'tit Bistrot de Saigon
6	Sapa Bar & Restaurant
7	Camargue
10	Ami Restaurant
11	Korean Food Restaurant
12	Le Chalet Suisse
17	Saigon Intershop & Minimart
20	Kem Bach Dang
21	Kem Bach Dang
29	Givral Restaurant
37	California Chicken
45	Dinner Cruises
50	Paloma Café
51	Vietnam House
53	Brodard Café
54	Augustin
59	Lemon Grass Restaurant

OTHER

1	Notre Dame Cathedral
2	CPO
8	Chi Lang Coffee Shop
9	Thai Airways
13	Hotel de Ville (People's Committee)
14	Revolutionary Museum
15	Municipal Library
19	Government Bookshop
22	Pacific Airlines
23	Phnom Penh Bus Garage
25	Vietnam Airlines & Malaysian Airline System
26	Cathay Pacific
27	Saigon Tourist
28	Hieu Sach Xuan Thu Bookshop
31	Municipal Theatre
32	Q Bar
34	Air France
35	Saigon Central Mosque
38	Apocalypse Now
39	Ton Duc Thang Museum
40	Hien & Bob's Place
42	Banque Française du Commerce Extérieur
43	Me Linh Square & Tran Hung Dao Statue
46	Small Motorised Boats for Hire
49	Tiem Sach Bookstore
56	Tax Department Store
61	Huynh Thuc Khang Street Market
62	Old Market

MAP 8

Dong Khoi Area

0   200   400 m

MAP 9

PLACES TO STAY	OTHER
1 Ky Hoa Hotel	2 Vietnam Quoc Tu Pagoda
6 Trung Uong Hotel	3 Hoa Binh Theatre
7 Phu Tho Hotel	4 Post Office
8 Goldstar Hotel	5 An Quang Pagoda
17 Thu Do Hotel	9 Cho Ray Hospital
18 Truong Thanh Hotel	10 Khanh Van Nam Vien Pagoda
20 Song Kim Hotel	11 Phung Son Pagoda
21 Trung Mai Hotel	12 Binh Tay Market
22 Phuong Huong	13 Cholon Bus Station
(Phoenix) Hotel	14 Cha Tam Church
33 Arc En Ciel	15 Phuoc An Hoi Quan Pagoda
(Rainbow) Hotel	16 Quan Am Pagoda
34 Tan Da & Van Hoa	19 Tan Le Uyen (Karaoke)
Hotels	23 Ong Bon Pagoda
35 Bat Dat Hotel	24 Dai La Thein (Toronto Karaoke)
39 Cholon Hotel	25 Post Office
40 Cholon Tourist Mini-	26 Electronics Market
Hotel	27 Thien Hau Pagoda
41 Caesar Hotel &	28 Dai Bac (Taipei Karaoke)
Andong Market	29 Nghia An Hoi Quan Pagoda
42 Andong Hotel	30 Tam Son Hoi Quan Pagoda
43 Dong Khanh Hotel	31 Cholon Mosque
& Superstore	32 Croissants de Paris
44 Hoa Binh Hotel	36 Nha Van Hoa (Disco,
45 Tokyo Hotel	Rollerskating)
46 Hanh Long Hotel	37 Tan Dong Thang (Karaoke)
47 Regent Hotel	38 Nha Sau Church

MAP 10

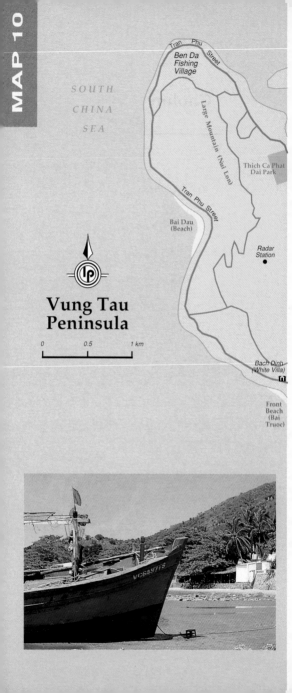

SOUTH
CHINA
SEA

Tran Phu Street

Ben Da
Fishing
Village

Large Mountain (Nui Lon)

Thich Ca Phat
Dai Park

Tran Phu Street

Bai Dau
(Beach)

Radar
Station

Vung Tau
Peninsula

0   0.5   1 km

Bach Dinh
(White Villa)

Front
Beach
(Bai
Truoc)

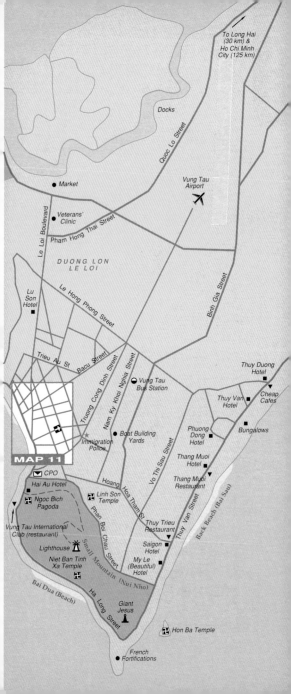

To Long Hai
(30 km) &
Ho Chi Minh
City (125 km)

Docks

Quoc Lo Street

Vung Tau
Airport

Market

Veterans'
Clinic

Pham Hong Thai Street

Le Loi Boulevard

DUONG LON
LE LOI

Le Hong Phong Street

Binh Gia Street

Lu Son Hotel

Trieu Au St

Bacu Street

Truong Cong Dinh Street

Nam Ky Khoi Nghia Street

Thuy Duong
Hotel

Vung Tau
Bus Station

Thuy Van
Hotel

Cheap
Cafes

MAP 11

Immigration
Police

Boat Building
Yards

Phuong
Dong
Hotel

Bungalows

Vo Thi Sau Street

Thang Muoi
Hotel

CPO

Hoang Hoa Tham St

Thang Muoi
Restaurant

Hai Au Hotel

Linh Son Temple

Thuy Van Street

Back Beach (Bai Sau)

Ngoc Bich
Pagoda

Phan Boi Chau Street

Thuy Trieu
Restaurant

Vung Tau International
Club (restaurant)

Saigon
Hotel

Lighthouse

Niet Ban Tinh
Xa Temple

Small Mountain (Nui Nho)

My Le
(Beautiful) Hotel

Bai Dua (Beach)

Ha Long Street

Giant
Jesus

Hon Ba Temple

French
Fortifications

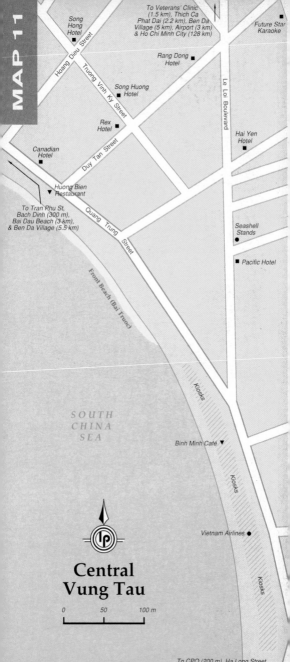

MAP 11

Song Hong Hotel

Hoang Dieu Street

Truong Vinh Ky Street

To Veterans' Clinic (1.5 km), Thich Ca Phat Dai (2.2 km), Ben Da Village (5 km), Airport (3 km) & Ho Chi Minh City (128 km)

Future Star Karaoke

Rang Dong Hotel

Le Loi Boulevard

Song Huong Hotel

Rex Hotel

Hai Yen Hotel

Canadian Hotel

Duy Tan Street

Huong Bien Restaurant

To Tran Phu St, Bach Dinh (300 m), Bai Dau Beach (3 km), & Ben Da Village (5.5 km)

Quang Trung Street

Seashell Stands

Pacific Hotel

Front Beach (Bai Truoc)

SOUTH CHINA SEA

Kiosks

Binh Minh Café

Kiosks

Vietnam Airlines

Kiosks

Central Vung Tau

0   50   100 m

To CPO (200 m), Ha Long Street, Road to Lighthouse (300 m), Bai Dua Beach (2 km) & Back Beach (4 km)